Young People Leaving Care

of related interest

Children's Homes Revisited
David Berridge and Isabelle Brodie
ISBN 1 85302 565 8

Social Work with Children and Families
Ian Butler and Gwenda Roberts
ISBN 1 85302 365 5

Punishment Under Pressure
The Probation Service in the Inner City
Bob Broad
ISBN 1 85302 090 7

Child Welfare Services
Developments in Law, Policy, Practice and Research
Edited by Malcolm Hill and Jane Aldgate
ISBN 1 85302 316 7

Residential Child Care
International Perspectives on Links with Families and Peers
Edited by Mono Chakrabarti and Malcolm Hill
ISBN 1 85302 687 5

Effective Ways of Working with Children and their Families
Edited by Malcolm Hill
ISBN 1 85302 619 0

Children's Homes and School Exclusion
Redefining the Problem
Isabelle Brodie
ISBN 1 85302 943 2

Issues in Foster Care
The Personal, the Professional and the Organisational
Edited by Greg Kelly and Robbie Gilligan
ISBN 1 85302 465 1

State Child Care
Looking After Children?
Carol Hayden, Jim Goddard, Sarah Gorin and Niki Van Der Spek
ISBN 1 85302 670 0

Young People Leaving Care

Life After the Children Act 1989

Bob Broad

Jessica Kingsley Publishers
London and Philadelphia

First published in the United Kingdom in 1998 by
Jessica Kingsley Publishers Ltd
116 Pentonville Road
London N1 9JB, England
and
325 Chestnut Street
Philadelphia, PA 19106, USA

Copyright © 1998 Bob Broad

Second impression 2001

Library of Congress Cataloging in Publication Data
A CIP catalogue record for this book is available from the Library of Congress

British Library Cataloguing in Publication Data
Broad, Bob
Young people leaving care: life after the Children Act 1989
1. Youth - Services for - Great Britain 2. Youth - Housing - Great Britain
I. Title
362.7'3'0941'09049

ISBN 1 85302 412 0

Printed and Bound in Great Britain by
Athenaeum Press, Gateshead, Tyne and Wear

Contents

List of Tables

List of Figures

for Ruby and Basil Broad, my beloved late parents

Acknowledgements

All the leaving care projects that agreed to participate in the research merit a very special thank you, because their responses form the research base for this book. In addition De Montfort University and the Royal Philanthropic Society, Kent (since late 1997 RPS/Rainer) also provided valued and considerable assistance. A special thanks is extended to Professor David Ward at the Department of Social and Community Studies, De Montfort University for his consistent support for this research project. I would also like to thank Gina Short for her help as librarian/ex-colleague, and John Gent, also at the Royal Philanthropic Society, for their much valued assistance, the latter especially regarding the *Leaving Care in the 1990s* survey, the forerunner of the survey in this book. I would also like to acknowledge Professor Colin Fletcher's and Dr. David Denney's, and Professor David Ward's comments on an earlier draft. I am especially grateful to all the following who were so kind as to find the time to act as readers for earlier sections: Lorna Whyte, Jane Greenhalgh, Barbara Fletcher, Julie Kent, Martin Hazelhurst, Sue Fowler, Peter Breathwick and Heather Loxley. A thanks is also extended to City Computing, London for its assistance with collecting and processing the data, to Andy Farringdon, also at De Montfort University, for advising me about SPSS for Windows, and to De Montfort University computer staff, Amanda Cook and Brian Darleston for their guidance. A particular thanks is also extended to NCH-Action for Children and to Helen Dent in particular for her support and permission to use some NCH material. A special thanks is also extended to those projects and areas which gave me permission to reproduce excerpts from their written material. These included leaving care projects within the London Boroughs of Wandsworth, Hackney, Sutton, Lewisham, Brent, and Hammersmith and Fulham, as well as the Mid Surrey Stepping Out project and the Royal Philanthropic Society, and Dudley social services department. I am also grateful to Wendy Thompson, at the Children's Society leaving care project, Derbyshire, for being given access to her Masters degree research study from De Montfort University into education and care leavers. To any others whose names I may have unintentionally left off this list and who helped me, thank you. My publisher has also been most helpful and offered guidance.

Finally a very special thanks is extended to my family, Denise, Jenny, and Jonathan Broad, for their love, support and understanding, especially during those periods when I was struggling with all the usual conflicting pressures of working full time, and being a husband and father of young children. Without all these people this book would have not been possible and my gratitude and love is extended to all of them.

Introduction

In discussing young people leaving care it is extremely difficult not to become drawn into the wide array of issues that face young people, especially those concerning young people leaving home. Important though such broad discussions are, this book is limited to discussions about young people leaving care set within the wider social context. Having established leaving care as the focus for the research and this book, a balance still had to be struck between a number of competing and complementary features. These included setting a balance between: the social context and practice content, the professional and the political, individual good practice and local authority policies, and, finally, between national and local developments, and the relation between all of them. In striving for such a balance, a particular understanding of the links between these features will reveal itself, namely that leaving care work and its associated political, managerial and professional activities do not operate in isolation from each other. Seen in this way it is folly, therefore, to describe leaving care work purely in professional terms. On the other hand, if only the political and policy debates are aired then this also presents a partial, and often unhelpful, picture to those working in the field. Next, a word about politics.

From 1979 to early 1997 Conservative governments were in power in the United Kingdom, during which time the Children Act 1989 was introduced. This book was completed soon after a new government, a Labour government, was elected in May 1997, much too soon for any new initiatives affecting young people generally to be announced and included here. At the time of writing, then, there was political uncertainty and unrealistically high expectations about changes to policies, probably further heightened by the 179 seat majority. Nevertheless, by examining the contents of its pre-election manifesto and first Queen's speech in May 1997, the book examines the issues emerging from the Labour government that could be relevant for young people leaving care. A suggested new agenda for young people leaving care, arising from the change of government, is discussed in the final chapter.

The book faithfully seeks to record the state of key leaving care developments in England and Wales between 1991 and 1997, set within the broader context of what has happened in the field since the Children Act 1989 was introduced. When parliament, through the Children Act 1989, placed a responsibility on social services departments in respect of helping young people leaving care, there were certain expectations. This book seeks to acknowledge those expectations as well as what has happened since, the needs of young people leaving care, and the work of leaving care projects. I have set out to undertake this ambitious task in the full knowledge that there will be important omissions.

Although the book contains many points about good practice, and illustrations of good local authority policies, it is not intended as a practical guide to practice. Such important and helpful practice guides are already produced by agencies working in the field. This book seeks to serve a different function to a practice guide by presenting further research evidence about leaving care work, reflecting on that and other evidence, as well as exploring policy and professional developments, and, not least of all, the practice consequences and recommendation that follow from the findings. How well this job has been done is for others, not me, to judge.

From one point of view it is a very comprehensive book, in that it describes and analyses leaving care projects that are working with over 3000 young people. In terms of subject areas covered, it has not been possible to go into depth about a number of related 'up and coming' research areas in this field. The area of health care for young people leaving care is not addressed at any length in this research (although perhaps it should have been), for the simple reason that at the time the research underpinning this book was conceived, health was not presented as a high priority for leaving care research. The fact that it has become an important issue can be shown by the increasing interest in the subject by the National Children's Bureau, the inclusion of health in the Social Services Inspectorate's national standards, and research being done elsewhere. For example, also based at De Montfort University, there is an action research health project about young people leaving care, in partnership with the Royal Philanthropic Society's Mid-Surrey Leaving Care project and East Surrey Health Authority (Saunders and Broad, 1997).

Although I am very aware that the issue of young people leaving care and parenting, and single parenting are issues which others have identified, and again seen as yet another important specialist area, it is not one that there was sufficient opportunity to discuss here, other than when the issue was raised by respondents. One could add to these health and parenting issues the specific health issues of HIV/AIDS, suicide and self harm, as well as those of poverty and offending. Some of those topics are discussed here, though not all of them, and, with the exception of poverty, none are discussed in depth. At some stage I had to stop. I had to decide what to include and what not to include. In the end I was guided by the views of those projects which kindly agreed to pilot the questionnaire, as well as my own gut feeling, about what was desirable, and pragmatically, what was possible, within the timescale and budget available.

Finally, this book is designed to make a positive contribution to all aspects of leaving care work, namely, the campaigning, lobbying, policy, professional and practice aspects. The energy for writing this book stemmed from my concerns, amongst many, that young people leaving care must get a better deal than they do at present. If this book makes some contribution to debates which might lead to any improvements for young people leaving care, then I will feel the effort will have been worthwhile.

Bob Broad
Leicester

PART ONE

Legal and Policy Perspectives

CHAPTER ONE

The Legal and Social Context for Young People Leaving Care

The main cause for concern is the considerable variation in the sort of assistance which can be expected, which is at present unacceptably dependent on geographical happenstance This wide variation in turn arises from the weak and confused state of the law in this respect...present legislation on continuing care for young people leaving local authority care is diffuse and misleading, and is by nature discretionary rather than obligatory. (Second Report from the Social Services Committee, Children in Care, 1984, referring to the Child Care Act 1980 (DHSS, 1984))

Introduction

The actions of young people leaving home or public care are guided by a wide range of factors, both internal, in terms of strengths, skills, and personality, and external, in terms of services, personal and financial supports, and facilities. It is because their actions and options are guided by these external factors, extending far beyond immediate child care concerns, that it is necessary to describe that legal and social context as well as the professional child care context. Therefore in this chapter, after providing an overview of the situation of young people in transition to adulthood, and given the major transition that young people must make from dependent child to becoming a young adult, the key social policy areas are detailed from a legislative perspective. Other pressing issues impacting on leaving public care, with a less direct social policy status than those presented here, and more concerned with 'the way things are done', namely the issues of children's rights and participation by young people in projects, are discussed in a later chapter. This chapter's aim is to provide the main legislative framework within which leaving care work takes place. Although there has been a change of government to a Labour government, in May 1997, it is much too early at the time of writing (May 1997) for any changes to be made to this framework. In any case, such is its history, depth, breadth and complexity that any substantial changes will take some considerable time to be introduced and take effect.

After presenting an overview of young people in transition, the chapter is in two parts: part one concerns children's legislation, and part two concerns other key legislative changes.

The key legislative areas affecting young people leaving care discussed here are:

- child care legislation: the Children Act 1989 – preceding legislation about leaving care, history and rationale
- education and the position for 16+s, given the low levels of in-care educational achievements
- welfare benefits, given the high proportion of young people leaving care without employment
- housing, given the inevitability of a move or moves on from care to other accommodation
- training and employment, given the considerable proportion of young people that seek, and in some cases obtain, one or other.

Overview: young people in transition

Being a young person aged between 16 and 21 growing up in England and Wales and seeking to leave home involves a range of financial, emotional, developmental, psycho-social and physical transitions. There is evidence that in the population as a whole the length of the transition from childhood to adulthood (i.e. the period of youth) is increasing (Jones, 1995) and becoming more complex. Jones describes youth as an extended period 'in which a gradual transition is effected between childhood and citizenship, mediated by the family and the state' (Jones, 1995:1). In order to successfully make the transition from being 'at home', however that is defined, to living away from home, requires the young person to have the following 'essentials': financial support and somewhere to live, coupled with a desire to leave home and the sort of resilient personality and friendship network which supports, and does not impede, independent living. If for one moment one assumed that this was a 'good practice' exercise for parents about what it would be desirable for young people to have in order to leave home to live elsewhere, it would most likely include the following: networks of support and friendships, good educational attainment level with anticipated enhanced employment prospects, good health, an earning potential, the right (i.e. agreed) timing for leaving home, and a certain maturity of personality on the young person's part. Financial issues are especially keenly felt in a climate of increased financial insecurity so far as the parents, as well as the young people, are concerned.

It would also be important to try to reach some sort of understanding, arriving at an agreement about when to leave home, where to move into, and with whom. There would probably be an expectation that the young person could return home if necessary, subject to further discussion perhaps.

This important transition, whose length is increasing as a result of reduced benefits for 16–17-year-olds and rising youth unemployment, has too often been regarded as a social problem, to be controlled by the family and/or eliminated through the provision of basic youth training schemes. It has not been regarded as a welcome and necessary right of passage worthy of government support, and perhaps this should not be surprising given the level of financial investment that is required. The fact that the problem is presented as one about who supports young people leaving home to live independently masks the real problem, which is about levels of youth unemployment (of which more later). After all, if a youngster leaves home and finds a job which pays for rent and living expenses, and does not come to the attention of any public service, then where is the problem?

However, the thrust of governmental policy, especially from the 1980s to the mid 1990s, has been to reduce the role of the state through reducing public expenditure and increasing individual, family and parental responsibilities. This social transformation, some would say social revolution, has taken the form of a change to the balance that previously existed between collective and individual rights and responsibilities. A statement by Sir Keith Joseph, a key member of the Conservative administration's cabinet in the 1980s, encapsulates that cabinet's ethos (quoted in Digby, 1989:90): 'In as much as personal responsibility has been eroded by a shift in housing, education, and welfare provision excessively to the state, we are trying to shift that responsibility.' Killeen (1992:201) strongly argues that since 1980 young people in the process of leaving home have been at the receiving end of this political shift which constitutes:

> ...a form of laboratory for the social policies which governments of the time have begun to introduce more slowly and cautiously to other sections of the population: the removal of wages council protection and reductions in legal pro-tection for those in work; an increase in discretionary welfare payments and a re-duction in basic benefits; a continued resistance to the idea that the state has a primary duty to protect the most vulnerable – such as the homeless. As the years have passed, the Government's agenda has become increasingly transparent; that once a person leaves the support of their parents' home their survival should be linked entirely to their playing an economic role within the market place. Those who remain unemployed are criticised...for missing the opportunities provided by the education system to adapt themselves to the requirements of employ-ers...those who choose to study...must increasingly look to parents or to part time and temporary employment for the money to pay for food and housing.

The fact that previous Conservative governments had introduced fundamental changes to the role of the state, placing more emphasis on the family to provide for its members, is not in dispute and it is not intended to reproduce here the evidence and arguments ably presented elsewhere (see, for example, Coleman and Warren-Adamson, 1992, in connection with social policies and young people). However, some basic statistics will help to set the scene about the changes to the situation concerning young people in Britain. For example, according to a British Youth Council's report (1996) young people in 1996:

- represent a significant but decreasing segment of the population – there are some 7,747,000 16 to 25-year-olds in the United Kingdom as of 1996
- are better educated than ever before
- make up a disproportionate number of the unemployed
- have low and falling wages
- appear to be under significant stress
- lead unhealthier life styles (especially concerning smoking and drinking)
- are finding it hard to set up home on their own.

In comparison with former times, and across a series of indicators, the position of young people in the United Kingdom is undergoing steady and ongoing changes. These changes significantly impact on young people seeking to make the transition from home or care to more independent living because the changes affect the capacity of young people to gain economic independence and therefore to pay for and live in separate accommodation. This is the critical point: the capacity to be financially independent. This then raises further questions, namely, at what age is this independence expected? How will it take place? Who will pay to support the young person making this transition? And, finally, what happens if, despite making the effort, it is not possible? The widespread difficulties about making this transition are summed up bluntly in a Coalition of Young People and Social Security (or COYPSS) report which specifically examined the options and opportunities available to young people from the age of 16 in their transition from school to the labour market. The report stated the concerns of many child care charities as being (1995:4):

- the transition from school to the labour market has become unacceptably difficult and complex, with young people facing a series of obstacles to gaining employment, education and training
- there is a lack of support for young people making this transition

- there is a lack of coherence and co-ordination between bodies responsible for aspects of the transition

- the options on offer to young people leaving school are limited

- many of the training schemes for young people are of poor quality and fail to prepare young people for employment or lead to jobs.

It is against this background of greater financial insecurity, major political changes and, one could add, ongoing changes to social services departments (SSDs), that the Children Act 1989 was introduced in 1991. As has been touched upon, this climate can be characterised by a political party, elected in 1979, committed to change. As will be demonstrated below by reviewing the key legislation, it wished to reduce public expenditure and direct taxation, increase the role of the state in terms of statutory policing powers but reduce its role in terms of social welfare provisions, and further reduce the powers of local authorities to raise revenue to extend services or to build additional social housing.

PART ONE: LEGAL AND SOCIAL CONTEXT – CHILDREN'S LEGISLATION

Background to the Children Act 1989

The drafting of the Children's Bill which then, with amendments, eventually became the Children Act 1989, took place within a certain political climate. Although difficult to fully appreciate and gauge now, to those working in the leaving care field there was a considerable build up of hope and expectation that the Children Act 1989 would make a real difference. For example, Stein writes:

> ...it is to be hoped that child care legislation in the 1988/9 parliamentary session will both strengthen and clarify the law to assist care leavers, and that the government will recognise the urgent need to review and reform its social security provisions for young people. For local authorities the most important issues raised by the research are those which identity their failure to behave as a caring parent and the possibilities open to them to do so. (1989:213)

It has been argued by Biehal et al. (1995) that there were three developments associated with the introduction of statutory changes to the leaving care legislation which eventually became incorporated into the Children Act 1989 legislation and which have subsequently accounted for the relatively high levels of publicity leaving care issues have received:

1. The first development was the force of the consistent evidence emerging from studies about the level of deprivation experienced by care leavers, and the problems they experienced when making the

transition from care towards independence (including Bonnerjea, 1990; Stein and Carey, 1986; Randall, 1988 and 1989).

2. The second development, especially in the 1970s and 1980s, was the way in which the messages of young people and those representing their interests became more vocal and formalised, especially through the medium of the National Association of Young People in Care (or NAYPIC), the Who Cares? Trust, and Black and in Care.

3. The third development is what can be called the professional child care lobby dedicated, in its various forms, to legislative reforms. In relation to aftercare, the term then used, these included the recommendations of the Social Services Committee Report on Children in Care or Short Report (DHSS, 1984). These recommendations were amended by the Review of Child Care Law (DHSS, 1985) and included in the White Paper 'The Law on Child Care and Family Services' (DHSS, 1987).

These three developments had social, legal and professional dimensions. The social dimension was and is concerned with the social context of the employment, housing, training, and education situation facing care leavers. Critically, it is also underpinned by the desire for young people to have further legal and social rights, to services and power holders. Such an agenda is still propounded by young people's groups, charities and lobby groups, of which there will be more analysis in Chapter Two. The Children Act 1989 simply could not deliver on this three-fold agenda, except in so far as it attempted, somewhat weakly and half-heartedly it now appears, to emphasise corporate, not departmental responsibilities. The legal dimensions and professional dimensions took forward the concerns of researchers and other academics about the shortcomings of the Child Care Act 1980 and research findings which pointed to the poor life chances of care leavers. Whilst the Children Act 1989 has been lauded as something of a victory in some quarters in relation to leaving care, upon closer inspection it seems that the gains are not as great as they are made out to be. However, before examining how it is different from the Child Care Act 1980, and the Children Act 1948, let us first look at the duties contained within the Children Act 1989 itself, to see what they provide for young people leaving care.

The main legislation: the Children Act 1989

The main legislation governing leaving care work is the Children Act 1989, the main principles underlying which are the promotion of the welfare of the child, work in partnership with parents, acknowledging the importance of families and the views of the child and of parents, and, finally, emphasis on the corporate responsibility of the local authority. The Children Act 1989 was introduced on the 14th October 1991. Prior to the Children Act 1989 the legal framework for leaving care work was the Child Care Act 1980. At the time of that 1980 legislation the social security legislation allowed 16- and 17-year-olds to receive social security payments and there were no lower levels of benefits for those aged under 25. It was also left as a discretionary matter for local authorities as to if and whether they defined young people leaving care as vulnerable, under the Housing (Homeless Persons) Act 1977.

The Child Care Act 1980's responsibilities towards young people leaving care, and the provisions of the earlier Children Act 1948, are summarised in order to highlight the level of differences between the sets of legislation over a 41-year period. Today a local authority's responsibility does not end once a child is discharged from care, and this has been the case in law for some considerable time. As can be seen from what follows, some of the responsibilities more popularly associated with leaving care and the Children Act 1989 originate from much earlier child care legislation, in some cases dating back to 1948, and possibly even earlier.

Duties concerning after/leaving care as contained in the relevant Children's Acts of 1989, 1980 and 1948

The Children Act 1989

- to advise, assist and befriend children who are looked after, with a view to promoting their welfare when they cease to be looked after (S24:1)

- to advise and befriend young people under 21 who were looked after by the local authority after age 16, or who were accommodated by or on behalf of a voluntary organisation and are known to the local authority to need advice (S24:2)

- to look after young people who qualify for advice: those who at age 16 were either in local authority care, or were provided with accommodation, including those compulsorily accommodated (young people on remand or the subject of a supervision order with a residence requirement) (S22:1)

- to advise the relevant local authority when a young person who they are advising and befriending moves to another area (S24:11)

- to establish a procedure for considering any representations, including any complaint, made to them by a person qualifying for advice or assistance about the discharge of their functions under this part of the Act (S26:3)

- it is the duty of the local housing authority to assist so far as this is compatible with that authority's own statutory duties (S27:2)

- to provide accommodation for any child in need who has reached the age of 16 and whose welfare is likely to be seriously prejudiced without accommodation (S20:3)
- young people aged 16 or over may be accommodated if they agree, despite their parents' objections (S20:11).

The Child Care Act 1980

- Section 28 of the Child Care Act 1980 stated that the local authority has a duty to advise and befriend any young person who was in voluntary care, unless the authority is satisfied that this is not required. This duty only applies to young people between 16 and 18 years of age who were in voluntary care on reaching 16.
- Section 69 of the Child Care Act 1980 gave the local authority the duty to advise and befriend any young person who was in the care of a voluntary organisation unless the authority is satisfied that this is not required or they have arranged for the voluntary organisation to offer aftercare.

The Children Act 1948

- Section 34 stated that a local authority was under a duty to advise and befriend anyone under the age of 18 who was, at or after his 16th birthday, in the care of the local authority or voluntary organisation, unless that organisation provides aftercare or the child's welfare does not require it.

- The authority was also placed under a general duty to provide aftercare at the request of a person under 21 who was in the care at, or at any time after, his 17th birthday but has now ceased to be in care. Later amending legislation phrased the duty as follows: The duty is to visit, advise and befriend him, and *'in exceptional circumstances' to give financial assistance.* (Children and Young Persons Act 1963 (S58), emphasis added)

COMMENT ABOUT DUTIES

Clearly the Children Act 1989 has extended the local authority duties, to a point. Yet the local authority had just two additional statutory duties placed on it in 1948 in respect of aftercare. Essentially, these duties focus upon advising and visiting young people after care, and these were not extended under the Child Care Act 1980. The extension of local authority duties towards young people leaving care as contained in the Children Act 1989 is a marginal one, with virtually no financial requirements being placed on local authorities. The list of powers is somewhat longer than the list of duties, and in respect of providing financial assistance, this has been downgraded over the years from a duty to a power.

Powers concerning after/leaving care as contained in the Children's Acts of 1989, 1980 and 1948

The Children Act 1989

- to advise and befriend other young people under 21 who were cared for away from home after the age of 16: young people accommodated by a health or education authority; young people in any residential care or nursing home (for a consecutive period of three months). This will include young people with a physical disability, mental illness or handicap, and those with educational and behavioural difficulties; young people privately fostered. (S24:2; 4; 5)

- to provide assistance in kind or, in exceptional circumstances, in cash, to any young person who qualifies for advice. Cash assistance may be subject to repayment and a young person or parent may be means tested unless in receipt of Income Support or Family Credit (S24:6; 7)

- to provide financial assistance connected with the young person's further education, employment or training. This power enables the local authority to contribute to expenses and the costs of accommodation so that a young person can live near a place where he or she is employed, seeking employment or receiving education or training (S24:8)

- education and training grants may continue beyond the age of 21 to enable a young person to complete a course (S24:9)

- to accommodate young people aged 16 to under 21 in a community home, provided the home takes young people who have reached 16, if they consider that to do so would safeguard or promote their welfare (S20:5)

- local authorities may request the help of other authorities, including any housing authority, to enable them to comply with their duties to provide accommodation (S27:1)

The Child Care Act 1980

Section 27 of the Child Care Act 1980 allowed the local authority the discretion to make contributions for accommodation and maintenance to assist with education and work. It applied to all young people leaving care between the ages of 17 and 21.

Section 29 allowed the local authority to offer advice and assistance (including financial help) to anyone formally in care (either statutory or voluntary care) after their 17th birthday up to the age of 21.

Section 72 allowed for local authorities to house anyone under 21 in a community home if it provided solely for children who are over compulsory school age.

The Children Act 1948

- In the Children Act 1948 (S20:1) the conditions that needed to be met concerning the provision of financial assistance aftercare were that the child be either 17 or more and no longer in the care of the local authority, or that s/he be 18 (whether or not s/he is still in care). In these cases assistance *could* be given at any time up to the young person reaching the age of 20 or towards the cost of accommodation and maintenance near the young person's place of employment, education or training.

- In respect of education, if a child was in care at any time after s/he reached the age of 17, grants *may* be given to that person while s/he is aged between 17 and 21 towards the cost of education and training.

- These grants *could* be continued even where the recipient had reached 21 if the course of study was still continuing or was later resumed after some interruption (Children Act 1948, S20:2; 3).

- The local authority had a power, not limited to children who were in or had been in care, to provide accommodation in a community home to persons aged between 16 and 21 who were working, seeking employment or studying nearby (Children Act 1948, S19).

COMMENT ON POWERS

There are then a considerable number of discretionary powers connected with leaving care work, as has been the case since 1948. On this key area of the legislation being, and continuing to be, *discretionary*, Stein and Carey's comments pertaining to the Child Care Act 1980 are still relevant today:

> …what its discretionary nature means in practice is not a developed aftercare service linked to local need, but sketchy, minimal and, in certain areas, non-existent provision…we would argue that until there is a universal system of mandatory grants covering maintenance fees and other costs then it should be a *duty* of local authorities to support young people on suitable courses. (Stein and Carey,1986:170–71, emphasis in original)

During the parliamentary session of 1988/9 the question of whose responsibility it was or should or could be for meeting the financial needs of young people leaving care as well as those who generally were without family support was discussed at length. In theory, had the government of the day agreed in principle to making financial provisions for young people leaving care, these financial responsibilities could have been included in the then Children Bill or through the Social Security Bill, discussing improvements in income maintenance. Yet the government of the day remained determined not to be seen as providing incentives to young adult offspring to leave the family home, conveniently ignoring the fact that the local authority is the legal parent to young people leaving care until they reach the age of 18.

In addition to the Children Act 1989 legislation there is comprehensive and helpful Department of Health (DoH) Guidance. What follows is a summary, in relation to leaving care or, as they describe it, aftercare.

Guidance notes about aftercare

Three general themes of preparation for leaving care are covered:

1. enabling young people to build and maintain relationships;
2. enabling young people to develop self-esteem;
3. teaching practical and financial skills and knowledge.

After leaving care most young people will continue to need some help, and the guidance notes (DoH, 1991) state that these may include any or all of the following examples:

- advice and information
- continued interest in young people's welfare, possibly by a person specified to advise and befriend the young person
- assistance in cash or kind
- return to care if necessary
- education and training (Education Department)
- accommodation (Housing Department and the SSD).

All these general principles, themes, points of guidance and general areas to be covered illustrate the considerable breadth of knowledge and skills that staff teams working in this area need to have in order to undertake their jobs effectively.

Guidance notes about leaving care guide, monitoring and financial responsibilities

In the guidance it is also stated that each local authority should provide written policies on leaving care which take into account the above principles and apply these policies to meet the needs of individual young people (DoH, 1991c). Each SSD is required to provide a written statement of its philosophy and practice on the preparation of young people for leaving care and the provision of after care support. Policy statements do not provide all the answers but they provide a framework for good practice and partnerships to develop. Policy statements need to specify corporate responsibilities, comprehensive, anti-discriminatory, flexible and informed by the views of young people themselves. Each SSD is also required to provide an easy-to-read guide to its services for young children when they leave care. Like the policy statement, this should include a brief guide to services available from other agencies.

A leaving care guide is to be produced and should contain information about: advice and befriending services available; financial entitlements from the local authority; the nature of help available from other agencies, including financial advice, in preparing young people for leaving care and supporting them when they have left care; details of youth counselling services; access to records policy and complaints policy and contact numbers for these agencies. It is further stated that it is desirable to monitor after care schemes and to evaluate them to see how effective they are, and that this should take place at regular intervals (DoH,1991:para. 7.61).

The guidance regarding care leavers' financial situation has been discussed at some length because of its intrinsic importance and because of the ways in which practice and policies have developed, as we shall see when the research findings are presented later in the book. It is recognised that after leaving care most young people will continue to need help which may include advice or information, a continued interest in their welfare, assistance in kind or cash, a return to care (these four are SSD responsibilities), education and training and accommodation. Thus the casework and welfare responsibilities remain with the local authority, but other responsibilities, also necessary for good parenting and survival, are much less clearly stated. In respect of financial assistance, the guidance states that:

> The primary income-support role lies with the Department of Social Security. However, local authorities may also give financial assistance to young people leaving care on account of their particular needs over and above those of other young people. (DoH, 1991:para. 7.69)

> Local authority powers to give assistance in cash or in kind are designed to meet the special needs of young people leaving care over and above the needs of other young people. They are not designed simply to duplicate the social security system, which is why the making of these payments is at the discretion of

the local authority... Local authorities will wish to note that any payments made to a young person under section 24 entitlement are not regarded as a part of his income or capital when his entitlement to Income Support, Housing Benefit, Community Charge Benefit or Family credit is being calculated. (DoH, 1991c:paras. 7.99 and 7.102)

It was clearly the intention of the legislation to put the main financial emphasis on the social security system and not social services. Yet, as will be illustrated later in this chapter, at the very same time the benefit system was being reduced in terms of its coverage, eligibility and levels, especially concerning the benefit entitlement of 16- and 17-year-olds.

Who qualifies for help leaving care under the Children Act 1989?

Section 24 does not only apply to care leavers but also to certain other young people who have reached their 16th birthday. Thus young people are entitled to help if they have been privately fostered, lived in an establishment run by a health or education authority for at least three months, been looked after by a local authority of a voluntary organisation, lived in a residential care home, nursing home or mental nursing home for at least three months. For the Children Act 1989 the definition of a child in need is:

- those unlikely to achieve or maintain, or have the opportunity of maintaining, a reasonable standard of health or development without the provision of services
- those whose health or development is likely to be severely impaired, or further impaired, without the provision of such services
- those who are disabled (S17:10)

Young people with disabilities

The guidance also states that local authorities must take account of the particular needs of young people with disabilities who, for the purpose of the guidance, are defined as 'blind, deaf, or dumb, or [suffer] from mental disorder of any kind or [are] substantially and permanently handicapped by illness, injury or congenital deformity' (S17:11) of the Children Act, DoH, 1991c). The term disabilities, then, is being used to describe what is now widely regarded as two different groups with different needs and problems: namely, those with physical disabilities and those with a range of learning difficulties. This is not simply a pedantic point but one which looks to this wide and, to my mind, misleading definition as one which fuses rather than clarifies particular needs. Nevertheless, the guidance states that in respect of these young people with disabilities, SSDs are required to ensure that they have access to information on special resources and services required to meet the particular needs of this varied group. They are also required to liaise with housing departments, education departments and health authorities. In discharging their responsibilities to these young people, local authorities also have to act within other legislation, particularly Section 2(1) of the Chronically Sick and Disabled Act 1970 and Sections 5 and 6 of the Disabled Persons (Services, Consultation and Representation) Act 1986. The latter are especially relevant because they are designed to ensure a smooth transition from full-time education to adult life for a young person who is subject to a 'statement of special educational needs'. Their intention is to require the relevant education department to obtain the view of the SSD as to whether such a young person is disabled.

The Children Act 1989 and approaches to anti-discrimination

The Children Act 1989 states that Britain is a multi-cultural society and that cultural background and beliefs are important. For each child and young person the importance of culture, language, racial origin and religion must be considered with other factors relating to their welfare (S22:5).

Under the Children Act 1989 the Local Authority has new duties to keep a register of children with disabilities and to provide services to same (Schedule 2, paras. 2 and 6). Existing powers already exist, under Sections 5 and 6 of the Disabled Persons (Services, Consultation and Representation) Act 1986, to carry out a disability assessment prior to leaving full-time education.

In the guidance (DoH, 1991c:107) under the heading of self esteem it is stated that:

> ...it is particularly helpful if young people are told as much as possible about their family background and about all aspects of their cultural and individual identity, e.g. race, language, culture, sex, religion and any physical or mental disability... (para. 7.52)

and:

> Young people with disabilities may also require a lot of counselling to enable them to accept themselves and to develop a sense of self-esteem. Gay young men and women may require very sympathetic carers to enable them to accept their sexuality and to develop their own self-esteem. And young people from ethnic minorities may need help – preferably from someone with the same background – to enable them to take a pride in their racial, cultural, linguistic and religious background. (para. 7.53)

It is also important to acknowledge the way in which this legislation interprets concerns about anti-discrimination. An anti-discriminatory approach would be one based on a recognition of systematic structural discrimination which recognises that dynamic action is required, underpinned by organisational targets and policies, and personal commitment. In respect of black young people, an anti-discriminatory approach is one based on acknowledging first and foremost, according to one's understanding, that racism is faced by most or all black people. The Children Act 1989 and associated guidance is concerned less with anti-discriminatory understandings and approaches than with encouraging non-discrimination, which is quite different, and to my mind a limited and dated understanding of anti-discrimination. The Children Act 1989 and associated guidance emphasises individual and not structural aspects, stressing that individual services be delivered in an 'appropriate way'. This is much more in line with an equal opportunity service perspective than anti-discriminatory practice, and this issue is taken forward in the book's chapter on anti-discrimination in leaving care work, as reported by projects.

In summary, as a whole the Children Act 1989 can rightfully be described as a major piece of legislation containing many progressive changes so far as children's services are concerned. Yet having described its provisions and the previous legislation governing after/leaving care, one can see that the act is a great disappointment so far as leaving care is concerned. This view will be examined and underlined further as the daunting scale of discretion shaping and directing leaving care practices and policies becomes all too apparent from the research. It is also vital to record here that developments in leaving care work are not simply guided by the Children Act 1989 but by other legislation to which attention is now turned, starting with education legislation.

PART TWO: LEGAL AND SOCIAL CONTEXT – OTHER LEGISLATION AND DEVELOPMENTS

Education legislation and developments

Since the 1980s the scale, direction and pace of change concerning all aspects affecting 16+s seeking education has been considerable. Schools, colleges, universities, the Training and Education Councils, and local education authorities have all been involved in one way or another. The Children Act 1989 makes the local authority as a whole responsible for promoting the welfare of looked after children (as opposed to children who have ceased to be looked after), starting with the Act's Guidance and Regulations.

The *Guidance and Regulations Volume 3 on Family Placements* (DoH, 1991c: 26) states that social workers are required to consider 'the applicant's attitudes and expectations in relation to education'. Furthermore any reviews of children in foster care have to consider the educational arrangements made for the child, and it is suggested that top priority should be given to continuity of education if children have to change placements. The point Aldgate *et al.* (1993) make is that these new requirements are in stark contrast to the absence of interest in official guidelines pre-1989. Their conclusion based on pre-Children Act research is that:

> ...there needs to be a change in attitude, both in social work practice and in training, so that the education of children looked after has high priority with both managers and workers. The view that children need to recover emotionally from bad life experiences before they can move on to new achievements must be challenged...educational achievement could be a factor in building confidence and self-esteem. (Aldgate *et al.*, 1993:33)

The majority of the literature concerning education and care relates to the education of younger school-age children being looked after and not the 16 or older age group of looked after young people, the group which is the concern of this book. Nevertheless, because the two groups are inextricably linked it is important to recognise the changing legislative framework and the concerns about it. The Education Reform Act 1988 and the Education Act 1993 were the first to switch power back from local education authorities to individual schools.

The *Education Reform Act 1988*, consisting of 238 sections, provided the most fundamental restructuring plan for education since the Education Act 1944. It conferred many new powers upon the Secretary of State and upon governors and head teachers at the expense of local education authorities. It sought to introduce competition in the provision of free education by reducing artificial restrictions on parental choice. According to one informed body, 'The changes to the distribution of power within the service, and the competitive influences operating on it, will rather come from the introduction of strong new forces working within established structures' (Advisory Centre for Education, 1989:1).

The relevant provisions of the 1988 Act were:

- the establishment of a national curriculum for all maintained schools
- the testing of pupils against attainment targets forming part of this national curriculum at approximately ages 7, 11, 14 and 16
- the delegation to governing bodies of all but the smallest schools of the control of school finance and staffing
- the establishment of a new category of grant maintained schools publicly funded but outside local education authorities control
- power to governors, upon a parental vote, to apply to the Secretary of State to become a grant-maintained school
- removal of polytechnics and colleges of higher education from local authority jurisdiction.

The law on exclusions, which will affect some young people, including those leaving care, was passed earlier, in Sections 22–26 of the *Education Act 1986*, and included:

- a clear delineation of powers between heads, governors and local education authorities

- a step-by-step guide to be followed by each local education authority

- the use of some safeguards to avoid arbitrary use of exclusion

- an independent appeals mechanism for parents of those pupils permanently excluded

- an independent appeals mechanism for governors in disagreement with the local education authority.

At the heart of the *1993 Education Act* was the government's desire to increase the size of the grant-maintained sector and further develop its managerial and financial structure. For that government the grant maintained schools are regarded as encapsulating all of the five great themes, namely quality, diversity, increasing parental choice, greater autonomy for schools, and greater accountability.

The 1993 Education Act was the biggest piece of educational legislation ever enacted in this country, (over twice the size of the 1944 Education Act) and as a result in the future the role of local education authorities is expected to be as enablers rather than providers of education. The 1993 Education Act is in six parts, all of which impact, directly or indirectly, on young people leaving care in some way or other. These six parts are concerned with responsibility for education, grant-maintained schools, children with special educational needs, school attendance, failing schools and miscellaneous items including school admissions and exclusions.

Section 261 abolished the category of indefinite exclusion as from September 1994, and it set a limit for fixed exclusions at an aggregate of 15 days in any one school term. Circular No 10/94 Exclusions from School (from the Department for Education) states that the purpose of these changes is to prevent exclusions lasting longer than needed, and to remove the uncertainty involved in indefinite exclusions. It is also intended that these arrangements for fixed period exclusions will give more flexibility to head teachers, so that normally head teacher would not normally use all 15 days in one exclusion period. The same circular suggests that exclusion 'should be used sparingly in response to serious breaches of school policy or law', although research by Berridge and Brodie (1997) points to developments in the opposite direction. They have found a 'dramatic' fourfold increase in exclusions from 3000 children in 1991 to 12,500 in 1995/6. They also found that younger children being looked after accounted for up to two-thirds of exclusions in one school, because of their emotional needs, and poor educational provision, co-ordination and support services for disadvantaged children (Berridge and Brodie, 1997:4).

Further and Higher Education

The Education Reform Act 1988 provided for greater delegation of budgets to newly constituted governing bodies for colleges of further education which from 1989 became independent corporate bodies, and the legislation also established two new funding bodies for higher education. Much greater pressure was placed on further education colleges to be self financing and competitive with sixth form colleges and further education.

In the circular *The Further and Higher Education Act 1992* (DFE, Circular /1, 1993), the establishment of the new Further Education Funding Council was described, which from 1 April 1993 took over the statutory duties in respect of the provision of full-time education for those 16 to 18. The Council also took over duties in respect of part-time education for those over compulsory school age and full-time education for those aged 19 and over.

The concerns of government regarding the education of young people in care and leaving care have been voiced through the production of occasional special circulars and reports.

Education Circulars and OFSTED

Circular 11/94 The Education by LEAs of Children Otherwise than at School provides guidance to local education authorities (LEAs) of education in school or otherwise, including pupil referral units. The aim is to return pupils to mainstream education as soon as possible. In May 1994 the Department for Education and the Department of Health issued a joint circular (DFE 13/94; DH LAC (94) 11) on the 'Education of Children Looked After', which reinforced the need for effective working partnerships between education and social services agencies. It was based on the assumption that satisfactory arrangements did not currently exist, and was one of a number of circulars issues at the time.

In respect of the education of children looked after a number of studies have pointed to the unsatisfactory situation about levels of attainment. The joint Social Services Inspectorate (SSI) and Office for Standards in Education (OFSTED) inspection report conducted in four areas in 1994 concluded, depressingly:

> The Education Standards achieved by the children [looked after] were too low. In primary schools more children achieved satisfactory standards than those of secondary schools where under-achievement was more widespread. A high percentage (25.6%) of the children at Key Stage 4 (14–16 years) had a history of poor attendance or were excluded from schools and did not have regular contact with education...social workers, teachers and carers did not give the children's educational progress and standards of achievement sufficient priority compared with the attention given to such matters as care, relationships and contact with parents. (SSI and OFSTED, 1995:3)

Importantly, the report also noted that the responsibility for the general educational oversight of the educational needs of this group was not clearly defined or located and stated that the changes from local education authority to individual school responsibilities was not sufficiently considered by social services departments when developing policies, strategic plans and procedures for the children. The effect of the macro education changes on 16–18 year olds outlined above is that the organisation and control of their education lies totally outside the control of their local education authorities. The other key effect of these changes, according to Jackson (1995), is that schools are now set in competition with each other and are reluctant to accept pupils who may cause trouble and are unlikely to improve their score in the exam league table. She then puts the position about the effect these changes of reduced local authority power will have on young people leaving care (Jackson, 1995:5):

> The stigmatisation which being in the care system carries combines with the reduced powers of local authorities to deny looked after children their rights to education. Many of them have to make do with a token five hours a week tuition. Many get nothing at all. How can they learn if there is no school for them to go to? They do learn of course-that they are of no importance and nobody cares about them.

In terms of information about looked after children gathered for that 1995 SSI/OFSTED survey across the four participating authorities, 360 (22.4%) were in the key stage 4 or 14–16 age group, and 202 (12.6%) in the post 16 age group. The report does not separate out this age group into separate age groups. Therefore it is not possible to make exact comparisons between the educational experiences of 16-year-olds being accommodated and those children, some 29%, according to Biehal et al. (1992) who move to independence at 16 years of age. What it is possible to say, however, based on the calculation that one-third of key stage 4 pupils are 16 years of age, is that an estimated 20% of the children in the OFSTED study were in the 16+ age group. A proportion of these 16+'s (estimated at 25% for the 14–16 age group) had a poor attendance record or who had been excluded. These broader changes to education are impacting on young people leaving care, although to what extent, for the over 16s, is difficult to establish precisely.

The more detailed requirements for all departments and agencies to co-operate with regard to young people with special educational needs and young people looked after can be found in the Children Act 1989, Sections 22 and 27; the Education Act 1993, Section 166; the Special Educational Needs Code of Practice (Department of Education, 1994a) and in Circular 13/94 (Department of Education, 1994b) which provides practical ways in which schools can secure advice and support from social services departments, social services personnel and foster carers.

Benefits legislation and developments

Since 1988 the social security system has been planned on the assumption that young people can look to their families for help until they reach the age of 18, when they are eligible for Income Support. Only when someone reaches 25 are they entitled to full rates of Income Support. *The Social Security Act 1986 and 1988* (S4) stopped benefits to 16- and 17-year-olds, and reduced Income Support and Housing Benefit levels to under 25-year-olds. It replaced the general entitlement to Income Support for young people aged 16 and 17 with a guarantee of a suitable offer of a Youth Training place. A small group such as single parents, young disabled people and carers were exempted. In addition, within the 1988 Act the Department of Employment provided an allowance of £15 per week for eight weeks where a young people had left work or training and could not find a training place. Partly as a result of lobbying, by Centrepoint and others, some changes were subsequently introduced to assist young people without family supports. Thus, albeit only in exceptional and discretionary cases of extreme hardship, young people can qualify for Income Support, which in any case only lasts for 12–16 weeks, according to the Social Security Act 1987, and the Credit and Income Support (General) Amendment Regulations 1989. In addition, the rate of Income Support for 16- and 17-year-olds living away from home *for good reason* was also increased to that given to 18- to 24-year-olds. Young people returning to the family home, relatives or friends are not entitled to Income Support.

Many young people leaving care have suffered both as a result of the abolition of householder status for under 25s and the withdrawal of Income Support, except in hardship cases which have to be proven, from 16- and 17-year-olds. There is evidence that care leavers find difficulty in completing training schemes (NACABS, 1992) and that applications for hardship payments include a disproportionate percentage, about 10 percent, of young people who had been in care (COYPSS, 1991). Three further changes to benefits introduced in the mid 1990s deleteriously affect a large proportion of care leavers.

The first change, about restricting severe hardship entitlements, followed the MORI (MORI, 1991) survey commissioned in 1990 by the Department of Social Security into 16- and 17-year-olds claiming Income Support under the severe hardship provisions. This study had found amongst other things that one in ten of the sample had been in care. The Conservative government tightened up the guidelines on severe hardship provision, with a view to achieving cost savings by the Department of Social Security. The emphasis on young people being required to have a more rigorous assessment and produce (written) evidence of hardship, combined with the existing delays in processing claims, produced further short term hardship, and homelessness whilst claims are being investigated and assessed.

The second change was the introduction of the Job Seekers Allowance in 1996, which further limits young people's entitlements to benefits. This allowance cut the period for which unemployment benefit is paid from one year to six months and is replaced at that point by a means tested benefit, namely Income Support. Job Seekers Allowance includes a requirement for people to sign the 'Jobseekers Agreement' confirming availability for work for 40 hours a week, and detailing steps taken to find work. There are harsher benefit sanctions against refusal to take a job or loss of job through 'own fault'. Young people aged 18 to 24 receive less in Income Support but the same unemployment benefit levels as their elders. These age based thresholds governing Housing Benefit and Income Support payments distinguishes those who benefit from 'adult legal capacity and independence' (Harris, 1992). According to Centrepoint (1997:7):

> There is also a[n]...obligation to sign a Job Seekers Agreement backed by a variety of sanctions. Officials will have the power to issue a Directive setting out what steps a claimant must take to increase their employability thus increasing the discretionary element of the system. Benefit sanctions will be extended from those failing to meet rules on being available for and actively seeking work, which are already sufficient, to those who refuse to sign an agreement or comply with the steps set out in the Directive. Severe hardship payments for those who break the rules will be much harder to obtain and even if awarded will not be given for the first two weeks of claim. Young people who refuse two training placements, reject jobs on the grounds that there is no training element or who leave two training placements will be subjected to a penalty of a forty per cent cut in benefit for two weeks.

With the Job Seekers Allowance benefits are paid in arrears, and this already causes severe problems with rent deposits and food purchasing, and Housing Benefit can take several weeks to process, which can make it virtually impossible to obtain certain accommodation (such as emergency bed and breakfast accommodation). The payment of housing benefit in arrears will greatly restrict access to the private rented sector for single people on low incomes. Thus the parent state requires these young people and others to prove that they are capable of independent living, while at the same time making it financially impossible for them to do so. As the National Children's Bureau (under)stated prior to these harsh changes being planned, 'Neither the social security legislation nor the child welfare legislation cater adequately for young care leavers' (National Children's Bureau, 1992).

The third concerns Housing Benefit introduced under statutory instrument (Department of Social Security, 1996). As a result, under 25s were no longer entitled to receive a full range of subsidised social housing. The only type of housing which will qualify is 'shared and non self-contained accommodation in the private rented sector'. Rent officers will now ask to determine the local 'single room rent' for the area, and this will set the limit for any rent used in the calculation of housing benefit for the under 25s. There is also a link to the Job Seekers Allowance in that young people should not be deterred from taking a low paid job by the fear of losing a large amount of housing benefit tied to a high rent. Although some categories of under 25s were exempt, including, for example, those living in specified accommodation where care, support or supervision is provided, these changes may directly affect young people living in supported accommodation, a most popular and expanding housing type for young people leaving care. These changes, according to SITRA News (SITRA Bulletin, February, 1996):

> ...are clearly aimed at encouraging landlords to convert self-contained accom-
> modation not bedsits and shared housing, despite the health and safety risks as-
> sociated with houses in multiple occupation... The result will be to ghettoise
> young single claimants in sub-standard private rented accommodation... The
> proposed changes will effectively exclude young housing benefit claimants
> from self-contained accommodation in the private rented sector.

All these changes emphasise the 1980–1990s Conservative administrations' ideological pursuit of the self supporting family, not forming a partnership with the state, but instead looking after and paying for the care of its young offspring until they obtain gainful employment. This approach deterred and frustrated even further young people's struggle to meet their intentions of 'moving to independence' without recognising the special situation of young people leaving care and other categories of young people, such as the homeless. This leads us neatly into to the vexed and complex subject of housing itself and the legislation effecting young people leaving care.

Housing legislation and developments

This section discusses housing legislation other than the aforementioned powers contained in the Children Act 1989. The Housing Act 1996, enacted in December 1996, replaced the Housing Act 1985 (which succeeded the 1977 Homeless Person's Act) so far as the statutory responsibility for dealing with the homeless is concerned. Yet a presentation of the Housing Act 1996, in isolation from the previous relevant legislation, will not make a lot of sense, in part because the impact of the Housing Act 1996 is still unknown. Thus the earlier acts' duties will now be summarised, in order for readers to fully appreciate the changes brought in by the Housing Act 1996.

Previously under the *Housing Act 1985* if a person was homeless, in a priority group and not deliberately homeless, a local authority must secure indefinite housing for that person and anyone also with whom they might reasonably expect to reside (S65:2, 1985 Act). The duty was mandatory, not an exercise of discretion by the local authority. The duty could be discharged by providing council accommodation, by transferring the housing duty to another housing association or in the private sector (S69:1, 1985 Act). Through the Housing Act 1985 homeless young people could be re-housed whether with or without an associated family.

The *1988 Housing Act* had made it more difficult for young people to gain access to low cost housing, with a reduction in protection for tenants and the ending of rent restrictions in the private sector. Although noting that age is not a criteria in itself for vulnerability, the 1991 Homelessness Code of Guidance for local authority listed the conditions, including those who have been physically or sexually abused and 'those leaving local authority care', under which a homeless young people *could* (note not *must* or *would*) be considered 'at risk' and therefore vulnerable. However 'even' Codes of Guidance, especially those which themselves are full of 'should be' not 'will be' phrases (the former a feature of much of the legislation in the leaving care field), are for guidance only and are not binding on local authorities, as we will see, to anywhere approaching the position where young people leaving care and therefore homeless can then secure housing. One survey revealed that only half of the responding housing authorities said that they would deem as vulnerable homeless young people with no parents and no support (Abrahams and Mungall, 1989:7). Yet the Guidance to the Children Act 1989 (para 9.82) states that the primary responsibility (for the provision of accommodation for young people leaving care) lies with the housing department of the local authority. The 1991 Homelessness Code of Guidance (para. 6.15) recognised this responsibility and stated:

> Thus whilst there is no formal correlation between the definition of vulnerability in the Housing Act 1985 and 'serious prejudice' (or 'need') in S20 of the Children Act 1989, the two might be expected to arise in similar circumstances and housing authorities will need to have regard to a social services authority's or department's assessment that its housing authorities have an obligation to provide a child with accommodation under 20 (1) or (3) of the Children Act 1989.

The 1991 Homelessness Code of Guidance (para 9.82) also had two let out clauses for housing departments:

> ...the Children Act 1989 requires the housing authority to respond to that request if it is compatible with its own statutory duties and obligations and does not unduly prejudice the discharge of its functions and the priority afforded to providing housing for young people leaving care *is a matter for local consideration.* (emphasis added)

The Housing Act 1996

In 1995 the previous government launched the White Paper 'Our Future Homes' and one of its key proposals was reforming the homelessness legislation and the Housing Act 1996 enacted those proposals. As with any legislation it takes time before the effects, here in respect of care leavers, are known. The main change to previous housing policy is that local housing departments no longer have a duty to provide permanent housing for priority needs homeless households. They are given a duty to advise and assist priority needs households who are homeless and to ensure suitable temporary accommodation (up to two years) is available. Because of this act's potential impact on young people leaving care, its main provisions and guidance are listed here:

- The Housing Act 1996 made no reference to young people leaving care but the Code of Guidance on parts V1 and V11 made a number of references to this group. This includes considering the housing needs of this group when setting age limits for waiting lists, planning and co-operation between housing and social services (S7:5), and consideration of the vulnerability of this group when setting criteria for priority need.

- The Act requires local housing authorities to keep a housing register of people or households who qualify for the allocation of settled (i.e. long term) housing. Priority homeless households will be placed on the housing register and unless they fall within one of the 'reasonable preference' categories specified under the Act or by the local housing authority they will be *given no priority in the allocation of permanent housing.* (emphasis added)

- Every housing authority is to have an allocation scheme which determines both priorities and the procedures to be followed in allocated housing.

- Local authorities have a duty to secure short term housing for those homeless and in priority need, and this includes young people who are vulnerable.

- The requirement to give reasonable preference to certain groups within the local authorities allocation schemes laid out in S167:2 of the Act in effect replaces the former points system for assessing housing need.

- Local authorities should consider certain factors or groups including 'those leaving or who have been in local authority care' when assessing vulnerability (S14:10, of the guidance); other criteria, for example, those with learning difficulties, would also apply to some young people leaving care.

According to First Key (First Key, 1996b), the guidance should encourage those authorities and those social services departments experiencing difficulties in making joint arrangements with their housing departments. It remains to be seen if and whether the Labour government elected in 1997 will change the direction of housing, and indeed other policies affecting young people leaving care.

Housing Issues and Leaving Care

In addition to changes concerning housing legislation affecting the homeless (and young people leaving care), a series of other major legislative changes introduced since the 1980s affect young people leaving care concerning entitlement to, and availability and affordability of, accommodation. Some of these changes have been about all important housing finance and not strictly about housing provision. These changes can be summarised as:

- 'the right to buy' policy under the Housing Acts of 1980,1984, 1985 and 1986 served to further accelerate the general reduction in the overall housing stock, and left the lower quality and less marketable properties for rent

- the abolition of the 1977 Rent Act protection and the protection of 'secure tenancies'. The council rents were brought into line with the private sector (i.e. increased)

- increase in Housing Association rents as a result of the shift from government funding to private loans (Local Government Association Act 1985; Housing Act 1988)

- changes in income support and housing benefit rules, and the introduction of age related benefit system (Local Government and Housing Act 1989, S81, Social Security Act 1986 and 1988)

- removal of Wages Council protection for under 21s (Wages Act 1986)

- abolition of 21 hour earning rule, preventing financial support for young people continuing studies (Employment Act 1988)

- removal of grants for rents in advance (Local Government and Housing Act 1989)

- implementation of a discretionary Social Fund offering loans repayable via benefit deductions (Local Government and Housing Act 1989)

- limitations of length of stay in temporary accommodation for young people under 26 (Board and Lodging Regulations 1985)

- in 1995 maximum housing benefit levels were set which encouraged landlords/ladies to increase rents (see Walentowicz, 1995).

The case is put by several commentators, (for example Kirk *et al.*, 1991; Jones, 1995; and Hutson and Liddiard, 1994) that youth homelessness, of which young people leaving care is a significant part, is an increasing problem for a variety of reasons. These include the increased emphasis on the purchasing of houses and the associated decline in the amount of rented property available, and for young people, affordable rented property. If young people must find independent accommodation and move away from home (if indeed they have one), then such accommodation is not only increasingly rare, but beyond their financial reach. As Doogan points out (1988:91), 'youth homelessness is but one symptom of the deteriorating economic position of young people that has its roots in the restructuring of the world of work.'

There are problems with the homelessness legislation for young people leaving care because the legislation does not apply until literal or threatened homelessness has arrived. This is not the main accommodation issue for care leavers. The question is more about access to accommodation, namely which route – the housing legislation or the Children Act 1989 legislation route – is the most appropriate for young people leaving care?

The toughest battles arise with the 16- and 17-year-olds about to leave care. If they start their search for a new home with the housing authority they may well be accepted as homeless and 'vulnerable as a result of…some other special reason' according to the earlier legislation that applied during the research period (S59: 1C 1985, Housing Act) or satisfy the council they are in 'priority need' (pregnant or physically disabled). However, if that authority uses its discretion (under S72 of the 1985 Act) to call on social services to exercise its functions, and it is satisfied under the 'child in need' interpretation of the relevant Children Act 1989 (S17: 10), both authorities will come under a duty to provide housing. The housing authority will say it has discharged its duty by arranging for social services to accommodate (S69:1 1985 Act) and social services will accept the duty and then ask the housing authority to discharge it (S27 1989 Children Act). The young people will be stuck in the middle unless both authorities devise tighter criteria. For example, if the young person starts at the local housing authority they may well discover the authority finding fewer young people 'vulnerable' because they can go to social services for housing and are thus not 'vulnerable'. Social services will say that the young people will not be prejudiced by failure of social services to provide accommodation because the local housing authority should accept them as 'vulnerable'. Again, young people will be stuck in the middle with both authorities disclaiming, rather than seeking to transfer, their responsibilities. As Hutson and Liddiard (1994:104) conclude in writing on youth homelessness:

> Crucially, however, it is evident that without a resolution of the acute shortage of housing and local authority funding that lies behind the interpretations of

the Housing Act and the Children Act, they are unlikely to have a significant impact upon the youth homelessness problem in the UK.

There is then a 'tough and getting tougher' housing climate in so far as housing for young people leaving care is concerned, again with all the accompanying unhappiness and deleterious effects this causes. It becomes even easier to understand the popularity of supported lodgings for this group in the light of these housing problems and restrictions.

Youth Training

Youth Training (YT) replaced the Youth Training Scheme (YTS) in 1990 as the primary training scheme for unemployed young people, and is planned to change again under the Labour government, at least according to its manifesto (Labour Party, 1997). An understanding of youth training's history and development is nevertheless vital to appreciate the critical part it plays in many young people's lives.

The YTS developed amidst growing concerns about rising unemployment about young people and after a succession of special training programmes developed by the Manpower Services Commission. The early Youth Opportunity Programmes or YOPS were introduced in 1977, not for all unemployed young people but only for the most disadvantaged, and the courses were usually for six months. In 1983 the Youth Training Scheme was introduced, not as a short-term scheme aimed at the most disadvantaged but made available to all unemployed young people to act as a bridge between school and work. In 1986 the scheme was extended to two years and was reinforced by the removal of entitlement to housing benefit and income support for those under 18 years of age. This removal of social security benefit entitlements for 16- and 17-year-olds combined with the encouragement being given to two year training programmes combined to discourage young people from moving away from home, thus having most awkward consequences for those not living at home, and being 16 and 17 years of age, such as young people leaving care. YT is mainly government funded and is operated through the increasingly commercial Training and Enterprise Councils (TECS) and local enterprise companies (LECs).

After its introduction in May 1990 Youth Training continued to guarantee a training place to all unemployed school leavers, with the rates to the young people continuing as under the previous youth training scheme, but the rate being paid to employers being reduced by a sixth, to £30.50 per week. If a young people refuses to take up a training place they do not receive the training allowance, and benefit has been removed for 16- and 17-year-olds. The stated aims of Youth Training are:

- to provide help for young people to acquire the broad based skills necessary for a flexible and self-reliant workforce
- to meet the skill needs of the local and national economy, including in particular the need for technician and craft-level training
- to provide participants with training leading to National Vocational Qualifications (NVQs), at or above Level 11 standard.

The provision of Youth Training Credits (YTCs) is another potential way of delivering training to young people as it aims to give 16- and 17-year-olds a voucher worth between £1000 and £5000 with which to purchase approved training from an approved trainer, usually a college of further education. The official national purpose of YTCs is to expand the training of young people, especially 16- and 17-year-olds, by motivating the individual to train to higher standards, encouraging employers to invest in training and establishing an efficient market in training (Employment Department, 1994). Other aims include minimising the number of young people entering jobs without training, and making a fresh start where Youth Training's local reputation is low. It is further claimed that YTC's will improve the position of trainees with special needs, by ensuring equality of opportunities. The funding of TECs is well beyond the scope of this book, except to say that there have been continual funding cut-backs to their work, and some local TECs have been forced to close due to shortage of income/funding. As well as the overall effect of such measures and incidents, funding shortages have had a particularly negative effect on young people with special needs, whether physically disabled or having learning difficulties. This issue has been discussed in parliament on several occasions, and raised by Baroness Sear. For example, in 1992 in a debate entitled 'Training and Enterprise Councils' information was provided to the debate that in one county alone, Somerset, some 500 17- and 18-year-olds were without training scheme places, and therefore receiving no social security. The inconclusive answer (Hansard, 1994) from the government minister at that particular debate was that additional funds were being provided to TECs in the following year, 1993, for a declining number of young people waiting to go onto such schemes. These schemes provide a very low rate of training allowance and have an increasingly compulsive element. The key to successful Youth Training Schemes should be their availability, their appropriateness and their quality. The research findings later in this book about youth training schemes do not point to increased availability or enhanced quality.

Concluding comments

The legislation affecting young people generally, whether about their education, housing and housing benefits, benefits generally, or youth training, is designed to reinforce the financial responsibilities of parents and reduce the role of the state in financing young people seeking and/or having to live away from home. Yet this dominant philosophy, at least from the early 1980s to 1996, to increase parental responsibility does not seem to apply to the corporate parent (i.e. the state), of young people leaving care. The legislation during that period was designed to reduce public expenditure and the role of the welfare state. There remains increased competition for these reducing public resources, especially in housing and education, and an underlying presumption that young people be given a very limited number of opportunities to try again, whether this relates to housing, education, or youth training. The direction of social policy has been away from the collective entitlements or services towards reducing entitlements, or the purchasing of individual service packages, with the social services departments as enablers not providers. This is already the case with the purchase of community care packages following assessments. Another example is for cash vouchers to be made available for young people at 16 to purchase the sixth form education of their parents' choice, whether in a school or sixth form college, or college of further education (*The Guardian*, 1996a).

Although the Children Act 1989 produced a most welcome new legal framework for leaving care work, by far the majority of the responsibilities, and all those requiring resource inputs, have power and not duty status, thereby allowing less scrupulous or caring local authorities to introduce minimal changes and still fall within the law. Some of the 1989 legislation, such as the provisions relating to financial assistance in general and those relating to financial support for young people leaving care for their education needs, are virtually the same as those contained in the Children Act 1948, the Children's and Young Person's Act 1963, and the Child Care Act 1980. For many years the broader social and financial context has been one which discourages and prohibits the very financial investments in services needed by young people leaving care. There are no immediate signs that the legislative and social climate is changing in these young people's favour. This makes the list of achievements described in this book all the more remarkable, but it points to the 'services as a lottery' scenario, reinforcing the view that whatever the political party in power, a fundamental review of leaving care legislation and provisions remains necessary, an argument which is further developed in the last chapter after the research findings are presented.

CHAPTER TWO

Research Messages and National Developments in Leaving Care

Introduction

The aim of this chapter is twofold: to summarise leaving care research and policy messages, and to record national developments in leaving care work since the introduction of the Children Act 1989. There has been a range of information produced about leaving care developments since the Children Act 1989 was introduced in 1991. This information stems from official publications, such as the annual Children Act reports (DoH, 1993; 1994; 1995) Social Services Inspectorate Reports, government sponsored research and developments (of the former see, for example Biehal *et al.*, 1995; regarding the latter, see First Key, 1996b, c, d), or independent research and developments, mostly from the voluntary sector (for example Action on Aftercare Consortium, 1996; Broad, 1993; Save the Children, 1995). All these sources complement each other to provide a valuable potpourri of information and provide a diversity of ideas. Although as a result of the Children Act 1989 the technical terms 'ceased to be looked after' or 'ceased to be accommodated' could be used to describe the young people in leaving care research including this study, the more succinct terms 'in care' and 'leaving care' are used instead. This is because the aforementioned technical terms are awkward, and they do not enjoy popular currency, either with projects which work with these young people, in research, or with the young people themselves. However, where the official literature, or other studies, use those terms, they will be included here and elsewhere in the book. There is a wide range of research evidence about leaving care work produced with government funded research usually being less critical, as one might expect, of the political dimensions of government policies. The first period chosen for analysis is the period immediately prior to the introduction of the Children Act 1989.

Leaving care research prior to the Children Act 1989

This section will examine research into leaving care work from 1986 up to 1991. Stein and Carey's seminal work (1986) raised and anticipated many of the key issues central to leaving care work and their study included not simply an analysis of the problems facing care leavers but also an analysis of the previous legal framework (Child Care Act, 1980), and the policy and practice framework, and shortcomings leading to recommendations for change and improvements. This book established a clear benchmark for all future research, described the campaigning history of leaving care work, local authority planning inadequacies, and pointed to the shortcomings of the legislation (then the Child Care Act, 1980).

Stone's research, based on a survey of leaving care schemes (1990), concluded that whilst most leaving care schemes provided accommodation, the staff profile of the teams suggested that they were not well placed to provide a wide variety of other services needed. Another conclusion was that further clarification of leaving care schemes' roles *vis-à-vis* residential services and existing provisions was also necessary, and that better planning between housing and welfare agencies was also necessary. Bonnerjea's work (1990) examined leaving care work in the London boroughs and concluded that 'for half the authorities in London there are neither borough wide policies nor individual plans for young people' and that 'leaving care plans for individual young people were so often ad hoc and were dependent on resources such as housing which was increasingly difficult to have access to' (Bonnerjea, 1990:41). She concluded:

> *in most local authorities in London there are no formal policies about leaving care.* It remains the responsibility of field social workers, sometimes with residential workers. It is not generally regarded as a separate activity that requires special training or departmental policies or monitoring procedures. However some local authorities have developed specialist provision, usually a small team of workers who work intensively with some young people or more broadly with all of them. The rationale for specialist provision seems clear: it can be justified in terms of prevention, it has clear benefits in terms of providing a systematic method for helping all care leavers leave care and for identifying problems early after they have left. Some broad preparation together with somewhere to go for help afterwards seems more important than prolonging residential placements or giving young people large sums of money to leave with. *It is paradoxically the ability to come back that seems the most important part of effective policies for leaving care.* At the same time that the rationale is clear and convincing, the practice is less clear. Local authorities that have specialist provision use different models, each with many advantages and lots of successes. *But there is as yet no local authority which in practice does smooth the way out of care for all young people, black and white, with and without young children.* (emphases added)

The *Patterns and Outcomes* report (DoH, 1991b:11–12) stated that the messages that came through from various studies were:

- care leavers often experience periods of semi-homelessness and frequent moves

- the ex-care population are heavily over-represented in the destitute young peoples groups found in inner cities

- even when granted a tenancy this group often find themselves lonely and unable to cope financially

- to be fully effective specialist preparation for independence units must have access to suitable permanent accommodation

- discharge to independence is occurring at increasingly younger ages

- of young people from ethnic minority groups in public care there is a grossly disproportionate number of those of mixed parentage

- there are fewer black than white children admitted for long-term care

- admissions with the aim of 'temporary care' are much more common for young Afro-Caribbean and African children than for any other group

- there are fewer compulsory admissions of black children.

Garnett's research was based on information about 135 young people leaving care based on interviews with their last social workers, and other data sources, following up the sample from the original six Child Care Now (Rowe *et al.*, 1989) authorities. Her main findings were:

- although other varied sums of money were made available none of the participating authorities paid a leaving care grant (although financial assistance could be made available under S27 and S29 of the 1980 Child Care Act)

- none had specific (i.e. specialist) provisions for the aftercare of young people

- more than half of the small group with continued befriending by social workers for two or three years after leaving care (two thirds of the group), with the majority within that group being women, had either moved into care in their teens and moved into independent lodgings, or been in care for many years and had many unsettled placements.

- there were two thirds for whom there were no firm plans to continue social work contact after they had left care (in some cases they were not seen as needing it because of other support elsewhere or chose not to want the support)

- a further group did seek latter help, mainly in connection with housing and benefit problems. (Garnett, 1992: 110–111)

Garnett made a number of important conclusions, which can be summarised here as:

- imposing additional duties on local authorities without a parallel increase in resources is unlikely to improve the position of young people leaving care
- extending social work duties whilst cutting back in other areas makes little sense since the success of many leaving care policies and schemes largely depends on young people's access to these other resources
- many local authorities will need to conduct a major review of their leaving care work and policies to comply with the Children Act 1989 requirements
- flexibility of service provision will be difficult to provide
- improved monitoring of services is required
- less disruptive movement in the run up to discharge from care is necessary if there are to be less placement breakdowns
- the common practice of discharging young people to foster care at an increasingly younger age combined with the lack of suitable and/or permanent move on accommodation to produce placement breakdowns
- there was often a lack of formal planning at the time the young people were discharged from care
- the majority of the young people had totally insufficient material means
- leaving care plans need to be longer term and better planned
- improving the life chances of these young people leaving care requires more than changing the process by which they leave care but the process could and should be less sudden and less stigmatised
- local authorities will need to do more preventive work with black young people leaving care, especially in predominantly white areas
- the ways in which befriending is interpreted and structured requires further planning and resources and less discretionary actions.

Biehal *et al.*'s (1992) study also makes an important contribution to this field. It consists of the findings of a survey of 183 young people from three local authorities, based on social worker completed questionnaire, and was the first published research from the 1990–94 leaving care research project conducted by Leeds University. The sample consisted of young people who were discharged from care prior to the introduction of the Children Act 1989 in 1991. The findings confirmed those of others in respect of 'their problems' whether concerning poor education, housing and employment situations. The research provided important findings, first then in relation to black young people leaving care. Thus (Biehal *et al.*, 1992:36):

- young people of 'mixed origin' were by far the largest sub-group of the young people from minority ethnic groups

- young people from minority ethnic groups were likely to enter care younger and stay longer

- proportionately more black young people remained in full-time education and, as a group, they were slightly more successful in gaining qualifications.

The more general findings from Biehal *et al.* were that:

- young people with special needs were particularly over-represented among the homeless in the sample

- one in eight of the young people already had children by the time they moved to independence or legally left care

- just under one-third of the sample (n=179) had moved to an independent living situation before their 17th birthday and nearly two-thirds had moved before their 18th birthday

- young people are having to manage on very low levels of income.

Leaving care research post Children Act 1989

The Save the Children (SCF) study of young people leaving care was largely conducted by young people themselves, guided by SCF staff and based on 77 interviews of young people leaving care and 21 staff interviews. As well as findings which confirmed those above about the appalling poverty of care leavers, a key findings was that many 'found care affected their health badly, linked to diet and mental health. Several were underweight and more women than men were not eating enough. Health preparation in care was inadequate' (SCF, 1995:36). The young people also found that the top-up payments by social services interfered with and reduced their benefits. The researchers made a large number of practice recommendations, the main ones being:

- young people of 16 and over should be entitled to benefit in the same way and at the same rate as those over 25 years

- social services must ensure care leavers under 21 years have enough to live on (minimum level, benefit at current over 24 years rate)

- youth training should not be (effectively) compulsory

- there should be a minimum wage for young people

- tapers on housing benefit should be altered to increase take home pay from low waged work
- social services must ensure young people get help to find work and understand employment opportunities
- social services must ensure proper finance and support is available from care to continue or return to education (at any level) up to 24 years
- social services must ensure that young people in and from care are supported and encouraged at school, and encouraged in education beyond 16 years
- there should be choices regarding housing and a minimum of £2000 leaving care grant is required to provide essential items and meet starting up costs.

The research's policy recommendations (SCF, 1995:39) were:

- the Children Act 1989 should be reviewed to ensure that the welfare of 16–21-year-olds in and from care is being promoted
- good practice should be identified by children and young people and shared nationally
- more resources should be made available from central government to ensure that duties and responsibilities under the Children Act 1989 are met fully and properly
- social services must ensure that young people make decisions and are involved in leaving care processes and that staff understand their definitions
- young people should be involved in the training of staff
- discrimination against young black people must be recognised and fought.

This author's earlier leaving care survey for the Aftercare Consortium (Broad, 1994c) was conducted with the aim of establishing the extent to which the Children Act 1989 had been implemented as well as examining the social context in respect of leaving care work. The survey collected data from 25 projects working with 1538 young people leaving care. It concluded that in nine areas of social policy effecting leaving care work there had been a significant deterioration. These concerned:

- the availability and accessibility of Housing Benefit payments
- the situation concerning income support for under 18s
- the extent and availability of community care grants
- the extent and availability of loans from the Social Fund

- the availability and level of education grants
- the availability of financial support during vacation periods
- the funding, availability and appropriateness of youth training courses
- financial support from social services.

The survey revealed that the *only* area of substantial improvement for leaving care work was the availability of supported lodgings, which was also the most common accommodation type being used. The survey's findings that young people leaving care were largely unsupported in the majority of social areas necessary for living led this author to conclude that 'leaving care work is unsafe in the hands of the Children Act 1989'.

Another post Children Act 1989 research study, Acting in Isolation (McCluskey for CHAR, 1994), set out to evaluate the effectiveness of the Children Act 1989 for young homeless people, a proportion of whom are young people who have left care. Its key findings were:

- social services departments are, in the main, failing to fully implement the Children Act 1989 for homeless 16- and 17-year-olds
- there were noted improvements in the areas of joint work with housing departments, joint policies, links with voluntary organisations and housing associations, publicity and audits of need
- there was a deterioration concerning undertaking of assessments, recording and monitoring, links with agencies other than those listed above
- there were inconsistent and complex assessment procedures
- homeless 16- and 17-year-olds faced problems at the point of access and were frequently being referred onto other agencies without...being assessed.

The report's conclusions were:

Acting in isolation, the Children Act 1989 has not been able to meet the needs of young homeless people. It has not altered or affected the crucial policy areas of social security, employment, training and housing that impinge on young people's lives...the solution to youth homelessness does not lie in one piece of legislation but requires *strategic action across a range of government departments*. This would tackle the key issues of youth unemployment, the need for improved and increased training opportunities, the shortage of affordable accommodation, and the restoration of income support for those under 25. (McCluskey, 1994:6; emphasis added)

Biehal *et al.*'s major study (1995) concentrates on professional/practice child care issues as well as discussing outcomes, and questions about which model of leaving care services might work best. It contains such a volume of research findings and discussion that it is not possible to summarise its findings here, and instead it will be referred to throughout this book. The book's particular contribution to the field lies in its recording of young people's experiences, its comprehensive analysis of the key issues, and its listing of helpful summary points at the end of each chapter. The three sets of interviews of the 74 young people were conducted between January 1992 and January 1994 (Biehal *et al.*, 1995:10–13), that is, post Children Act 1989 implementation in October 1991.

Morris's research and policy review concerns disabled children leaving care. After criticising much of the research about leaving care for excluding discussions about young people with physical disabilities, Morris (1995) raises many critical issues for this group, including:

- for many disabled young people leaving care the issue is more one of *barriers to leaving care* rather than support after leaving care

- these young people can and do easily fall between children's and adult services in the world of community care and purchaser–provider developments

- if genuine needs-led assessments, not resource-led assessments were carried out, this could result in access to services which meet their needs and prove an 'empowering experience' as they move into adult services

- whether disabled children who 'leave care', or seek to, are simply moved to adult residential care, and given no other options.

She concludes that preparation for adulthood for this group is especially important; otherwise they will be consigned to 'perpetual childhood' (Morris, 1995:80–82).

The limited published research into leaving care work in Northern Ireland suggest that six months after leaving care a much higher percentage of young people leaving care (about 50% of the 110 young people in the sample) were living with their relatives than housing authorities, compared with other research in England, especially the Leeds research.

The report's conclusion about the young people in other respects and especially the support they received after leaving care is similar to other research, namely:

> Almost half the young people left care without any qualifications, a seventh had last attended schools for young people with special needs and about a fifth had enrolled in technical colleges or colleges of further education since leaving

secondary school. By the six month period only an eighth were said to be involved in full time education…only a tenth were currently engaged in full time work and a quarter were employed…over a third were in government funded youth training projects…three quarters of them were dependent on income support or training allowances and were living on less than £40 per week. Almost none of the young people received financial support from social services or other sources. (Pinkerton and McCrea, 1993:34)

In relation to inter-agency working, research across the London boroughs by Centrepoint (Strathdee, 1993) confirms earlier findings that co-operation between social services departments and housing departments is given a greater priority than with homeless young people as a whole. This is hardly surprising given the very low priority to homeless young people! Nevertheless, the research did come up with other interesting findings, for example about local authorities' having or intending to recoup costs from other local authorities from whom young people had originated. This is a major issue for local authorities, and this author is unaware of whether this issue has been legally adjudicated on, rather than, as seems to be the case, the situation being discussed on a local case by case basis. The other key finding of that research by Centrepoint was that 20 (or 65% of the sample) of the local authority social services departments stated that they used bed and breakfast accommodation for care leavers, but under what circumstances was not described. Stein has also produced a review of what is known from local research studies about the effectiveness of leaving care services within the context of service delivery by projects (Stein, 1997).

Research then has focused on the experiences of the young people and the responses of local authorities. It has consistently discovered the extent of continuing poverty of young people leaving care, as well as pointing to the discretionary nature of the services provided, the steeply declining social work support that exists post leaving care, the suddenness of the discharge from care, and inadequate resources in the housing, education, employment and training fields. It is to the official reports about, and proposed responses to, these problems to which attention is now turned, before looking at broader lobbying and professional developments.

Official reports and responses

In the first Children Act 1989 report published one year after that Act was introduced (DoH,1993) it was reported that:

Only some 50 per cent of local authorities (surveyed) had developed formal written policies on preparation for leaving care…that staff in half the authorities in the country did not have a clear framework…is a cause for concern. (HMSO, 1992:71)

It will be recalled that this is a very similar percentage to that found by Bonnerjea two years earlier, prior to the Children Act 1989 being introduced. The first Children Act 1989 report (DoH, 1993) recorded that good practice concerning preparation for leaving care could be found in various settings prior to the implementation of the Act and, in relation to written policies, that about a half of authorities had developed formal written aftercare policies. The report's chapter on leaving care developments concluded that:

> While much progress has been made…it is clear that the overall picture remains fragmented and patchy. The fact that a substantial proportion of authorities have still to formally address the expanded aftercare responsibilities on them by the Act is a cause for concern. Without clear statements of policy or service provision, staff have no agreed framework within which a consistent service to young people who seek their help and support can be provided. (DoH, 1993:73)

The Children Act Report 1993 (DoH, 1994) did not have a separate chapter entitled leaving care and information about this subject was contained within a chapter entitled 'Children looked after by local authorities'. The Children Act Report 1993 again places an emphasis on supporting improved preparation for independence initiatives for young people leaving care, and supporting the University of Leeds research and training initiatives. The same report also describes a Social Services Inspectorate study which is 'due to be published in 1994' about local authorities leaving care policies, but to my knowledge this has not been published. According to the Children Act Report 1994, leaving care services 'continue to improve' and the situation of young people leaving care experiencing a range of serious social and economic problems can be reversed by providing effective preparation for leaving care and continued support after young people have left care (DoH, 1995a:7). The report then concludes '…much needs to be done to ensure that young people receive a comprehensive and effective service.' Unlike the national situation in respect of children being looked after, there is no data presented about the numbers and situation of young people leaving care in either the Children Act 1993 or 1994 reports. The absence of such data, whether about assessments, or numbers leaving care, or services offered, or about service monitoring, are worrying features of these official reports.

Since 1981 and prior to the Children Act 1989, aftercare information was contained in the annual *Children in Care of Local Authorities* publications (DoH, 1981 annually to 1991), the governing legislation being the Child Care Act 1980. Since the Children Act 1989 a new series of publications entitled *Children Looked After by Local Authorities* (DoH, 1995b) has replaced that series.

Having looked at leaving care research and policy findings, and begun to examine official reports and responses, it is now necessary to consider the lobbying, campaigning and professional developments about leaving care work, and to consider the terms in which these developments describe the issues, whether or not they are a problem, and if so to whom? The key issues to consider are what type of changes are campaigners or professionals or researchers calling for? How realistic are they?

- Are they simply calling for more resources to be put into the area?

- Are administrative changes being called for? (i.e. better procedures, more assessment criteria)

- Are different systems, models and policies for dealing with and helping young people being called for?

- Do some see the solutions as simply being couched in political terms?

- Can any group be identified which considers that improvements are not necessary?

- Are they looking to better staff training as providing the appropriate avenue for improved services?

- Is a mixture of several or all of the above approaches or understandings required?

These leaving care developments are divided into two groups: those concerned with lobbying and campaigning, and those focusing on professional developments. The former are produced in Table 2.1.

Lobbying and campaigning

Table 2.1 National leaving care campaigning and lobbying developments
1991–1997

Date	Group(s) involved	Focus/event
1991	Young Homeless Group/Centrepoint	Publication about homelessness and leaving care
1992	After Care Consortium	National conference. Aftercare One Year On
1993	After Care Consortium/ National Children's Bureau	National conference. Improving Policy and Practice in Aftercare Work
1992	CHAR: 'Plans, No Action'	Report about the housing needs of care leavers and local authorities' responses to the CA 1989
1992	First Key	Publication of DoH backed survey of SSDs

1992	Social Work Today publication	Major campaign to improve services/change legislation
1993	After Care Consortium/ Royal Philanthropic Society	Launch of *Leaving Care in the 1990s* research publication
1992/3	NAYPIC/NSPCC/childcare	Campaign to improve services
1992/3	NAYPIC/NSPCC/childcare	House of Lords debate
1992/3	NAYPIC/NSPCC/childcare	Television *World in Action* programme
1993	Centrepoint	Launch of *On the Streets* briefing paper
1993	Who Cares? Trust	*Not Just a Name* report of the views of young people in foster and residential care
1994	Community Care magazine	Sustained media campaign especially concerning the monitoring of care leavers
1994	Centrepoint/ Community Care	Launch of *A Word from the Streets* research report
1995	First Key	Briefing paper for all parliamentary group on children leaving care
1995	Save the Children Fund	A video entitled *Does Anyone Care?* promoting a stronger Children Act 1989
1995	100+MPs	Signing of early day motion for the statutory monitoring of greater support to care leavers
1995 (6/11)	Mr Paul Flynn, MP, introduces House of Commons debate	Reply from the parliamentary Under-secretary of State for Health (then John Bowis)
1995	First Key/Parliamentary group on children leaving care/ Action on Aftercare Consortium	House of Commons December 1995: lobbying meeting following an earlier briefing paper
1996	Junior Health Minister and representatives from the field plus 'a care leaver'	As a result of 6 November 1995 debate there was a meeting with various parties ('very little came of it sadly', I was informed)
1996	Action on Aftercare Consortium: Too Much Too Young report	Report looking at the failure of social policy in meeting the needs of care leavers

February 1997	NCH Action for Children	House our Youth 2000 campaign, including young people leaving care
February 1997	Labour Party: announcement by Tony Blair (prior to the election result)	A leaving care 'summit' to tackle homelessness for care leavers
May 1997	Labour government elected	?

Comment

The prime purpose of the various lobbying groups in the leaving care field has been to improve the lot of the young people leaving care in order that they are no longer being abused, or perceived as victims or as a 'problem', either to themselves, their families or others. Where there are differences between the various lobbying groups these have been about which is the most effective way of achieving these aims to help young people leaving care. Effective lobbying and publicity is also designed to attract additional funding, especially if it is a voluntary organisation, and the effect on the client group involved and the agency of 'emotive lobbying' continues to be a sensitive issue, especially for child care agencies. Most of the lobbying has sought, through professional, rational, and 'shaming' moral arguments, for the guiding legislation to be strengthened, planning to be improved, and for more financial support be provided. When leaving care lobbying has called for additional resources to be made available, or when a reassertion of children's rights is called for, government has usually ignored these calls and become intractable, and local authorities defensive. It is also recognised that such legislative changes on their own, (i.e. without additional ring-fenced funding also being made available), and planning changes, would only further frustrate the change makers and make little substantial impact. It is too early to say whether the policies of the Labour government elected in 1997 will improve matters, and the last chapter contains more discussion on this matter and possible ways forward in leaving care work.

There have also been a significant number of professional and policy developments designed to improve services to young people leaving care, and the key ones are summarised below. Occasionally it is difficult to see where the professional developments differ from the lobbying activities above. In terms of the questions raised above about identifying the assumptions underlying the changes being called for in the professional sphere, they can be clearly understood as leaving care having the capacity to improve as a result of internal changes, such as better models and standards specification, without needing either more resources or major policy and legislative changes or both.

Key professional and policy developments affecting leaving care 1991–7

First Key, the national leaving care advisory service, continually promotes improvements to leaving care services. It does this in a variety of ways. It organises conferences, provides consultancy services, liaises with the Department of Health, distributes written materials, produces the Key Notes newsletter, and actively involves care leavers in its work. It has also co-ordinated the production of national leaving care standards. Its problem is one of having a national brief with ever reducing core funding. Alongside this hard working agency can be placed a range of other important professional initiatives in the leaving care field. As can be seen, they range from those which argue for additional resources, and stronger legislation, through to those which put the case that better planning and higher standards provide the answer, without addressing the resources question.

1992 After Care Consortium National Conference: Aftercare One Year On

This conference was organised with the specific intention of establishing what progress had been made since the legislation was introduced one year earlier. The junior health minister gave the key address, with additional inputs from Stein, a young person representing NAYPIC, and several practice workshops. The conference was written up (Roberts, 1993) and there was a modicum of publicity, predominantly from the social work press. The message from the practitioners and young people at that conference was that there were many examples of good practice with young people leaving care but the Children Act 1989 was weak, allowing cash strapped local authorities, if they so wished, to avoid fulfilling their responsibilities.

1992 National Foster Care Association: After Care – Making the Most of Foster Care

A report on the significant contribution that is made by foster carers regarding leaving care. This was a most important report presenting the views of foster carers.

1992 First Key: The Agenda

This excellent 'starter' publication is a practical introduction to the Children Act 1989, presenting different models of leaving care provision and pointing to key issues to be addressed to make the legislation 'come alive.'

1992 Department of Health: Looking after Children Assessment and Action Records

This project at Bristol University provides a complete package for assessing, planning and reviewing the experiences of all children for whom statutory agencies have undertaken responsibility.

1993 After Care Consortium/National Children's Bureau: Second National Conference

This conference was organised in order to present an overview of national leaving care developments and promote good practice. The emphasis of this conference was to provide a national overview of leaving care (Broad, 1994a), and to bring discussions about equal opportunities (Whyte, 1994) and the contract culture (Hardman, 1994) centre stage, with additional practice and policy workshops. These were on partnerships, the contract culture, and children's rights. This conference had limited publicity.

1993 Welsh Social Services Inspectorate: Inspection Report

This report examined leaving care work in three Welsh authorities 13 months after the Children Act 1989 was introduced. None of the three SSDs inspected had produced a policy statement on young people leaving care. The report stated that it was a matter of concern that some vulnerable young people were living in unacceptably poor bedsit accommodation.

1994 Social Services Inspectorate: Raising the Standard – The Second Annual Report of the Chief Inspector

On children leaving care the report acknowledged the positive ways in which some local authorities have responded to their new duties for some children, but the report contained 'worrying evidence that the intentions of Parliament regarding some groups of children in need were not being met in a good number of areas' (SSI,1994c:30,31).

1994 Social Services Inspectorate: Publication of Corporate Parents – An Inspection of Residential Child Care Services in 11 Authorities

In its examination of the extent to which children in homes should receive care which helps prepare and support them into adulthood the report concluded that 'five authorities had adopted a strategic approach to the provision of leaving care services and the others had identified it as a significant area requiring development'... Inflexibility of budgets and lack of identified money for leaving care services was reported to limit the level of support which staff could provide for children preparing for independence. Finance...contributed to their being looked after for longer than necessary' (SSI, 1994a:59).

1994 Social Services Inspectorate: Agendas for Action Arising from the National Residential Child Care Inspection 1992–1994 (Social Services Inspectorate, 1994b)

This set of briefing papers was aimed at reinforcing the corporate nature of local authorities' responsibilities towards children being looked after and noted that most SSDs had made a clear commitment to work with other agencies in providing services to meet the needs of children leaving care. This practical publication placed considerable emphasis on a training and action plan approach to perceived problems.

1994 Royal Philanthropic Society: Production of a Resource Guide for Local Authorities (Smith, 1994)

This part Department of Health funded publication contains chapters on interpreting the legislation, developing an effective project model for aftercare, housing options, ways of helping with training and employment, staff training, and monitoring.

1995 Support Force for Residential Child Care: Code of Practice for the Employment of Residential Social Workers

This comprehensive code of employment practice arose from the Committee of Enquiry into children's homes chaired by Norman Warner and contains very detailed information about the selection, development and management of residential staff.

1995 Leeds University: Provision of Training Pack for Staff Working with Young People Leaving Care

This extensive, informative and user-friendly loose leaf publication is an easy to use training pack for leaving care staff.

1996 First Key: the Production of National Leaving Care Standards

In 1995 First Key organised a National Standards Working Group with all the major agencies invited to discuss and specify a set of leaving care standards. Seventeen standards were produced covering leaving care policies, practice guidance, continuous planning, financial support, integrated voluntary/specialist provision, a comprehensive staff training strategy, production of a leaving care guide, an interagency framework, joint working arrangements, and complaints, representation and monitoring procedures.

1996 DOH: Production of Further Circular Guiding Local Authorities to Produce Comprehensive Children's Plans

Following the Audit Commission's Seen But Not Heard report's recommendation that central government should take the lead in raising the status of children's services (Audit Commission, 1994), The Children's Services Plans draft circular (draft LAC{95}) was issued to meet the point that children's plans should be joint, mandatory, and published.

1996–97 The 'National Voice' Project: First Key

This initiative aims to organise young people who are in care or who have been in care to provide a national voice about how young people leaving care are treated and to help change and improve their situation.

Social Services Inspectorate Inspection of Leaving Care (SSI, 1997)

This major report is based on an inspection of nine local authorities. It highlights local good practice, and reports that there are several areas of particular concern including that of young people's health, the monitoring of leaving care services, service planning and reviewing, family placement issues, and policy issues. The report is mostly qualitative and in its summary it lists the many developments that are still needed to improve matters up to an acceptable standard. The report lists many suggestions to improve matters based on practice from inspected areas.

Conclusion

For such a relatively small client group there has then been a considerable amount of activity as well as a steady stream of research about leaving care work providing similar messages, namely of extensive, deep seated, and mounting problems and uneven modest gains concerning young people leaving care. Whilst the lobbying and professional development work has been conducted steadily and in earnest, there has been and continues to be a dogged disinterest and resistance to introducing any legislative changes, including those which place a duty on local authorities to provide financial support for young people leaving care. Whilst this might be regarded as acceptable to those who view the social security system as the proper place for providing financial benefits, that system is not doing so. The lack of automatic benefit entitlement to 16- and 17-year-olds combined with the woefully low payments to others means that the system is hostile to young people leaving care, especially at that age. The key issue of the poverty of young people leaving care, and indeed other young people in need, is one which still has still to be addressed.

The only substantial contribution that has been made by government to leaving care work since the Children Act 1989 was introduced in 1991 – apart from important, though inadequate, levels of funding to First Key, and the funding of research (Biehal et al., 1995), and other small development grants – is yet more professional input, namely inspection work set against standards. The fundamental assumptions, namely that young people leaving home, including those leaving care, should largely fend for themselves, effectively with nil state support, have remained unchanged. At a macro level, then, those working in the field, armed only with more training ideas, standards, and research findings, still face an ongoing uphill task. This is especially the case for the 'corporate parent', whether central government or the local authorities, still needing to make the flexible, financial, and professional investments that are necessary to support these young people. Yet much creative work is going on locally despite the overall bleak social policy context, and the grim and consistent research findings outlined in this chapter. So it is to the practice and policy research which forms the backbone of this book to which attention is now turned to examine the work with young people leaving care to record those projects' energetic commitment to working with young people leaving care.

PART TWO

Research and Policy Findings

CHAPTER THREE

The Research Project: Aims, Methods and Scope

Background to the research

In 1993, when I was working in a senior research and development capacity in a voluntary organisation, a similar, though much smaller, questionnaire study was conducted to the one underpinning this book. At that time the agency concerned (the Royal Philanthropic Society) published a directory of leaving care projects, on behalf of the London and South East Leaving Care Support group. Although the majority of the projects involved in that group were from London and surrounding areas, a proportion were from other parts of England, as well as Wales. In 1992 a questionnaire was sent to all 48 of projects listed at that time, with returns being forthcoming from 25 or 52 per cent of the sample. The findings of that survey, based on data collected during 1993, were published under the title of *Leaving Care in the 1990s* (Broad, 1994c). The sample consisted of all known leaving care projects published in that directory at that time. The research produced for this book is based on a much extended version of that questionnaire survey.

In the last chapter the key research findings for leaving care were reviewed both pre and post Children Act 1989. In this chapter it is relevant to record the methods used by others and the scope of their work in order to establish the nature of the research base for leaving care work in England and Wales, before moving on to describe this study's methodology in some detail.

Methodology and scope of other leaving care research

Stein and Carey's seminal work *Leaving Care* (1986) was a qualitative study which documented the experiences of a group of 45 young people through interviews. Lupton's work (1985) was based on intensive semi-structured interviews with 20 out of a possible 46 young people, plus statistical information from Hampshire social services department about all that authority's care leavers at the time. First Key's study of black young people leaving care (First Key, 1987) was based on interviews with selected staff taken from 12 projects, with contributions from 54 young people and workers. Stone's study (Stone, 1990) was based on a postal questionnaire to 20 local authority and voluntary organisations, interviews with project staff and young people, and 75 young people who had recently left care. Stein's *Living Out of Care* (Barnardo's, 1990) was based on background data collected from 65 young people at a project, and semi-structured interviews with young people and staff at three different points in time. *Making the Most of Fostercare* (Fry, 1992) presented a nation-wide survey of 207 foster carers completing a postal questionnaire. The influential *Patterns and Outcomes* publication (DoH, 1991b) summarised messages from research drawing, for leaving care work, on earlier local studies. The Save the Children Fund's research project (SCF, 1995) was a small scale study but was distinguished by its very full involvement of young people at all stages of the research production. Jones's book *Leaving Home* (1995) was based on a wide range of statistical data gathered from previous studies about homeless and other young people who were no longer living at home. The sampling frame for Garnett's study *Leaving Care and After* (National Children's Bureau, 1992) was the 308 young people who were reported to the *Child Care Now* survey (Rowe *et al.*, 1989) as 'leaving at 16+.' *Leaving Care in the 1990s* (Broad, 1994c) was based on a postal questionnaire of 26 leaving care projects, mostly based in the South East and London areas of England. Biehal *et al.*'s study *Prepared for Living?* (NCB, 1992) was based on social worker completed questionnaires on 183 young people from three local authority areas, and in *Moving On* (Biehal *et al.*, 1995) the study was based on a total of 426 interviews with 74 young people. In 1997 the Social Services Inspectorate published findings of its inspection of nine leaving care projects.

This brief review shows that the majority of research into leaving care work has consisted of in-depth, qualitative and local studies, making national comparisons impossible. What it has produced, as we saw in Chapter Two, is something equally valuable from the perspective of good practice and local policies, namely a wealth of rich and varied research material, on which national recommendations have been made. Essentially then this research has drawn on interview schedules or questionnaires, and conducted by researchers, with the notable exception of the Save the Children research which closely involved young people in the work.

What else does this review of research methods into leaving care show? It reveals, generally, the paucity of large scale research funding for this area of work, and the emphasis, therefore, on local qualitative studies and 'cases', in the past funded and conducted either by local authorities themselves (e.g. Oxfordshire, Leicestershire and Cambridgeshire) or by voluntary organisations with their 'lobbying on professional and policy issues' hats firmly on and quite rightly so. The consequence of all this is that, whilst acknowledging the statistical and data gathering difficulties in the child care world, there continues to be a lack, some would say an appalling lack, of comparable local, national or even nation-wide data about the nature and extent of leaving care work in England and Wales.

This raises the question about whether this local/good practice emphasis matters. It is argued here that it matters for a number of important reasons. It matters to the young people because they lack national data to compare their situation with others elsewhere about how they are treated. It matters because it symbolises a lack of concern, and lack of priority, for this group. It matters locally, for example, about how many young people leave care from such and such local authority because otherwise how do we know who they are and where they are? How are they to be assessed and helped? It matters because the absence of national reliable data leads to uninformed debates about national statistics. It matters ultimately because knowledge is power and the lack of one leads to the denial of the other. Finally, and perhaps most important of all, it matters because the treatment of young people leaving care (and in care) is a political and social scandal, at least as much as it is a professional policy and practice issue.

Aims of the research study

In general terms, this research study set out to record what is happening to young people leaving care and leaving care work in England and Wales since the Children Act 1989 was introduced. This is done by drawing on data from leaving care projects covering the period from 1991/92 to 1996.

The more specific aim of the study is to record and analyse three key different but linked social arenas affecting young people leaving care: relevant national social policy developments, professional leaving care policies and procedures, and good practice initiatives. A comparison of developments in leaving care work, from 1991 to 1996/7, will also be made.

In Relation to the First of the Above Social Policy Aims:

- to identify the nature and direction of social policy changes which largely determine the position of care leavers, and indeed all other young people, especially those not living at their parental home. These changes include the critical areas of financial support, accommodation, education, training and employment to young people aged 16+.

In Relation to the Second of the Above Professional Policy Aims:

- to compare the findings with the 1993 study in order to establish whether and how the situation of care leavers is changing (i.e. getting better/worse/remaining the same)
- using broadly similar questions to the 1992 study to reach a unique position of comparing 1992 and 1996/7 data about the

implementation of the Children Act 1989 (i.e. to provide a 5 year national overview and review of leaving care work)

- to analyse the many recommendations writers and practitioners and others have made about leaving care work since 1989.

In Relation to the Third of the Above Practice Aims:

- to identify the key practice issues in leaving care work drawing on the views of leaving care practitioners and managers
- to identify examples of good leaving care practice and policies and, if they seem localised and isolated, to look at how these can be more widely applied.

Methodology

The aim of producing a national study from which generalisations could be made pointed to a postal questionnaire format. The bulk of the projects used for this study were those which featured in the 1994 Royal Philanthropic Society leaving care directory, complemented by my own knowledge about the whereabouts of other leaving care projects. Voluntary organisations such as NCH-Action for Children, Barnardo's, the Children's Society, and Save the Children Fund also provided me with the names and addresses of leaving care projects throughout England and Wales. The research was also publicised and other leaving care projects were invited to contribute to the research. I became increasingly committed to the position that this study would not be yet another snapshot local study (valuable though they are), which critics, looking for a reasons to dismiss or minimise findings about this sensitive area of public policy, could mischievously seek to discount, as 'just' local findings.

Having chosen this approach it was vital to analyse the data in a more rigorous way than had been possible with the 1992 study. SPSS for Windows 95 (version 6) software was used in order to produce statistically quantifiable data. Throughout this book the term 'estimated numbers' is applied to describing the number of young people attending the leaving care projects or in different accommodation types etc. In terms of collecting information about young people leaving care there are two critical factors.

The first is that where they exist at all local authority and voluntary organisation leaving care monitoring systems are not precise, and the second factor is that the position and circumstances of each young person leaving care can and often does change frequently, sometimes monthly, other times weekly or even daily. To take one example from having worked in an agency undertaking this sort of work, it proved extremely difficult to record the housing situation of young people leaving care each time the situation changed. Instead, it became more relevant and practical to note retrospectively the number and type of such changes.

Given the extent of young people's 'resettlement problems' and, initially at least, the transient situation of the young people whilst they seek some sort of stability, and the underdeveloped (with notable exceptions of course) central monitoring systems, leaving care projects and social statisticians and researchers find themselves entering the world of estimates. This is the case in most other studies, it might be added. Yet it seems particularly poor in the world of leaving care.

The figures used here are calculated estimates based on the actual information the leaving care projects had at the time the questionnaire was completed. It is in that light that they are presented to you, the reader, as accurate so far as respondents could tell at the time. It is, of course, your final judgement as to whether using calculated estimates makes any significance difference to the policy findings and discussions.

Other data

A considerable amount of information was gathered from reading reports from a large number of leaving care projects and national organisations. Thus at a distance it was possible to keep abreast of both the very real issues facing leaving care projects, and national developments. Where good practice examples or good policy examples were not available from the questionnaire returns, these were obtained by directly approaching leaving care projects for the information. In some instances these were provided by leaving care projects which had participated in the questionnaire survey, but this was not always the case.

This study falls short of the demands of methodological pluralism if that term is taken to mean multiple or at the very least a triangulation of methods, preferably evenly weighted. On the other hand, if methodological pluralism can allow for methodological pragmatism, suggesting the gathering of a range of data whose findings are rigorously tested against other in the field, then this study's totality and substance is rather more than the sum of its questionnaire parts. Its genesis, namely an intent to produce a statistically credible and rigorous study about national leaving care developments, largely determined its methodology.

The collection of other data and policy information about leaving care developments has also produced a policy and practice research study. This data included projects' and organisations' service agency agreements, monitoring information, examples of particular areas of good practice, case studies, and leaving care guides and complaints systems. The primary purpose of obtaining such data was to complement the questionnaire data and 'bring it alive' through written accounts of projects' good practice or policies. This extra data provides an important illustrative function, as well as a check on the themes emerging from the questionnaire returns.

Although I am someone who often advocates collaborative and qualitative research methodologies (for example Broad, 1994b, and Broad and Fletcher, 1994), this was not seen as essential or possible for this study. Normally qualitative methodologies are used to seek 'depth rather than breadth' of research findings in order to 'get below the surface' to use Fletcher's (1974) phrase. First, this was research conducted with a single pre-established focus about recording the state of leaving care work, primarily at a policy level in England and Wales, as seen through practitioners' eyes. There had previously been many valuable in depth local cluster studies (Biehal *et al.*, 1995; Stein and Carey, 1986), and studies where the views of young people were paramount (Save the Children Fund, 1995), and the view was taken here that these types of studies did not need repeating.

Furthermore, because it was central to the research to collect comparable data, something which the 'one off' studies, by definition, can not do, it was regarded as vital to retain, broadly speaking, the same questions as had been asked of a smaller group of respondents in the 1992 study. Although not possible to set up initially, on reflection it was nevertheless a mistake not to have a research steering group which would have been helpful in a host of ways.

Research stages

Stage 1 — Preparatory Stage:

- collect data about number and whereabouts of leaving care projects from across the country. There were some 75 projects listed initially, but upon further investigation only 61 were working with young people leaving care. Others, for example, were working with young homeless including a proportion of care leavers. A number of social services departments were also contacted, for the names of leaving care projects, and this produced further projects which formed part of the final 61 teams. It was finally decided to stop collecting questionnaire data from teams in the summer of 1996

- decide on the sample frame. This was simply all those leaving care teams that could be identified, and who agreed to take part in the study, and showed an interest

- design and pilot a questionnaire, taking into account the key point that this survey is partly a replicate study, and thus the questionnaire needed to cover the same areas as those which informed the 1992/3 study

- having selected the projects, all of them were telephoned personally and asked if they would be willing to participate in a leaving care survey

- follow up letters were sent to each project to thank projects for agreeing to participate.

Stage 2 – Data Collection:

- over a period of nine months 46 projects returned their questionnaires for analysis

- for all the closed questions data was coded and entered into the computer using SPSS PC for Windows software

- for the open ended questions about, for example, use of complaints systems, all the examples were extrapolated from the written questionnaire, coded, and then grouped together and analysed.

Responses to questionnaire

The questionnaire was sent out to 61 leaving care projects and responses were received from 46 projects. Using a questionnaire format and knowing the advantages and disadvantages that are characteristic of questionnaire surveys, it was the aim to gather a wide range of responses from a large number of leaving care projects working in England and Wales in different types of authorities. Initially 49 projects responded to the invitation to participate, but three of them could not be included in the survey because, upon further enquiry, their client group was not young people leaving care but others such as homeless families or a children's rights service. Therefore the decision was taken not to include them in the 1996 survey. Also, because the 1996 survey set out to be a survey based entirely on recorded active leaving care practices and policies, and informed opinions based on practice, it was decided not to send the questionnaire, as had been done in 1992, to other educational or campaigning groups, for example groups working with homeless young people.

Having settled on the responses from 46 leaving care projects working in 43 different areas with an estimated 3308 young people, a high degree of representativeness is claimed about leaving care work at the time the study was conducted. Nationally an estimated 10,000 16- and 17-year-olds leave care to live independently each year (National Children's Bureau, 1992). At the time the study was conducted in 1996 (i.e. before unitary reorganisation) there were 106 local authorities in England and Wales. Therefore the survey has obtained the views of leaving care projects working in 41 per cent of all local authorities. This does not account for a third of all young people leaving care in 1996 (i.e. taking

3308 from 10,000), as seems possible at first sight, because for this study, age breakdowns were not asked for/collected. Therefore both older and younger leaving care age groups are likely to be included in projects' responses, and there is a discussion about the estimated average age of the young people on the survey's sample in the next chapter.

The 75 per cent questionnaire return rate (by 46 leaving care projects) is an exceptionally high response rate for a postal questionnaire. This is twice the number of projects which took part in the earlier 1994 survey. The high return can be accounted for by considerable attention paid to detail about potential respondents, including simple things like keeping records of changing addresses and telephone numbers, or project names or changes to staff. In addition each project was contacted by an assistant, in the first instance to enquire whether projects would be willing to take part in this survey. In discussions it became clear that projects probably had at least three agendas which explain their willingness to complete and return the questionnaires in such high numbers:

- a willingness to contribute to research 'for the general good'

- to demonstrate all the work that has gone into developing their good practice/policies

- to use it as an opportunity to contribute to a wider campaigning and policy improvement debate about leaving care work across England and Wales.

Research scope

There is one important qualifying comment about using the data from two periods in time from similar but not identical projects. It is not possible or claimed here that the two sets of respondents are the same, and, therefore, that the findings from the 1996 survey are directly comparable project by project. Rather, the view was taken that the 1992/3 findings provide a sound basis for comparison, but not a perfect fit. Although it would have been possible, data is not compared project-by-project with those same projects who participated in the 1992 survey or conclusions made about their changing local situation. The reason for this is that the main aim of the research was to stand back and look at the big picture and not the local picture, and hence the basis for these intra and inter period comparisons, whilst factual, is presented for more contextual and thematic reasons.

The issues of national and representative findings

The absence of an accurate national overview about leaving care (compared with, say, national crime and/offending rates) fulfils two important functions. It hampers national government or national associations (such as the Association of

Directors of Social Services) or institutions with some sense of a national overview or brief (such as the Social Services Inspectorate, or, less so, First Key) which set out to record and/or improve matters nationally. This absence of any national material also conveniently fulfils the function for national government, other institutions, and the responsible government departments of avoiding the issue. This includes, at its strongest, the avoidance of public duty and responsibility, and any meaningful response or commitment to the consequences that flow from the findings being widespread and significant, and not local and insignificant. 'It is only a small sample' is often the response (quite rightly some might say) followed quickly by 'the findings are now out of date and (by the way) things have now improved', or other variations thereof. In a climate of privatised services and continued financial cut-backs in local authority budgets, it is perhaps understandable that any identified unmet need is seen first as yet another cost, and only second, if one is lucky, as an important service gap to be filled.

How often have published valuable local studies, often involving post-graduate students' work, in leaving care or case studies in other social welfare areas ended with the comment that the findings are limited to the project or case study under consideration? That is, it is not possible to generalise because of the (small) size of the sample. Whilst this must be the case in those circumstances, from a statistical standpoint, it is nevertheless a source of regret at times, given the actual and the potential implications that can often flow from these small scale works. In the leaving care field the Welsh Social Services Inspectorate 1993 report into leaving care work was conducted in three social services departments, and based on a two month inspection (*Community Care*, 5 August 1993) but the findings were presented as if they were typical of practice elsewhere with broader lessons to be applied to other authorities. The converse is also the case. Some national reports acknowledge that their findings can not be 'widely representative' because of the small numbers involved. For example, in the introduction to the *Focus on Teenagers* publication (DoH, 1996a) the limitations of the report are recognised in terms of 'their experiences should not be assumed to be widely representative', but then goes on to state that the studies have 'important messages' because they are the 'first to look specifically at the deployment of local authority services in relation to teenagers and the outcome of these efforts' (DoH, 1996:1). This is an example where messages are presented as having universal or extensive application though not claiming to be widely representative.

Though small scale studies cannot claim to be representative, they can nonetheless provide extremely rich data (see, for example, Fletcher, 1974, on observations in a GPs surgery; or Broad, 1991, on inner city probation work). Virtue does not lie in size alone but it is only by conducting research across a number of areas, or groups, and preferably at different points of time to provide that extra dimension, that it can have both important practice/policy messages *and* claim to be representative. Biehal *et al.*'s study is an excellent example of a well designed and constructed study, based on an depth survey of 183 young people, and as one of the four *Focus on Teenagers* studies has many invaluable messages for other leaving care schemes.

So what are the claims of this study in terms of representative findings? The study reports draws on the findings of the questionnaire returns from 46 leaving care teams. These teams are based, as is described elsewhere in the book, in many different places within England and Wales. The largest number of geographical leaving care areas, via teams, previously covered in any research study into leaving care is 26 (Broad, 1994c). Apart from that survey, much shorter than the one used in the current survey, in depth work in this area has been focused on two or three local areas (e.g. Biehal, *et al.*, 1995; Stein and Carey, 1986), or, through the 1996 Social Services Inspectorate inspections, nine areas. It is against the background of these local and regional inspection studies, and of long-standing complaints about and dissatisfaction with the non-availability of a national picture of leaving care work, that this work is presented to readers. Although it is not claimed that it provides a total national picture of leaving care work, it is a start in that direction. It must also be recognised that this study's disadvantage is that it does not carry the amount of rich qualitative data that others' work, especially that of Stein and Carey (1986), contains. What the study *does* provide, in addition to the quantitative data obtained from the questionnaires, is illustrations of cases and good policies and practice. In most cases the latter are based on practitioners and, to a lesser degree, this author's assessment of what constitutes 'good practice'. This approach is derived from the proposition that the best way to establish good practice is based on examining what practitioners do as they work sequentially with similarities and differences, explorations and eliminations. Seen from this perspective, studying good practice becomes more of a mid-point analysis, namely a study of good practice cases, rather than a definitive example of good practice universally defined and agreed upon.

CHAPTER FOUR

The Leaving Care Projects and the Young People in the Study

Introduction

Having set out the research aims, scope and broader social context, the purpose of this chapter is to focus on policies and practice, beginning with the description of the leaving care projects and the young people in the study. The first thing to say is that the sample group of 46 projects produced a considerable amount of data, something like four times that produced from the 25 projects responding to the 1993 survey. By drawing on both sources it has been possible to produce comparisons about specific issues, and although some is provided in this chapter about project staffing and the young people, the analysis regarding the education and housing situation of the young people is contained in the following chapters on those specific topics.

The leaving care projects in the study

Project Types, Responses and Location

There are three types of leaving care projects described in this book:

- *Type 1 – local authority projects*: these are normally 100 per cent local authority funded; 14 such projects (or 30% of the sample) responded to the questionnaire

- *Type 2 – joint local authority/voluntary organisation projects*: these are normally jointly funded by the two organisations; 17 such projects (or 33% of the sample) responded to the questionnaire

- *Type 3 – voluntary organisation projects*: these are funded in a variety of ways; usually 100 per cent local authority funded if a 100 per cent contracted out service, and/or sometimes funded by different local authority and central government grants, and/or sometimes a project can be funded from a regional or national charity's central budget plus minor voluntary contributions or donations. The same range of funding sources for voluntary organisation projects can also resource joint projects; 15 such projects (or 37% of the sample) responded to the questionnaire.

For the 1993 survey there were responses from 12 local authorities (or 48%), 4 joint local authorities/voluntary organisations (or 16%), and 9 voluntary organisation projects (or 36%).

As was the case in 1993, in this research all the leaving care projects work with young people leaving care, with 90 per cent of them having 'leaving care project' or something similar in their title. Ten of the respondent projects were based in the South East of England (outside London), nine in London boroughs, six in the South West of England, five in Wales, seven in North West England, four in the North East, and five in the Midlands. The projects came from across the full range of county, borough, city and metropolitan authorities and areas. The research was conducted during 1996, before the local government reorganisation in 1997 which resulted in new unitary authorities being created in some areas of England and all of Wales.

Project Start Dates

Five had begun before 1986, 12 started between 1986 and 1989, 12 between 1990 and 1991, and 17, the majority, as one would expect given the introduction of the Children Act 1989 in October 1991, had begun since 1991. There has continued to be an evenly distributed growth of different project types, whether voluntary organisation, or joint, or local authority, throughout the period covered by the questionnaire.

When adding the number of voluntary organisations to the joint voluntary organisation/local authority projects there are exactly twice that number of projects started since 1991 compared with local authority projects. The most recent starting date for any new project in the survey was 1994, when five new projects began, one local authority, two voluntary organisations, one joint project, and one joint private/voluntary organisation project (the only one from the sample with any private component).

Staffing and caseloads

The survey set out to chart current staffing numbers in leaving care work, any changes to staffing numbers, the numbers of young people using the projects, and the subsequent ratio of staff to users in order to gauge the growth or otherwise of leaving care projects, as well as workloads. The 1993 survey also asked respondents questions about staffing and caseloads, providing a valuable basis for comparison. For the year 1994/5 the projects in the survey estimated that they worked with a total of 2783 young people, whereas for the year 1995/1996 the same projects worked with an estimated total of 3308 young people, representing a 16 per cent increase. For the 1992 survey, the 25 respondent projects, (compared with 46 projects for this current survey) worked with an estimated 1538 young people in 1992, compared with 968 for the previous year, 1990–1991. Table 4.1 sets out this information in greater detail.

Table 4.1 indicates that staff numbers within respondent projects have barely changed between 1994/5 and 1995/6, with a total increase across all 46 projects of just 10.75 staff (full time equivalent). During the same period the number of young people increased by an estimated 525 overall, or an estimated two additional young people for each staff member. The average staff group size was five per team, with teams ranging from 12 to 1(!) in size. The ratio of young people to each staff member for 1995/6 was 15:1, for 1994/5 it was 13:1, and, by re-examining the data from the earlier survey, other comparisons could be made, with even lower ratios, 12:1 and 11:1 for 1992/3 and 1991/2 respectively. In 11 cases the caseload changes between 1994/5 and 1995/6 were in excess of 50 additional young people, and in two cases changes over 60 were recorded, of 110 and 75, *additional* cases during the one year period.

Table 4.1 Staffing levels and caseloads: a comparison of 1991, 1992, 1995 and 1996 survey figures[1]

Subject	1991–2 (25 projects asked)	1992–3 (25 projects asked)	% change between 1991 and 1992	1994–5 (46 projects asked)	1995–6 (46 projects asked)	% change between 1995 and 1996
Total number of staff	89	128	+30%	214.75	225.5	+5%
Mean number of staff	3.5	5.12	+31%	4.66	4.83	nil[2]
Team caseload: total no. of young people	982	1583	+36%	2783	3308	+16%
Team caseload: mean no. of young people	39	61.25	+35%	63	74	+15%
Ratio of young people: each staff member	11:1	12:1	+1%	13:1	15:1	+13%

1   44 projects responded to the 'staffing and young people 12 months ago' questions, and there were 45 answers to the 'current young people total' question (1).

2   All figures rounded. For the percentage change between 1995 and 1996 the figure was 0.17 per cent, and is recorded as nil.

Changes to Projects Caseload 1994–1996
FINDINGS

As can be seen in Table 4.1, there has been an average overall caseload increase of 15 per cent young people between 1994/5 and 1995/6. There were also examples from individual teams where the number of young people referred to their project had reduced over the previous year (seven teams) or where they had remained the same (five teams). Leaving care projects were asked to briefly explain why there had been a change in the number of referrals to their project during the previous year. The question was phrased in this way to allow for explanations about increases or decreases (or indeed numbers referred remaining the same) to be included. All the explanations given by leaving care projects were collected, analysed and placed into those three sub-groups, namely, those where there were more referrals, those where there were less, and those where there were the same number of referrals and caseloads. Having established the numbers and type of caseload changes, in the first instance the reasons for caseload increases were then further grouped into increases arising from factors outside the project's control or from those within the project's influence.

First, then, there are the explanations (n=38) given by respondents for increases in the number of young people with whom projects were working in 1996 as compared with the same period 12 months earlier.

Explanations for increased referrals to leaving care projects

Reasons Beyond the Project's Control
FOURTEEN EXAMPLE TYPES TAKEN FROM THE 22 EXPLANATIONS GIVEN

- more new referrals from local teams: five examples

- increase in self-referrals: three examples

- new policy introduced: one example

- increase in local number of 16–17-year-olds: two examples

- more effective use of referral procedure: one example

- change of project's role (more long term work expected from the team): one example

- increased numbers of young people leaving care who moved into the area from other areas: one example

- more young people in care with local authority: one example

- less direct referrals but more young people returning to area after not managing/not receiving support from receiving local authority: one example

- growth of numbers of young people in need: one example

- more homeless young people, especially 16- and 17-year-olds: two examples

- project under pressure to take local authority's under 16s as foster care places for under 15s not available: one example

- more long term work expected from the team: one example

- more young women needing help: one example.

REFERRAL INCREASES: CASE EXAMPLE

How one leaving care team's referrals increased 27 per cent in one year. One leaving care project was a London borough whose numbers of young people had increased by 53 over its previous year's figure of 140. The explanation for this increase lay in the external changes imposed by the purchasers, namely the local authority's own leaving care team's service agency specification, which extended the eligibility of the service from 17–21 from the previous year to 21–25-year-olds entitled to aftercare support and advice. Such was the volume of this increase that the team in question was seriously considering how it could possibly work in any effective way with these additional numbers.

Reasons Within the Project's Influence (n=15)[3]

- more housing attracting more referrals: two examples

- more accommodation: two examples

- better referral system: two examples

- more staff so able to take more work: two examples

- intensity of support: two examples

- increase in workload as a result of negotiation with local authority: two examples

- greater publicity: one example

- new project taking extra work to gain credibility: one example

- more advocacy than awareness raising: one example

Explanations for decreased referrals to leaving care projects (7 provided)

- changed assessment of need by local authority means less young people entitled to service

---

3   There was one case where the reason for the extra referrals was for both internal/external reasons.

- smaller staff group, forced to work with less young people: one example
- referred more but can only work with highest priority cases, meaning that the in-need under 16s: two examples
- more young people choosing to stay with local authority rather than voluntary organisation leaving care team: one example
- locum post-holder in post not a full time person: one example
- procedural restructuring of services to encourage one-route referral system: two examples.

There were just five explanations given for there being no changes in the numbers of referrals made. The main reason for these five leaving care projects not experiencing any changes were, in the case of four of them, that they were voluntary organisation projects whose limits were established by a fixed housing stock.

Whilst it is undoubtedly the case that the development work of leaving care projects, to produce additional housing and extend services to young people leaving care, accounts for a proportion of the increases, the more substantive explanation *lies outside the projects' control*, in the form of increased demand from a range of young people, only a proportion of whom seem to be local young people who have ceased to be accommodated.

There were also two cautionary tales about projects' survival. First, there was one voluntary organisation project which was closing down because the local authority was no longer purchasing its services. Second, there was another, possibly unusual, case in that the young people leaving care when faced with choosing between the larger and relatively well resourced local authority leaving care team, and the smaller less well resourced voluntary organisation project, attended the local authority team rather more, which contributed over time to the decline and subsequent closure of the voluntary project.

Nevertheless, despite the occasional closure there is a definite degree of 'demand overflow' on leaving care projects from elsewhere, for example those arising from the demands of homeless young people. Although important, this 'demand overflow' trend should not be regarded as the only explanation, and the firm impression gained, confirmed in the requirements set out in service agency agreements, is that more is expected from leaving care teams than before. If this analysis is correct then the problem which follows is how will projects meet this increasing and continual demand with less resources? This important question is discussed further in Chapter 10 and the final chapter.

Staffing and Caseloads by Project Type

Generally respondents' answers – whether about leaving care policies, the state of education for young people leaving care or across a wide range of issues – were not distinguishable by project type. This might seem surprising given the different position and size of the different project types. Had the questionnaire asked more questions about professional practice, and given the different roles leaving care projects often have in the three sectors, it is almost inevitable that such organisational differences would have appeared in the responses.

Yet there were some significant differences about staffing and caseloads as recorded by the different project types, and these are presented in Table 4.2.

Table 4.2 Staffing, caseloads and implications by project type

Issue	Local authority projects (n=14)	Voluntary organisation projects (n=15)	Joint projects (n=17)	Practice/policy implications arising from reponses
Project caseload (average no. of young people)	118	50	59	with ever increasing caseloads, from the time of the 1992 survey, service quality will become even more of an issue
Staff size (average)	5.2	5.1	5.0	local authority projects under particular pressure
Ratio of young people to staff	23:1	10:1	12:1	significantly different staff time available for the work-quality of service will be affected without changes being made to: • numbers/nature of inputs i.e. young people • and/or staff numbers • and/or level/quality of service offered

As we also saw earlier, so here in Table 4.2 the caseload/staff ratio differences between different project types are significant and, although to some extent this may be simply explained by the slightly different functions of some projects, this cannot fully account for them. The more likely explanation is that since local authorities have the prime responsibility for offering support and guidance to young people leaving care, it is to them and their projects that the young people are normally initially referred and where the greatest increases will occur. For the local authority leaving care teams there was an increase of 19 per cent in the caseload between 1994/5 and 1995/6, compared with just 6 per cent for the voluntary organisation teams. The jointly run teams recorded a 17 per cent caseload increase during the same period. So despite the steady decrease in the numbers of children looked after by local authorities during the 1980s and 1990s, for example between 1991 and 1995, the numbers declined from 59,834 as of 31 March 1991 to 49,000 as of 31 March 1995 (DoH, 1996b). This has not resulted in less young people being referred to leaving care projects. Many of the reasons given for caseload increases were given earlier in the section explaining the changes, as seen from the projects' perspective.

It is possible that these changes are also associated with the fact that more young people are leaving care at an earlier age, 16 and 17 in many cases (see Biehal *et al.* 1995, on this point), in some considerable need, and placing additional demands on the system, than has previously been the case. The newer leaving care projects set up since the Children Act 1989 was introduced may now be catering for an increasing number of younger people leaving care. This continuing increase, in proportional terms, in young people being referred to projects may also be associated with the changes to, and the steady decline in, residential child care services, and variations in discharge arrangements. A further factor, and one which at least one leaving care project brought to my attention, was the increase in the number of over 21-year-olds being referred for services. If it is the case that leaving care projects are also soaking up the older youth homeless referrals as well, then the picture becomes even more complex.

The young people in the study
The Young People's Characteristics[4]

Respondents indicated that their projects were working with an estimated 3308 young people of whom 1620 (or 49%) were males and 1687 (or 51%) were females. This compares with 51 per cent males and 49 per cent females for the 1993 survey, so the change is not significant.

The Ethnic Origin of the Young People in the Study

There were 2579 young people described by respondents as white (making 78% of the total figure), 449 black (14%), 100 Asian (3%), with 191 (or 5% of the total) whose ethnic origin was classified as 'other', making a total of 3319 young people whose ethnic identity was identified. The difference and margin of error between the grand total of young people with whom the projects work (3308)

---

4   Not all the projects provided information about age breakdown at the time of the move to independence and so exact age breakdowns cannot be provided.

and the ethnic origin figure provided (3319) is less than 1 per cent at just 0.3 per cent. Although invited to do so if they wished, projects did not use or add other ethnic categories, such as mixed race or Afro-Caribbean.

The *Patterns and Outcomes* report (DoH, 1991b) concluded that if departments do not know how many children from black and minority groups they are looking after, or their cultural and linguistic background, it is most unlikely that they will be able to provide for them appropriately. There are no comparable figures from the 1993 study concerning ethnic breakdown of the young people attending the leaving care projects because of incomplete replies from that study. It is also difficult to make comparisons with other leaving care studies either because the issue of ethnic origin was not addressed and/or ethnicity data not collected or because the categories of ethnic origin are different from that used in this study. For example, in the *Moving On* study (Biehal *et al.*, 1995) the term 'mixed heritage' was used to describe young people, one of whose parents' ethnic origin was different from the other's. For example, one parent of a mixed heritage young people was black (further sub-categorised as Afro-Caribbean) and the other parent was white. Nevertheless, in that study of 183 young people 25 (i.e.14%) were described as being black, Asian, or mixed heritage. In this 1995/6 survey, if one also takes into account that an additional 191 (or 5%) were categorised as 'other', then the proportion of those of mixed ethnic origin amounts to 22 per cent of the total figure. Either way, whether including that 'other' category or not, the proportion of black and Asian young people described in the study is far higher than the proportion in England and Wales as a whole, according to Social Trends (1995).

What these figures do confirm from some earlier studies (for example, see Barn, 1990) is the continued over-representation of ethnic minorities, but especially black young people, in the public child care system. Policy questions about why this is the case and the practice issues that arise from this finding are picked up throughout the book, especially in chapter nine under the heading anti-discriminatory work.

The Occupational Status of the Young People in the Study

Of the number of young people whose occupational status was identified (n=2905) the two largest groups were those who were unemployed, accounting for 1497 or 51.5 per cent of the sample, and those young people in further/higher education, who accounted for 508 or 17.5 per cent of the sample. Figure 4.1 provides a breakdown of the different occupational status of the young people at the projects.

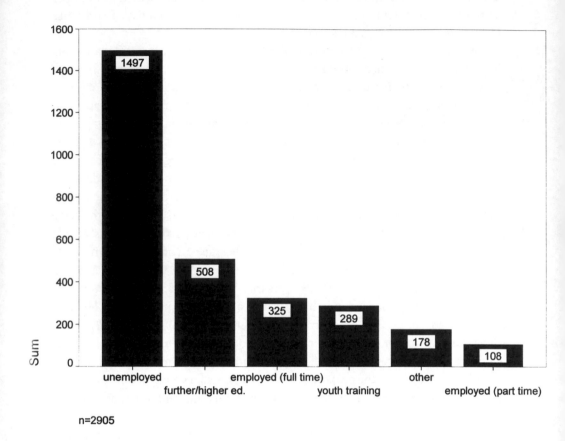

n=2905

Figure 4.1: The occupational status of young people leaving care (n=2905)

A very low proportion of young people, 11 per cent, were in full time employment, with only 4 per cent in part time employment. Some 897 young people or 27.5 per cent of the total were either attending a youth training course or in further and/or higher education. Let us see how these figures compare with the 1993 survey. Table 4.3 provides the details.

When comparing the two survey periods it can be seen that there has been a 2.5 per cent increase in the percentage unemployed. Furthermore, whilst recording that the proportion of young people attending youth training courses has slightly reduced in the current survey, it is important and pleasing to note, in comparing the two survey periods, that there is a 2 per cent higher proportion, albeit still only 11 per cent, of young people from the 1996 survey in full time employment.

Table 4.3 The occupational status of young people leaving care: comparing the 1992/3 and 1995/6 survey findings

Occupation type	1992/3 survey figures and percentages	1995/6 survey figures and percentages	Percentage change between 1992/3 and 1995/6 surveys
Employment–full time	77 (9%)	325 (11%)	+2%
Employment–part time	36 (4%)	108 (4%)	same
Youth training	114 (13%)	289 (10%)	-3%
Further/higher education	162 (19%)	508 (17.5%)	-1.5%
Unemployed	418 (49%)	1497 (51.5%)	+2.5%
'Other' category	52 (6%)	178 (6%)	same
Total no. of young people	859 (100%)	2905 (100%)	n/a

Yet these two occupational tables should not be interpreted as being all negative about care leavers, but rather illustrative, albeit to an extreme extent, of other social policy issues about the position of young people in the 16 to 19 age group trying to make the transition to some level of independence. A considerable number more, 905 (or 27.5% of the total), of the young people discussed in this research were occupied attending a youth training course or further/higher education or in part time employment, than the 11 per cent who were in full time employment. This finding can be compared with the social and economic trends in terms of the much lower proportion of young people going directly from school into work (Wallace and Cross, 1990; Jones, 1995), the steadily increasing proportion of working class young people, especially in the 16–18 age group attending transitional youth training and other training schemes (Social Trends, 1994), and the increasing proportion of young people attending further and higher education since the advent of the expansion of those sectors.

Jones (1995) has examined these structural changes in some considerable detail. She argues that there are four elements affecting young people seeking to leave home and live in independent households. These four elements, which all affect young people's 'access to the rights and responsibilities of citizenship', are access to an income from employment, access to the state safety net of social security, access to family support, and access to independent housing (Jones, 1995:9). After discussing these elements she concludes (p.11) that as the safety net of state support is being withdrawn from young people, so parental support has become increasingly important.

The context for all occupational status and employment issues, including youth employment, has changed quite considerably since the 1980s. Compared with 1986 – when young people aged 16–24 made up 23 per cent of the workforce, in 1996 young people made up 17 per cent of the workforce (British Youth Council, 1996). This change is due to a fall in the total number of young people and a greater proportion of young people being in further and higher education. Of those under 20, 19.5 per cent are unemployed with 22.per cent of men and 17 per cent of women in this age group affected (Trades Union Congress, 1996). In 1993, taking the 18–24 age group, 23 per cent were unemployed compared to a rate of 14.5 per cent for all ages (Department of Employment, 1993). There are also unemployment differences not only in terms of geography but in terms of ethnicity with one study, not atypical in the field, reporting that for black people the unemployment rate is double the national average (Hutson and Liddiard, 1994:50). Unemployment is also linked to issues about the claiming of benefits, and under 25s account for more than one in four of all those unemployed and claiming benefit and one in six of all long term unemployed claimants (Youthaid, 1996).

Given the vital importance of financial and employment issues, the survey also asked projects' perceptions about employment to see whether they considered matters were changing, for better or worse. These answers were then compared with those from the 1993 survey.

Project Perceptions about Employment Opportunities

Table 4.4 Project perceptions about full time and part time employment opportunities for young people leaving care[5]

Subject area	1992/3 situation improved a little or significantly	1995/6 situation improved a little or significantly	1992/3 situation remained the same	1995/6 situation remained the same	1992/3 situation worsened a little or significantly	1995/6 situation worsened a little or significantly
Part time employment possibilities	12.5%	13%	21%	28%	67%	46%
Full time employment possibilities	8%	4%	21%	13%	71%	70%
Average percentages	10.25%	8.5%	21%	20.5%	69%	58%

5   In 1995 an average of 6 or 13 per cent of all respondents did not answer the above questions which explains why the percentage totals do not equal 100 per cent.

As Table 4.4 reveals, on average only a very small proportion, 8.5 per cent, of 1995 respondents considered that there had been any improvements in employment prospects. This is an even smaller average improvement than the small 10.5 per cent average for 1992/3. A much larger percentage of respondents, 46 per cent in relation to part time employment opportunities and 70 per cent in relation to full time employment opportunities, considered that the position had worsened either a little or significantly in the previous two year period. On average, for full time and part time employment opportunities 20.5 per cent considered that the position had remained the same during the two year period.

Whilst fully recognising that young people 16+ have a variety of potential occupations after leaving school, only one of which is employment, nevertheless young people leaving care, and the projects working with them, need some genuine encouragement in this area for unemployment not to become a permanent burden on themselves, their families and friends and the community as a whole. This remains one of the most challenging areas for young people leaving care and the need for demonstration projects, and centrally funded initiatives, could not be greater if young people are to be given hope for the future.

Conclusion

From the material presented in this chapter it can be seen that leaving care projects are taking on more referrals, and that local authority leaving care teams have by far the most challenging staff/young person ratios of 23 young people for each staff member. The majority of the projects, 63 per cent, have started since the Children Act 1989 was enacted, but a significant proportion, 37 per cent, had begun prior to that date. This does not suggest the sort of rapid growth in local authority projects that is sometimes assumed. In addition there has been very little growth in leaving care projects since 1994, and there are also reported cut-backs. The steady growth in the numbers of young people attending the projects can in part be explained by a growth in referrals and other factors external to the projects concerned. A significant proportion of the team's young people are black (14%), which is a higher percentage of the general black young people's population as a whole in England and Wales. The 46 leaving care teams are working with a group of financially dependent, and mostly unemployed, young people, but also a percentage who are at further and higher education training courses, or employed part time. Projects reported that the position regarding employment opportunities was worsening significantly, which confirms a longer term trend reported in the 1993 survey. This chapter has recorded the emergence of leaving care teams and not their rise and fall, although this may also happen if the financial situation gets much tighter. It has also pointed to some of the increasing challenges facing young people leaving care and the people who work with them, which are discussed further in the rest of this book, beginning in the next chapter, with education and training.

CHAPTER FIVE

Access to and Support for the Education of Young People Leaving Care

Introduction

Generally the role of education, in terms of providing opportunities for developing self esteem, building social relationships, friendships, and obtaining qualifications leading to enhanced job opportunities cannot be emphasised enough. In relation to qualifications Banks, for example, found in a large study of 5000 young people that qualifications earned by the age of 16 '...proved the best single predictor of the direction that individuals' careers would then take' (Banks et al., 1993:230) We have already seen that the school, further and higher education sectors have been the subject of considerable change since 1980, moving towards the notion that schools are competing businesses, often with an increasing number 'seeking the best and rejecting the rest'.

In respect of research concerning education and young people *in care*, government's own report concluded that 'The care and education systems in general are failing to promote the educational achievements of children looked after' (SSI /OFSTED:1995:3). That very detailed report then went on to explain the particularly difficult emotional circumstances facing young people in care whilst also making the point that their educational needs were not fully understood by teachers and social workers. Given these young people's situation, of personal and institutional disadvantage, the importance of education in these young people's life, and the absence of any positive research (as far as I am aware) in this area, it follows that the situation concerning the education of young people leaving care is particularly crucial, especially given the poor in-care educational experience they will have likely had. However, there has been little research in to the educational situation of young people leaving care (Jackson's work, 1995, is a notable exception), although it is a developing field of interest, and a continuing one for the *Who Cares? Trust*. The question therefore raised here is: will the education of young people leaving care also emerge as both a critical area and one found wanting? In short, will it replicate some of the structural shortcomings concerning in-care education experiences, especially in terms of professional and financial supports, or will there be examples of emerging good practice? It is known that young people leaving care are already dealing with a wide range of practical and emotional changes, and 'endings', whether about their foster carers, their social worker, their school, or their family. Yet another change on to further and higher education is yet another major transition in their lives, and the presence or otherwise of personal and financial supports will be crucial to whether they can make that transition.

It is also important to recall, from Chapter One, that the legislation concerning the funding of education of young people leaving care is weak and there has been little commitment to this important area, for many years in fact. The legislative requirements remain discretionary as 'may do it' powers, as opposed to a 'must do it' duties. These powers are contained in the Children Act 1989 (S24:8; 9), and are essentially the same as the power contained in the Child Care Act 1980 (S27), and even the Children Act 1948 (S20:1). The developments recorded in this chapter should be set against this low key background, so far as responsibilities to provide financial supports to care leavers post 16-year-olds are concerned. The other key issue concerning financial supports available to young people leaving care attending further and higher education is whether the financial supports should come from the social services as well as from the social security system.

This chapter will first concentrate on the research findings from the survey relating to the educational situation of young people leaving care with particular emphasis on their financial situation. Then there will be a review of the limited research which has examined the reasons for young people leaving or staying in further and higher education, concluding with examples of ways in which improvements can be made, drawing on current initiatives.

The educational situation of the young people

An estimated 508 young people or 19 per cent of the sample were attending either further or higher education, and this is exactly the same proportion as was the case in the 1992/3 survey. In the 1996 survey, and of this 508 figure, 208 of the young people were attending local authority projects, 200 were attending joint projects, and the remainder, 100, were attending leaving care projects run by voluntary organisations. One in seven of the young people attending local authority or voluntary organisation leaving care projects were in either further or higher education, compared with the joint projects where the figure was one in five. Data was not gathered about the educational content of local authorities' leaving care policies. It is possible to undertake an informed analysis about education and leaving care from other data collected first from the questionnaire about respondents perceptions about financial support for education, and from elsewhere.

Financial Support for Further/Higher Education

Table 5.1 Respondents' perceptions of their local education support/services in relation to leaving care work

Questions asking respondents to gauge changes between 1994 and 1996	Percentage and numbers who considered the situation had worsened a little or significantly	Percentage and numbers who considered the situation had remained the same	Percentage and number who considered the situation had improved a little or significantly
Provision of financial grants from local authority for education and training post 21 years? (Children Act 1989, S24:9 power) (n=31)	26% (8)	58% (18)	16% (5)
Availability of financial grants from local authority to young people under 21? (Children Act 1989 S24:8 power) (n=35)	25% (9)	61% (22)	14% (5)
Financial support during vacation periods from local authority to young people on further/ higher education courses? (n=35)	26% (9)	63% (22)	11% (4)
Average percentages	26%	60%	14%

Research findings

For this 1996 survey again projects reported a (further) significant deterioration in the education situation facing young people leaving care, whether attending further or higher education and whether part or full time. This applied almost equally whether concerning the provisions concerning financial support for under 21 (Children Act 1989, S24:8) or over 21 year olds (S24:9). The 1993 survey also revealed a worsening of the situation concerning funding for education, over the years 1991–92.

As can be seen from Table 5.1, and across the three potential education support areas, an average of some 26 per cent considered that the situation had slightly or considerably worsened, compared with an average of 14 per cent of those who consider that the situation had slightly or significantly improved; 60 per cent of respondents considered that the situation concerning certain specific local education supports for young people leaving care had remained about the same for the period in question. Other sources confirm that the base line for such support is extremely low and inadequate (for example, see Audit Commission, 1994; Biehal *et al.*, 1995). In this survey an already poor situation is not improving, and is perceived as getting worse when one looks at the responses other than those indicating the position has remained the same. If we consider the deterioration in other financial support sources, some of which have already been raised and some of which will be discussed in due course, then the position for young people of finding financial support for their advanced or non-advanced education looks extremely worrying.

It is symptomatic of the considerable challenges facing leaving care projects and local authorities that 'education' as a topic accounted for just four examples of project achievements, accounting for less than 3 per cent of the total number of 176 achievements listed as discussed in the later chapter on young people's participation and achievements.

Further and higher education: the only examples of education achievements given by projects were:

1. 'Enabling consumers to access further and higher education at the project and at various main sector colleges'.

2. 'Initiatives in attempting to provide employment/career opportunities for young people via negotiations with local colleges/training and enterprise council'.

3. 'Better networks with education providers'.

4. 'Record number of young people pursuing further and higher education' (estimated by this one project as constituting 25% of the occupation of all the young people attending that particular project).

These examples are especially interesting when it is considered that in only one of these four examples (the second one) did the project concerned indicate that there had been any improvement in funding for the sector. In other words, for this minority of projects the increase in activity in this area was not associated with any additional monies being made available, but rather a continuation of low or nil funding. It is also of note to recall from the general survey results about the 'occupation' of the young people in the survey, as reported in the preceding chapter, that after 'unemployment', the greatest number (508) of young people leaving care of the sample (n=2905) were those attending further and higher education. Yet the fact that it was listed the fourteenth main problem area facing leaving care projects, and as discussed in the later achievements and problems chapter, both confirms its 'problem status' and the lack of progress in the area of funding further and higher education. The following case study illustrates the serious and complex nature of the problems.

Case Study
'Joan's education: aged 17

Joan was taken into care when she was eight after her father deserted the family and her mother could no longer cope bringing up the four children on her own. After leaving care at 16, Joan moved to a county town near London, and returned to full-time education after spending a year in employment. A seemingly simple desire to return to education and a commitment to meet course requirements was not sufficient. Joan had to overcome extraordinary difficulties to sustain her course of study.

Prior to being accommodated, she had been in full-time education studying for GCSEs (General Certificate of Secondary Education). Shortly after her 16th birthday, she moved into privately rented accommodation and she decided that she would like to fulfil a life long ambition to gain a place at university. Aware that she would be required to pay for her education after her 19th birthday and that there would be implications for receiving benefits as she got older, Joan initially hoped to be able to complete her course work and take her GCSEs at the same time as other students were doing their retakes. After discussion with local colleges it became obvious that this would not be possible. At this time it seemed likely that she would be required to spend two years studying for her GCSEs.

After advocacy help from a voluntary organisation and much negotiation and an interview, a college offered her a place to study 5 GCSEs over a one year period. Joan was assisted in making a successful application for Income Support under the Severe Hardship rules. She was also successful in obtaining Housing Benefit. (Note: both of these supports have since been reduced/removed.) Even then she was not eligible for funding from her local education authority for an education maintenance allowance, although her level of income fell within the appropriate bracket. That allowance can only be assessed based on parental income and she is estranged from her parents and there is no separate criterion to assess young people living independently from their parents.

> As a result of advice from the voluntary organisation a financial assessment was undertaken as a result of which Joan now receives a 'top up' from social services, during term time, of £19.85 per week. She needs to supplement her income through part time work, but each £1 she earns above the first £5 is deducted, £1 for £1, from her benefit.
>
> Returning to full time study has been very stressful in other ways. Living in privately rented accommodation, Joan is without the support of family members. If, as is hoped, she does start university in the autumn, she will then be 18. In the second year at university, when she becomes 19, she will no longer be entitled to receive either Income Support or Housing Benefit. Basic estimated living costs for one academic year are in the region of £4000 to £6000. Although in advance of that time the voluntary organisation will present Joan's financial case, previous experience suggests that the local authority will not make additional funds available.

Joan's case illustrates problems which the East Midlands Leaving Care Forum (EMLCF) has recognised, and it has argued that what is needed are the followingbefore any agreements with young people about meeting their educational needs (EMLCF,1995):

- all alternative sources of funding should be pursued including education grants, the department of Social Security, parents, access funds, bursaries and charities
- young people to be expected to make reasonable attempts to contribute financially (e.g. by vacation employment). This should not interfere with their ability to pursue education or training
- funding/support should be agreed for the duration of the course and received periodically (e.g. six months)
- the level of any payment should fall within existing policy guidelines about financial support to young people. These use the Income Support levels as a base line.
- Negotiations should be undertaken with the education departments to promote the needs of care leavers in terms of access to local authority funding
- the resource implications of a positive policy should be relayed to central government departments of health and education.

Factors which help and hinder the education situation

As for the four examples given above, generally it was also found that there was no statistical link between the numbers in further and higher education and projects' perceptions about the state of educational support funding. Neither was there any statistical link between numbers attending further and higher education and the project type. The former finding may come as a surprise to those who might expect that the levels of attendance by young people leaving care at further and higher education courses are associated with the availability and level of their local educational support grants. Indeed the project with the most young people, some 92 receiving further or higher education, recorded that the position concerning the availability of three types of potential education support had worsened considerably in the two year period from 1994 to 1996. Yet there were also projects where the converse was the case. There were other scenarios which complicated the picture further, confirming that educational attendance for this group is not simply associated with the existence or absence of educational support grants alone, but rather is a result of a combination of individual, local and funding factors. This combination of factors requires further investigation, and this is well beyond the remit of this study. So instead the limited evidence that exists about young people's educational progress elsewhere will be examined.

Thompson's (1995) study of education and young people in and leaving care points to the considerable financial and personal problems facing this group at the further and higher education stages. Her main findings about education and young people leaving care, based on a sample of 157 young people from eight projects, were that 22 or 8 per cent of the sample were either in full time or part time education, compared with 7 per cent here. She provides valuable detailed information which makes an important contribution to the field. She found, for example, that of nine young people that took up post-16 education all five who stopped lived in independent accommodation, and not in foster care. She also found that the reasons given for stopping education were financial *and* emotional ones, and not academic. Furthermore, it was found that of the small number in higher education, just five in fact, three had gone there direct from a foster placement, and all of those had their foster placement kept open for them at weekends and during the vacations. When the young people in the study were asked what supported young people in their academic studies, they pointed first to their own skills and abilities, next to the social services help (both financial and advice/support), and next to leaving care projects, residential care workers, and then school, family and foster carers (Thompson, 1995:38–46). She concluded that although half of all the respondents continued their education beyond the age of 16, half of these did not continue due to financial reasons (Thompson, 1995:46). These reasons stemmed from the high costs of living independently. She also discovered that it was usually the case that financial support was available for those who went into higher education if the young person was accommodated at the time (Thompson, 1995:58).

In another study (Humberside County Council, 1996) it was also found that there was very low take up of further education or training by young people leaving care. Although the precise reasons for this were unclear, the fact that one in ten of the group had already moved into independent accommodation before their official school leaving age not only alarmed the researchers but did little to help with their further education aspirations! The researchers concluded that much more importance needs to be given to a prompt and thorough assessment of educational need at the point of referral to social services.

Overall from the research, if one totals the numbers of young people in a financially dependent state and therefore described in the survey as unemployed, or in education, or attending youth training, or in part time work (which also normally attracts benefits payments subject to certain hour limits), then the figure becomes 2402 or 83 per cent of the total. It is this consistent and very high level of financial dependency which is so keenly felt by the young people and the projects working with them, and may seem of most financial significance to those local managers, and local and national politicians who regard themselves as burdened with financial responsibilities. Such is the importance and scale of these financial issues that they are dealt with in a separate chapter, Chapter Ten. Here, however, it is necessary and appropriate to examine the more specific issue of the availability of educational grants for this age group.

The state of discretionary educational grants

As has already been demonstrated, the provision of educational grants or other sorts of financial support for young people leaving care seeking education is yet another discretionary matter so far as the legislation is concerned (Children Act 1989, S24:8; 9 applies). Table 5.1 showed that such financial educational support as there is for this group, is at worst deteriorating, and at best remaining the same from a low baseline of provision.

The recording of respondents' views about this worsening scenario is supported by other evidence about the declining levels of discretionary education grants as a result of research conducted by the National Foundation for Educational Research. This wide ranging national study collected and compared statistics of English and Welsh local education authorities' discretionary awards for each of the three academic years from 1990 to 1993 plus the planned discretionary awards for 1993/94. The report's main findings in relation to the 16+ age group which lead up to the 1994 period, the earlier of the two year period which respondents here were asked to consider (National Foundation for Educational Research, 1994:1–8), were:

- the average value of a Section 2 further education award for non-designated courses of higher and further education, mostly for full time study, was £900 per annum

- the average value for EMAs (educational maintenance allowances), although not strictly discretionary awards since they are paid to pupils and students under special regulations for 16–19-year-olds in full time education, was £450

- the number of further education discretionary awards is projected to be about one-third higher in 1993/4 than in 1990/91. The average value of such awards in 1993/94 is projected to be about one-tenth less in real terms than in 1990/91

- overall expenditure on discretionary awards by LEAs in England and Wales is projected to decline by about 8 per cent in real terms between 1990/91 and 1993/94

- the average value of an award in 1992/93 was about 6 per cent below the 1990/91 level, and projections for 1993/94 suggest that the average for that year will be about 13 per cent below the 1990/91 level in cash terms – this is a decrease of about a quarter in real terms

- there has been an increase in demand for discretionary awards since 1990/91 from 16–19-year-olds because of increased staying on rates for 16–19-year-olds, and colleges offering a wider variety of courses

- the majority of LEAs either had introduced or were planning to introduce stricter conditions of eligibility for and level of maintenance

- there was very little consistency among authorities' policies for discretionary awards: there is no such thing as a typical LEA discretionary awards policy

- overall expenditure on discretionary awards for 1993/94 by metropolitan authorities is projected to decrease by about a quarter in real terms compared with 1990/91, whereas for non-metropolitan authorities there will be much less of a decrease.

As the case study highlighted, Joan was turned down for an educational maintenance allowance because the allowance requires parental income to be assessed, and Joan is living away from home. How can you estimate the income of the local authority, as parent? And why should this be necessary? Thompson found that there was minimal financial support for the education of young people leaving care, and she found that despite *all* the young people in her study stating that they had receive some financial assistance from social services, this was in the main for setting up home, and had been one-off casual payments and not an educational grant. Biehal *et al.* recorded that those who did make the move into education or work or training were from more stable care backgrounds, the majority in foster placements, and disproportionately female (Biehal *et al.*, 1995:80). Biehal *et al.*'s and Thompson's work appear to confirm the view that the increasing trend of later entries into care, between 11 and 13, is also a further positive predictive factor concerning future educational achievement and fulfilment.

This survey suggests that post-16 opportunities are dependent upon the ability of young people to fight their own corner, or being lucky enough to have an effective advocate. There is no evidence to suggest that their post-16 futures are shaped by consistent local authority policies which recognise the needs of young people who are separated from their parents. The actions and deeds of the local authority as corporate parent seem largely irrelevant, in complete contrast to the situation in a settled family. The local authority seems to be acting largely as the absent and poor parent, with government providing the inadequate role model.

Setting education standards for leaving care

The East Midlands Leaving Care Forum (EMLCF) has called on the Association of Directors of Social Services to take a strategic direction over this matter, along with the other key bodies in respect of the funding of 'non-advanced' and 'advanced' education for young people leaving care (EMLCF, 1995:12). Similarly, the First Key National Standards Working Group's document National Standards in Leaving Care (First Key, 1996a:15) has also called for funding to be made available which takes into account the young person's needs in term and vacation time, and which should involve department planning and support. The Social Services Inspectorate's standards for leaving care (reported in Childright, 1996:15) emphasise the importance of education for young people leaving care, and, in relation to funding, states that 'the finance and accommodation to support young people in training and education take account of the full length of the education programme and different grants and benefits available'. This appears a highly ambiguous statement and can be regarded in one of two ways. Either it is a low expectation as a standard taking into account the poor state of affairs outlined above. Alternatively, it could be designed simply to report on 'what is', that is, a realistic standard rather than a standard of what could or should be, in this critical field. It raises the fundamental question once again of how can there be any, or any decent, national or indeed enforceable standards if policies are framed in a discretionary manner and locally driven?

The fact that the Social Services Inspectorate's standard 10 – employment/education/training – is the last of the ten sets of standards listed is hopefully not an indication of its perceived importance. However, it could be that its placing is intended to reflect the corporate nature of the financial responsibilities in this field, in contrast to the earlier standards which are concerned almost exclusively with social services responsibilities. More than that, the standard points to not being the responsibility of the social services but of the education department if practice falls short of the standard, whatever the description of that standard actually means! Even the Social Services Inspectorate leaving care standard about education, in its fuller version (SSI, 1995) stating that 'young people leaving care are identified as eligible for funding from the local education authority with the social services department supporting accommodation...', does not take the funding shortfall any further, but simply provides a mechanism for identifying what is already known, namely that young people are eligible but not entitled as a right to be fully funded for their further and higher education.

Tackling educational problems

What follows are examples and summaries of three quite different approaches by local authorities to dealing with the educational problems of young people leaving care. All three originate from local authority education, not social services departments. The first one, in the London Borough of Wandsworth, plans to integrate and improve services within existing systems and budgets (as far as one can tell), and the other two, in Leeds and Manchester, are separately funded education initiatives. What is described builds on existing initiatives involving the local social services and education departments which are not described here.

Many if not all local authorities are not unaware of the problems, and what follows is a summary of the inspection findings of one local authority, the London Borough of Wandsworth, into leaving care education, and its plan of action to deal with the problems. In its action plan the strategic nature of the required response, and the links between social services, education and carers, are clearly spelt out.

Tackling Educational Problems Locally (1): the London Borough of Wandsworth Example

What follows is a summary of one local authority's published 'snapshot' inspection survey of the quality of education provided for children looked after, both in residential and foster care (London Borough of Wandsworth, 1995).

> In order to improve the quality of education received by children looked after, and raise the standards of attainment achieved by them, a closer partnership must be developed between the education and SSD. Schools, carers, and social workers each have distinct but complementary roles in helping to ensure that the current slow progress made in primary schools is accelerated and built on, and is not lost as pupils progress through the system. (London Borough of Wandsworth, 1995:11–12)

SUMMARY OF INSPECTION FINDINGS

Before summarising the report it is necessary to explain, for those unfamiliar with the Special Education Need (SEN) code, that the five stages described here refer to a *process* of identifying needs. Also, experience shows that only the most tenacious parents ensure that they receive the support their statement recommends.

Most of the findings described here are also found in national reports, namely:

- A high proportion of pupils, particularly those of secondary school age, are under achieving.

- Many have a long history of poor attendance and exclusion rates are high.

- A disturbingly high percentage of those at key Stage 4 (aged 16+) are being educated in Pupil Referral Units (PRUs).

- Amongst the group as a whole, 54 per cent were identified as being at one of the five stages of Special Educational Need (SEN) and 18 per cent had a statement, as compared to an estimated 20 per cent and 2 per cent respectively of the population as a whole.

- *Where well focused individual education plans were being implemented, educational and behavioural targets are more effectively addressed.*

- Assessment and record keeping systems maintained by schools are on the whole adequate but information was often lost when pupils transfer to another school.

- Where records are lost or not passed to the new school promptly the disruption to pupils' education was exacerbated.

- Partnership between the schools, social workers and carers varied considerably from excellent to poor. In a number of cases schools were better supported by carers in relation to behavioural rather than educational goals. Greatest concern was expressed by schools over poor communication in relation to pupils in short stay residential centres.

- In many cases the fact that a pupil is looked after is not specifically noted by schools, unless problems arise. This limits their capacity to respond sensitively if crises arise and denies them the opportunity of being proactive and of ensuring that the particular needs of this vulnerable group of young people are met. (London Borough of Wandsworth, 1995:2–3, emphasis added)

Table 5.2 is a summary of the action points arising from that report.

Table 5.2 Leaving care educational issues:
the action plan of one local authority

Key Issue	Action by
Strategies should be implemented to reduce the high instance of unauthorised absence and exclusions associated with pupils looked after and their over representation amongst pupils educated otherwise than at school.	Education department
The quality development officer (working with parents) should ensure that systems are developed that maximise carers' involvement in the statementing and annual review of children for whom they are responsible.	Education department
Schools should be required to maintain an accurate list, reported termly, of those pupils who are looked after.	Education department Schools
Systems to be established to ensure that data held centrally is accurate, accessible and regularly updated.	Social services
In-service training for carers and workers to include information on aspects of education that have a bearing on their role and facilitate improved partnership. Parallel information relating to SSD's review systems etc. should be included in INSET for teachers with designated responsibility for children looked after.	Social services Education department
Close links should be established between children's homes/family resource centres and schools to ensure that the educational needs of pupils in short stay residential care situations are met.	Social services Carers Education department Schools
Schools should establish systems that allow them to act proactively in relation to children looked after so that under-achievement, absence and behaviour problems can be addressed in the early stages.	Schools
Where pupils are identified as having special educational needs, focused individual educational plans (IEPS) should be drawn up to address the issues. Plans should accompany a pupil if transferred to minimise discontinuity.	Schools
Educational records should be sent to a pupil's new school at the earliest opportunity. Copies of key educational documents should be sent to pupil's carer, particularly when a pupil has been excluded permanently or when no new school has been identified when a pupil has been taken off role. Carers should be responsible for the inclusion of these records in the pupil's educational profile.	Schools

Tackling Educational Problems Locally (2): the Manchester City Council Example

The Manchester Teaching Service (MTS) was established in 1989 by Manchester City Council to work actively towards meeting the educational needs of children looked after by the local authority and otherwise known to the social services department (MTS,1995).

As at 1995/6 the service was composed of 29 full time teachers, approximately 15 sessional staff, 4 secretaries and its own administrative centre. Organisationally, teachers function within teams with a specific remit to work to particular operational areas of social work practice. These include residential centres, the youth justice service, foster care and services for children living with their own families. The service states that in its direct work with a significant proportion of the 1100 children and young people looked after by the local authority:

> ...it has rapidly developed as the central agency through which the local authority's responsibility for 'educational parenting' is discharged, not only in the context of its specific work with children in partnership with their families, carers, residential and field social workers, but also through its capacity for developing information systems and for networking across the full range of education and social work agencies... Each of the five operational teams...take some responsibility for children and young people who are looked after within these [foster] placements. In particular one team is wholly dedicated to stabilising foster placements where there is considered an imminent risk of breakdown due solely to educational placements. Other teams provide a direct educational service to those children and young people who are considered at equal risk, due...to other pressures. (MTS, 1995)

The MTS report states that its teaching service provides a complementary service (to social services) which reduces the overall incidence of children and young people being separated from their natural families and significantly minimises the risk of breakdowns within specific care placements for those children and young people looked after. Of 218 referrals to the teaching service where the families were assessed as being directly at risk of breakdown due to educational factors, 195 placements were maintained and there were just 23 breakdowns. The report concludes:

> In almost all local authorities...the general absence of education as a strategic consideration within social work systems inevitably reduces their quality and operational effectiveness and also creates quite false patterns of demand for those services. This has served to perpetuate some of the most entrenched and intractable difficulties of the public care system in addition to fostering the educational disadvantage and underachievement of those within it. (MTS, 1995)

MANCHESTER TEACHING SERVICE: FINANCIAL COSTS

The financial costs also confirm the view that investing in prevention is financially as well as personally sound. The total 1995/6 budget is given as £884,115 and finances 29 full time teachers, 15 sessional teachers, 4 administrative staff and all supplies and services supporting 220–300 children in schools. This same amount is listed as equivalent to paying for 8 young people in secure accommodation or 14 children in high costs outside community homes with education/therapeutic placements or 20 children in local authority residential care. At the time of writing the service was under review, and may be absorbed as part of a wider departmental review, but it is still important to describe.

Another way of providing for, guiding and co-ordinating the education needs of young people looked after, and those who were known to social services (including young people who were looked after), is to develop an area-wide resource with corporate roles and responsibilities, such as has developed in Leeds. This initiative is sufficiently innovative and important to merit more detailed description and is included here as a further educational policy pointer.

Tackling Educational Problems Locally (3): the Leeds Example

The Leeds Education Support Team was set up to monitor, safeguard and promote the educational interests of all young people looked after by the local authority or who are known to the social services department. It does this in a variety of ways (Leeds City Council, 1996), including:

- provision of in-school support (a 14 teacher team)
- provision of a series of complementary half day education programmes with small 6/7 young people groups
- liaison with schools and the various agencies within the local education authority (or what is left of it!), helping schools compile their education plans and ensuring that information is available to them about social services and care plans
- education surgeries and advice sessions, to try to avoid crises situations
- membership of the inter-agency community assessment panels
- special educational needs advisors
- work experience/liaison with local employers (links into and is part of 'complementary education' above)
- college links with the local leaving care team – provision of special open evenings
- careers/employment seminars involving the business community

- team members are members of adoption panel in order to highlight educational concerns

- annual high profile 'well done' receptions, locally sponsored

- the development of a 'family of schools concept' which actively promotes the pooling of resources at both high school and primary school levels

- the writing of a 12 week course on educational matters for social services personnel and foster carers. The aim of the course is to increase the confidence and effectiveness of personnel to safeguard and promote the education of young people looked after. The course is accredited by CCETSW and the National Colleges of Further Education at NVQ levels 11 and 111.

Key issues involving education

Drawing back a little from the details, the fact that such a high number, 518 young people, were attending some form of education or training points to the importance of several key issues involving education:

- there is an education need for a proportion of young people leaving care as well as a keenness to obtain more education by the young people themselves, underpinned and reinforced by the high levels of unemployment for this group

- youth training has become virtually compulsory for young people to receive certain benefits

- payment to support oneself whilst attending at an educational institute can be considerable, when one considers the accommodation, fee payments and living costs involved

- The high number of young people without a full or part time work and, therefore, especially in need of support and financial assistance to survive is really quite remarkable, when one also takes into account that the majority of these young people are, at the same time, going through a major emotional and physical transition.

Practice/policy pointers in further and higher education

The evidence about successful access to and sustaining further and higher education and support points to the following key factors:

- the young person's individual capacities and qualities

- the need for a thorough educational assessment at the point of referral

- the availability of financial support (and not necessarily in the form of an educational but rather a social services grant)
- the type as well as the nature of the placement at post-16
- the quality of support available
- establishing whose responsibility it is to fund young people in further and higher education
- following an educational assessment, establishing whose responsibility it is to secure a place in further and higher education for young people
- establishing whose responsibility it is to support young people in further and higher education
- financial support by local authorities to foster parents for weekend and vacation foster places to be kept open
- most 16+s are badly in need of relationships and life skills which educational settings provide.

Recommendations for change

Education for young people leaving care is necessary because of the earlier dysfunctional and disruptive educational experiences of so many young people in care. It should also be seen as an investment in young people, to prevent the other sorts of problems, for example homelessness and unemployment, that so many young people leaving care often face.

There needs to be a review of education funding and planning for any significant improvements to occur. For the proper education and funding of education for young people leaving care what is needed is higher financial investment, as well as a greater emphasis on departmental liaison, information and planning.

Specifically, there needs to be a reversal of the following funding changes that have taken place:

- the withdrawal of housing benefit payments to students
- the freezing, then reduction, of maintenance grants from local education authorities
- only a very limited number of courses attract mandatory awards for fees and exam fees (i.e. those at undergraduate level)
- students aged 19+ are ineligible for income support unless the course is less than 21 hours a week; in April 1996 this was reduced to 16 hours, thus putting a further financial squeeze on young people leaving care in this situation.

Other recommendations about improving education and leaving care, from McParlin (Royal Philanthropic Society/National Youth Agency, 1995) include the setting up children panels within local education authorities, persuading local authorities to publicise GCSE results for children looked after, initiating a profile of further/higher education, and promoting the idea of independent visits.

The issue of education is a critical area of concern for young people leaving care and, as with housing or supported accommodation, to which attention is now turned in the next chapter, it has similar interrelating political, policy, financial, planning and practice elements which makes good consistent practice difficult.

CHAPTER SIX

The Housing Situation of Young People Leaving Care

Introduction

The last chapter concentrated on the education of young people leaving care and reported the research's findings about that vital topic and made recommendations for change. Earlier, the limited scope and strength of the legislation concerning leaving care and the Children Act 1989, and the impact of wider social trends detrimental to young people seeking to make the transition to independent living, were identified. This chapter will concentrate on yet another vital topic, that of housing, or rather providing supported accommodation for young people leaving care, because the issue is not simply one about 'bricks and mortar'. It begins with a summary of the main housing findings drawn from earlier leaving care research and then moves on to presenting the survey findings, making comparisons with the earlier survey findings. Next, the findings to the 'project achievements and problems between 1994 and 1996' question in the questionnaire are presented here because housing featured strongly, being described as the foremost achievement category and second in the problems lists overall. The chapter concludes with a series of policy and practice pointers to clarify the different accommodation types available, and to emphasise key practice and planning issues. The overall aim of the chapter is provide research evidence about the changes in leaving care provision and practice, and to examine the consequences of the same. Since the relevant housing legislation has already been discussed in some detail in Chapter One, it will not be repeated here.

Garnett (1992) found that leaving care plans were often based on short term considerations leading to unsatisfactory and temporary accommodation. Biehal *et al.*'s study (1992:43) found that young people leaving care experienced 'accommodation problems, including temporary accommodation, drift and homelessness'. There is also evidence (see CHAR, 1995) that young black people continue to be over represented in the homelessness figures as a result of racism. Additionally, and according to evidence submitted to the 1996 Inquiry into Preventing Youth Homelessness, two-thirds of young people leaving care experienced homelessness (CHAR, 1996:56). The three main reasons given in that enquiry for that situation were the (young) age at which the most care leavers make the transition to independence, their disadvantaged position relative to other young people, and the lack of adequate support and preparation that they receive (CHAR,1996:56). In a general sense these findings, though alarming, are not new. This author's earlier survey pointed to the range of accommodation in which young people leaving care lived and, amongst other things, noted the increased popularity of supported lodgings. Many other studies have reported on both the unsatisfactory situation in general regarding the availability of housing, and inadequate housing finances for young people (on this point see Darke *et al.*, 1994; Kirk, 1996), and in particular for young people leaving care (see Stein and Carey, 1986; Young Homelessness Group, 1991; McCluskey, 1994).

The securing of appropriate affordable accommodation, with support offered, is absolutely vital for young people when they leave care, if they are to make the transition to a more independent living a satisfactory experience, preparing them for the future. To some the term 'appropriate' means a long term or permanent tenancy with either a housing association or local authority. For others it could mean more temporary accommodation, such as supported lodgings where a young person will normally live with a family and receive support, from the landlord/lady and a social worker and/or project worker. There are many further accommodation alternatives available, some of which are desirable and some of which are not appropriate in terms of the rent or setting. The issue of young people leaving care is also about the timing of the move, the suitability and maturity of the young person wishing to live independently, and the supports available, as much as the bricks and mortar issue. The following is a summary of the principle housing types available for young people leaving care.

Types of supported and non-supported accommodation available
Accommodation for Young People Leaving Care Includes:

- *local authority and housing association tenancies*: these are provided more often, according to the questionnaire data, in urban unified local authorities than in county areas
- *voluntary sector schemes* which provide accommodation and support to young people leaving care and homeless young people. This is provided by Housing Associations working with voluntary organisations (such as Barnados or NCH-Action for Children). The type of accommodation can include floating support, self-contained bedsits, or shared houses
- *private accommodation* in the form of bed and breakfast accommodation, for emergencies, or, in other circumstances, private hostels are options,

although because of their varying quality it is potentially dangerous (and I do not use that term lightly) if used unchecked and unmonitored

- where young people can safely *return to family or relatives*, they may be provided with emotional support and contact networks even if accommodation can not be provided

- if it is appropriate and if sufficient finances are provided, *extended stays in foster or residential placements* can provide additional stability and deliberately delay the often premature 'preparation for independence' phase which 'kicks in' at 16 in many cases (see Biehal *et al.*, 1992:9)

- *supported lodgings schemes* have expanded since the Children Act 1989 was introduced and essentially they offer temporary lodgings with live-in support. To succeed, supported lodgings schemes require dedicated staff time to set up, appropriate referrals and suitable young people, an efficient Housing Benefit scheme to part fund the costs, quality vetting, support and monitoring structures, and clarity about how supported lodgings contribute to the local authority policies regarding leaving care (so they are not provided as a 'cheap afterthought' but as a real option)

- it makes sense for there to be contingent *emergency housing strategy in place and accommodation available* and direct access hostels and bed and breakfast facilities of some sort will be required from time to time though not always appropriate because there can be inappropriate client groups (such as older alcoholic men) living there as well

- *foyer accommodation* and training/employment can be made available to young people leaving care, although no specific reference was made to this form of accommodation being available and/or used.

Young people leaving care live in a wide variety of types of accommodation and all the leaving care projects' work described here, as with other research in this field, concerns young people predominantly drawn from the 16 and 17, and 18 to 21 age groups (although there were indications of some 15-year-olds as well as over 21s attending leaving care projects). At the time of moving to independence and legal discharge, the questionnaire returns indicated that the majority of the young people were in the under 18 age group (see note 4, p.82). For ongoing work with these young people the age breakdown should be slightly different. The London Borough of Brent, for example, estimates that the percentage of its young people aged from 15 to 17 is 19 per cent, and the remainder, 81 per cent, are between 18 and 21 years of age. Of course the precise age balance of young people within projects will vary according to different circumstances. In the Royal

Philanthropic Society (1995), for example, the average age for all the young people attending its projects at that time was 18.

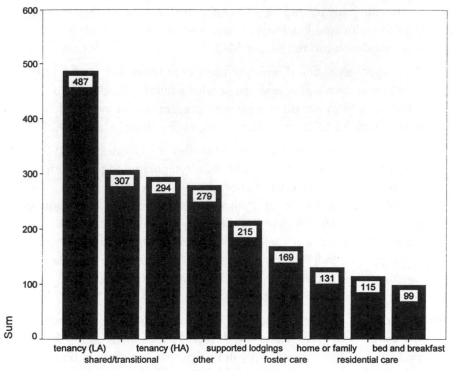

Figure 6.1 The housing situation of young people leaving care in 1996 (n=2096) [123]

1   The 'other' category totalling 279 consisted of young people living in a range of other accommodation or being homeless. The full breakdown is as follows: council/voluntary organisation accommodation = 38; hospital = 12; hostels = 32; other council accommodation = 15; unknown = 14; purchasing a home = 15; on remand = 3; at a penal establishment = 15 for those sentenced to in excess of 3 months, and if previously claiming Housing Benefit, they lose their entitlement to that benefit; at a mother and baby unit = 5; homeless = 25; living in project accommodation = 15; living out of borough = 4. The category 'private tenancy' was not listed by any project.

2   As has already been recorded, this survey describes the situation of some 3308 young people leaving care, and yet the housing situation of only 2096 young people was provided. The explanation for this discrepancy is that five of the participating leaving care teams did not complete the housing section in the questionnaire. This was the only omission of this scale in the entire research project, and probably reveals a shortcoming concerning local authority monitoring systems, although I have never before come across such omissions about housing data. The other associated explanation could be that the data was too time consuming to obtain for the large numbers of young people attending the projects concerned. The 1993 leaving care survey concerning 1538 young people contained housing data on only 987 young people, which does suggest a more widespread and systematic and ongoing data collection problem, rather than a local hitch.

3   It is not possible to provide a breakdown by gender or ethnic origin or special needs because that level of detailed information was not requested, or available.

The young people's actual accommodation will now be described. Then, after an analysis of that accommodation, there will be a comparison between those figures and the findings of the 1993 survey in order to answer the question 'how, if at all, have things changed, and why'? In the light of the comparisons made, the survey's leaving care projects' housing achievements and problems will be examined. The young people's (n= 2095) accommodation situation is presented in Figure 6.1.

Summary of Findings from Table 6.1 about the Housing Situation of the Young People's Housing in the Survey (n=2096)

The detailed findings in percentage terms and rank order, and illustrating the point that young people leaving care live in an ever widening range of accommodation types, are as follows:

1. local authority tenancies: 23 per cent

2. shared/transitional housing: 15 per cent

3. housing association tenancy: 14 per cent

4. private/bedsit /other /public care housing: 14 per cent

5. supported lodgings: 10 per cent

6. foster care: 8 per cent

7. home and family/friends: 6 per cent

8. local authority residential care: 5 per cent

9. bed and breakfast: 5 per cent

There were some differences between projects concerning the types of accommodation available and provided. These can be summarised as follows.

Differences in Accommodation Provided by Different Project Types

- the two most popular housing types for the *local authority projects* were local authority tenancies (average of 27 young people per project), and housing association tenancies (average of 12 young people in such accommodation)

- for the *voluntary organisation projects* the two most popular accommodation types were 'other' (averaging 7 per project) and shared/transitional housing (averaging 5 per project)

- for the *joint projects* housing association tenancies, shared/transitional local authority tenancies were the most popular accommodation types, accounting for an average of 6 young people for each type at each jointly run project.

This average, of 27 young people at each local authority project having a local authority housing tenancy, compares with an average of 3 young people who attended voluntary organisation projects, and 6 young people attending joint projects. The considerable differences cannot be explained simply in terms of the differences in average numbers of young people at the projects, which was 125 for local authority, 48 for voluntary organisation, and 59 for the jointly run leaving care projects. It can be more satisfactorily explained by the different levels of availability of such accommodation by project type, as well as project rationale. On average, one in every 4.6 young person attending a local authority project had a local authority tenancy, compared with one in 16 young people attending a voluntary organisation project, and one in 10 young people attending the joint projects. It is also the case that some of the larger metropolitan authorities have ongoing options on local authority tenancies (as witnessed in the content of some of the local authority Children's Services Plans that came to my attention). It also begs the question about what accommodation can be offered outside the local authority team framework and what real 'choice' of accommodation faces young care leavers in the smaller and predominantly county and country areas with teams run by the voluntary sector. Further research would be necessary to investigate the reasons beyond those already given for these differences.

Let me now turn to the housing situation of the young people in question compared with the 1993 survey before analysing the two results of the findings, and making comparisons with the youth housing market as a whole (see Table 6.1).

Comparing findings with other research

As we have seen, the most popular type of accommodation for young people leaving care is housing which offers the stability of a housing tenancy of some sort. Some 37 per cent were in tenancies, compared with 30 per cent in the 1993 survey. The 1996 restrictions on housing benefit have the aim of reducing the level of entitlements, therefore making it more difficult to retain such tenancies in the future. The figures for young people having tenancies are higher here than others have found to be the case. For example, Biehal *et al.*'s study of 74 young people leaving care (1995:36) found that just 20 per cent of the sample were in tenancies, with the most popular type of accommodation (accounting for 22 per cent) being hostel accommodation. Yet on the other hand the figures here reveal only the slightest increase, of 3 per cent, for local authority tenancies. This compares with a much higher, 16 per cent, increase in the numbers of young

Table 6.1 The housing situation of young people leaving care: 1993 and 1996 survey comparisons

Housing type	1992/3 survey figures and percentages (25 projects)	1995/6 survey figures and percentages (46 projects)	Percentage change from 1992/3 to 1995/6
Local authority tenancy	197 (20%)	487 (23%)	+3%
Shared/transitional housing	187 (19%)	307 (15%)	-4%
Housing association tenancy	103 (10%)	294 (14%)	+4%
Private/bedsit/other/ public care housing	169 (17%)	279 (14%)	-3%
Supported lodgings	243 (25%)	215 (10%)	-15%
Foster care	56 (6%)	169 (8%)	+2%
Home and family/friends	n/k	131 (6%)	n/k
In local authority residential care	n/k	115 (5%)	n/k
Bed and breakfast	32 (3%)	99 (5%)	+2%
Total	987 (100%)	2096 (100%)	n/a

n/k = not known

people attending projects during the same period, making the point that the demand on accommodation is far outstripping the increased supply of housing tenancies.

Although still popular, supported lodgings are also less popular than in 1993. Although in this 1996 research supported lodgings still account for 215 (or 10%) of all housing, this is much less than the 25 per cent figure from the 1992/3 survey. This significant change is most likely connected with the decreasing availability of multiple finance sources required for that type of accommodation.

There also seems to be more diversity in accommodation types according to these 1996 research findings. Thus, in this survey foster care accounts for housing 169 (or 8%) of the young people, and home and family (i.e. relatives) 131 (or 6%). Both local authority residential care and bed and breakfast, accounting for 115 and 99 young people respectively, each represent 5 per cent of the total number.

Although there was no specific question about housing with family/friends for either of the two surveys, the fact that projects listed young people as having this option, and the level of the responses they indicated, may suggest that this is a 'growth area' and one being more closely considered than before. It would be most interesting to take this issue further, which is one associated directly with the Children Act 1989's emphasis on encouraging partnerships and contact with existing families, in order to greater emphasise their responsibilities, to establish whether or not it represents a growing trend.

Bed and breakfast accommodation, occasionally necessary for a crisis situation but not normally regarded as generally suitable for vulnerable young people, only accounts for some five per cent of all housing. This represents a slight, but not significant, increase compared with 1992/3. Yet five per cent of the total represents some 99 vulnerable young people living in largely unregulated and unsupervised accommodation. This is still too many young people living in this type of accommodation if it is not simply being used for emergency accommodation. If this is the case, then the slight increase in the use of this type of accommodation is still of concern.

Temporary accommodation still accounts for between 44 per cent and 50 per cent of all accommodation, if one includes in that figure bed and breakfast, supported lodgings, shared/transitional, and private/other types of accommodation, as well as making some allowance (between 0–6%) for home/family/friends types of accommodation. It is a common but unsatisfactory situation that such a high percentage, nearly 50 per cent, of the young people in the 1996 survey are living in temporary rented accommodation. There can be cases where temporary accommodation is regarded as appropriate by the young person and the social worker, even if viewed as unacceptable to those pursuing permanent housing rights for all young homeless and young people leaving care. With such a high percentage of young people moving into such unplanned accommodation, the level cannot be regarded as acceptable. Nevertheless, the provision of temporary rented accommodation is also an understandable and a realistic practical option, if it is presented as an option and not all that is offered to young people. However, the Housing Act 1996 has effectively removed the entitlement to permanent housing for the homeless, and on the occasions when young people leaving care find themselves in this situation, and if they are older and no longer regarded as being entitled to leaving care services, or 'in need,' then they will only be offered temporary accommodation, if they are offered anything at all. For Housing Associations the situation regarding foyers, and young people's rights is an especially keenly felt one in that sector, traditionally espousing tenants rights in that in a foyer the young people, as tenants, are only being offered temporary accommodation with conditions attached. Ongoing changes to individuals' entitlements resulting in them only having the right to temporary accommodation, and to little else, diminishes and weakens to the point of oblivion the view that the state has a comprehensive responsibility to provide proper housing, supported or otherwise, for young people leaving care as a right.

There is then an overall emergent trend of both more young people being referred to leaving care projects by local authorities, and of those that are being referred, being worked with more intensely whilst they are in either foster care or residential care settings. In a sense, leaving care projects have always worked in this way, and it is not being claimed that the number of recorded foster care placements, 169 or 8 per cent of the total housing, representing a 2 per cent increase over 1993, or residential care placements with 115, or 5 per cent of the total, represents extra referrals or cases at an earlier stage. However, it is just possible that we may be seeing a slight change in the balance of responsibility for leaving care planning between foster care, residential care and leaving care teams, with the planning taking place more at the pre-leaving care stage, and for a more sustained period, than was previously indicated by the 1993 findings. This additional momentum of pre-leaving care planning, or preparation work as it is more commonly known, if this is happening, is again in line with long-standing good practice calls for more preparation work with young people about to leave care.

This research study slightly differs from other studies in respect to types of accommodation for young people leaving care in the sense that it records housing types for an unspecified period post leaving care. Other leaving care research, where housing was examined, has tended to record the first accommodation after discharge from care (for example, Biehal et al., 1992; Pinkerton and McCrea, 1993). This makes 'like with like' comparisons of post care accommodation types from this study virtually impossible, especially when one considers the number of subsequent moves that are regarded as often taking place. Overall and given that a period of time has elapsed since leaving care, it is encouraging to note that the single largest accommodation type is local authority tenancy which accounts for 23 per cent of the sample. This figure is considerably higher than the closest equivalent figure from other research, at 12.5 per cent for example from the Leeds study (Biehal et al., 1992:13). Additionally, if one includes housing association tenancies, the 'young people as tenant' figure from this study is 37 per cent. This is a direct proportional increase, compared with these combined tenancy figures from the 1992/3 survey (estimated at 30%). It is also a testament to the closer relationship between social services and housing departments. It may also be the case that a range of shorter, not long term tenancies are being used, with a higher turnover of young people.

Yet drawing on additional data from elsewhere it is possible to develop a further explanation for this increase in tenanted accommodation which centres on the proportion of young people who stay on in local authority tenancies. A local study in one London borough (Mills, 1994) of 75 young people who had left care and who were living in local authority accommodation via a local quota system found that the vast majority, 48 or 64 per cent of the sample, were still tenants in the same accommodation they had moved into some two to five years previously. This is a good record of stability offered by one local authority to those assessed as not requiring intensive support. Perhaps if support was offered the percentage of those remaining after five years could have further increased. All of the young people in this sample had been housed by the mechanism of a social welfare/independent living assessment and housed by means of the local authority's housing quota system used by that borough. By far the majority of this accommodation was single bedroom, and a substantial amount in three/four floor council blocks. In the majority of cases the young people were not working full time, and their rent was paid through the housing benefit system to support them, and they were in receipt of income support payments. A very small proportion (10%) of the young people were in rent arrears. Being in arrears with the rent meant that the young people could not move on from their accommodation until the arrears were settled, and Mills argues (1994:41) that this was a further contributory factor to their stability of accommodation. Yet there remains the general question about how these overall findings compare with research on other young people leaving home. There are significant differences.

One large study of 5000 young people found that 87.5 per cent of 16- to 17-year-old males, and 86 per cent of 16- to 17-year-old females were still living in their family home (Banks et al., 1993). Another large study, the Scottish Young People's Survey (SYPS), was a two part survey of young people who had left home. The data about some 4000 young people who had left home at 19, as analysed by Jones (1995), offers some, though certainly not a precise, basis for comparing findings about accommodation types. *First and foremost, 65 per cent of the young people in the SYPS were still living at home at 19 years of age. Here, for the leaving care group, even including living with friends as well as family, the figure is just 6 per cent.* Also in the SYPS survey, whilst over a third had left their parental home by the age of 19, 23 per cent of these had returned and were back in the parental home within a short time, emphasising, if this is needed, the point that leaving home should be a flexible, not a one off experience. The largest two types of accommodation for those living away from home, in the Scottish survey, were those living in private rented accommodation and in student hostel accommodation, accounting for some 9 per cent and 7 per cent of the entire group respectively (Jones, 1995:104). The second student hostel group was not mentioned by any of the leaving care teams, and this directly links to the levels of financial support, and early schooling experiences, as was discussed further in the last chapter on education. Without a good educational background being provided for young people in care, then further and higher education will be unattainable, and the option of a student hostel neither possible nor relevant.

Alongside these macro developments and concerns about housing, and in a hostile financial climate to young people living away from home, especially leaving care, it is also vitally important to record and celebrate the considerable number of remarkable housing achievements listed by the leaving care projects. These are now presented as evidence, with qualifications, of increased housing activity in the past few years. These achievements are taken from the answers to question 28a in the questionnaire 'What have been the project's six main achievements between 1994–1996?' The housing problems faced by projects, in response to the same question, are presented immediately afterwards.

First of the 244 overall achievements listed, the highest category was indeed housing with 64 achievements listed. The other achievements are fully discussed in the later chapter on participation and project achievements and problems.

Housing achievements between 1994 –1996

This section could easily be subtitled 'a tale of increased levels of individual enterprise and lack of corporate activity' given the nature of the responses. Whilst it was apparent from the comments by projects and on the questionnaire that the demand for suitable housing constantly outstripped its supply, nevertheless there were a surprising number of housing achievements listed. There were 64 housing practice and policy achievements, the highest single achievements category, and this constituted 26 per cent of the total number of achievements listed (n=244).

By far the most common type of housing achievements was in connection with the provision of *increased number and range of supported accommodation* for young people through establishing partnerships or other arrangements with housing providers. Incidentally, in the majority of cases the very same projects that listed housing achievements also listed housing problems in the 'problems' part of the question, as we will see shortly. Within the practice examples given small scale progress is recorded. For example, over the two year period the establishment by one project of two shared properties for six young people leaving care and homeless is an achievement. However, even acknowledging that not all the young people attending these projects seek housing, when one considers that the average number of young people attending each project was 74, this small scale incremental approach to bringing on stream additional housing, whilst welcome, is no substitute for comprehensive enhanced joint social services / housing policies and schemes for young people leaving care. It is individual enterprise compared with corporate provision. The achievements are presented as separate practice and policy sections.

Housing achievements – practice and policy examples

Practice Examples:

- established partnerships with the council housing department and voluntary sector
- development of semi-supported housing for young people preparing to leave care
- developing a range of high quality well maintained accommodation for young people with various degrees of support
- shared housing project established
- establishing housing agreements with a top housing association
- supported lodgings scheme with 11 providers established
- substantial increased number of affordable self contained flats available to care leavers as 'move on' accommodation
- short term private accommodation found and financed when necessary
- high occupancy level as a result of good relationship with all city boroughs.

Policy Examples:

- development of protocol with city council with respect to homeless 16–17-year-olds
- the appointment of a young homeless policy co-ordinator for 16–17-year-old homeless young people
- the appointment of a supported lodgings worker
- further development of protocol with the housing department *re* care leavers and especially young homeless people
- the establishment of local authority and housing association tenancies for young people
- establishment of shared housing project in partnership with housing association and local authority
- increased nomination rights for young people for local authority housing
- substantially increased number of affordable self contained flats available as 'move on'.

Projects took the view that there were both achievements in housing provision, in terms of additional short or longer term provision, but at the same time there was both an increase in young people attending the projects and a declining housing availability overall, in terms of volume, suitability and financial support. This achievement build on the 1992/3 survey finding that 'housing' was also the main practice achievement then as well. Initially it was unclear why housing was the main practice achievement again. It was unclear, for example, whether or not this achievement and reported activity was a 'distorted' finding, resulting from a low housing base some years ago, or whether it represented continued growth of activity based on a reasonable level of existing stock. Whilst it is the case that there was a relatively low housing base for young people at leaving care teams in 1992, this does not detract from the increased numbers of housing units, and the precise figure is unknown, that have since come on stream. Nevertheless, it must be noted that the housing policy examples given by respondents were ones more accurately concerned with improving protocol and liaison, important though that is as a first stage, rather than leading to increased numbers, variation in stock or access to it.

It is also significant that in relation to a question about housing achievements with young people leaving care, at the policy level, as indicated above, there were several answers about developing policies for 16–17-year-old homeless young people, not care leavers as such. Undoubtedly there are very similar problems for both in terms of the consequences of family breakdown, yet there are also differences, not least of all in terms of the legislative base for each group. There was also some suggestion from young homeless projects, not included in this survey, that they do not often know, or are told, whether the homeless young person has previously been in care, but that improved policies for homeless 16–17-year-olds would also pick up on young people leaving care.

The achievements and problems question also revealed that there were a considerable number of housing problems for projects as they strove to meet increased demand and expand housing services with insufficient resources. 'Housing' was the second highest problem listed, accounting for 35 or 15 per cent of all the problems listed (n=233).

Housing problems between 1994–1996

Also in answer to question 28a, the projects were asked to list their problems as well as achievements. 'Housing problems' were the second highest category of problems, second to local authority planning. There were 35 housing problems listed by leaving care projects, many of them of a similar nature, and the following is a list of some of the specific examples provided. Essentially, the answers centred on three areas: lack of suitable accommodation, lack of sufficient accommodation, and lack of affordable accommodation.

Housing problems – specific practice examples

Practice Examples:

- lack of move on accommodation
- reduction in local authority bed spaces
- identifying appropriate range of accommodation and support at 18 suddenly seen as less needy
- lack of accommodation for 16–17-year-olds/department unable and/or unwilling to keep young people in children's home after 16
- young people have unrealistic expectations of independence
- existence of suitable accommodation for young people with mental health needs
- increase in 'large estate' offers (although housing offers still coming through)
- danger of loosing private rented sector accommodation (although not used much anyway, but essential at times of crisis)
- reduction in bed and breakfast accommodation
- access to private sector accommodation worsened
- attempting to move the department towards supported housing at 16 and not permanent housing.

A bleak picture emerges of 35 of the 46 projects stating that housing problems were the second main problem that faced them in the 1994–96 period. The explanation for this problem centres squarely on lack of adequate resources from local authorities or housing associations to provide accommodation for young people leaving care. Possibly the most important finding is that the housing problem may be at crisis point for projects, especially outside the local authority, which do not receive an allocated amount of housing from local authorities. Furthermore, even for those within local authorities the survey suggests that such 'protected' allocations are being reduced, both in terms of quality and quantity.

Turning now to these wider housing policy points, let me present the findings about local housing and accommodation development concerning supported accommodation and bed and breakfast in the leaving care projects' local areas, as seen by the projects themselves. Questions about changes to the local housing situation were limited to those used in the 1993 survey, and were limited to just two types of accommodation: bed and breakfast and supported lodgings. The findings, therefore, do not relate to wider housing changes.

Projects' Perceptions about Supported Lodgings and Bed and Breakfast

In terms of supported lodgings accommodation, which accounts for 215 or 10 per cent of the total housing type, 51 per cent of respondents reported that its availability had improved a little or significantly, and 27 per cent considered the position had remained the same. However, when it came to supported lodgings' affordability, only 5 or 13 per cent considered the situation had improved a little or significantly, and 64 per cent considering that the situation had remained the same between 1994–96. In other words, supported lodgings accommodation had become increasingly available (and used by 10% of all the young people) but decreasingly affordable.

In relation to the availability of bed and breakfast accommodation, and taking into account the finding that just 99 or 5 per cent of the total number of young people whose housing situation was recorded (n=2096), it is significant to record that 30.5 per cent of respondents considered that the situation concerning the affordability and the availability of this type of housing had worsened a little or significantly, with the majority, 64 per cent, considering that the situation had remained the same.

The housing needs of young people leaving care extend far beyond bed and breakfast and supported lodgings accommodation, and what follows is an account of these needs, and the policy consequences which then follow.

Housing needs of young people leaving care

As a result of the security of tenure in the private sector being reduced by the 1988 Housing Act, and through the introduction of 'assured shorthold tenancies', private landlords can now set market rents and tenants no longer have the right to an assessed fair rent. In view of this development even more difficult decisions have to be made every day about housing resource availability, how to meet the different needs of the young people, and how to access affordable public and/or private accommodation, other than that provided by the local authority, which, of course, still has to be paid for.

Apart from affordability and availability, the major housing issue is what support is available for young people in housing. The notion of support for young people leaving care is a key issue whether the young people are in foster care, temporary, permanent or semi-permanent accommodation, the familiar argument being that, allowing for exceptions, these young people will not succeed in making the transition from care without a great degree of support being offered, available, and given as appropriate. Whilst it is acknowledged that a proportion of these young people will be receiving support, the finding that such a high proportion of the young people were living in temporary accommodation, including tenanted accommodation and not supported lodgings, begs the questions, how are these young people receiving support? How often? And from whom? Floating support is one of the answers to this question and increasingly a way of providing support to young people leaving care: in floating support the accommodation can change, but the support moves around with the young person.

The advantages of floating support are that, from the young person's point of view, they are offered a flexible package of practical help, especially in the early days of their tenancy. Floating support is where the young person 'stays put', with the support gradually reducing and moving away as the young person gains more skills in independent living. From the Housing Association's point of view they are guaranteed a rental income (conditional on Housing Support levels not falling) and the agency receives an ongoing supply of supportive accommodation which is self contained. Support to tenants can cover the entire range of practical and emotional needs. The Special Needs Management Allowance (or SNMA) system introduced in 1992 was payable for intensive housing management but not care and support. However, that system has now been replaced by another framework, and the critical care and support elements remain very difficult to fund. Financial security for housing associations can exist where an agent (for example a voluntary organisation) offers intensive housing management under a management agreement. Some housing association provide floating support themselves and therefore do take a financial risk.

Housing policy pointers for young people leaving care

Professional, flexible and informed support is just one essential element of the housing and support services that should be available to young people leaving care. The individual type and level of needs suggests there should be wide ranging housing options available to take into account the individual's own needs, capabilities and requirements, and financial support available. The problem is that the availability and type of financial support seem to be the guiding principle.

According to Kay (1994), young people leaving care (as with other young people but much more so) need the following:

- a choice of accommodation – a range of accommodation that meets their changing needs
- skills – acquired before leaving care
- planning – a coherent and flexible approach which emphasises planning in partnership and with contingencies in mind
- help – in the form of support and information
- money – in the form of an adequate level of income

- non-bureaucratic systems for service delivery – with systems being led by the needs of the young people, not the demands of institutional structures

- to be heard – the need to involve young people in decision making and listen to them

- social need – the need for a home not just a house

- relationships – the importance of continuity of relationships to assist in young people maintaining their accommodation.

The list vividly illustrates the point that services for young people leaving care should be comprehensive as well as requiring corporate funding and planning, based on a common and responsive understanding of funding entitlements, as well as a partnership between local and central authorities about required funding levels.

Wider housing initiatives

Other housing developments regarding young people leaving care have been recorded as a result of two large conferences in the 1990s at which good practice was discussed and shared (First Key, 1994) issues under discussion included ways of developing partnerships with housing associations, the opportunities provided by foyers and rent deposit schemes, special needs accommodation, supported lodgings schemes, and working with housing departments. The term 'foyers' can and does have different meanings, but at its simplest the term is taken to mean a form of temporary (or transitional) accommodation attached to training, employment, and support which can range in size from 30 to nearly 100 units of accommodation, Foyers, seek to deal with the problems of unemployment, homelessness, and the social isolation of young people. To my knowledge, whilst there has not been any serious suggestion that foyers provide the universal solution to these problems (i.e. replacing national policies), however inadequate they may be, they can offer one further option for young people by providing accommodation and employment and support which complements existing structures and approaches.

There have also been more specific initiatives, one of which is connected with supported housing.

1. A specific initiative has emanated from The National Foster Care Association's (NFCA). 'My Place' scheme, launched in the mid 1990s, is an integrated preparation, housing and aftercare scheme. It aims to help care leavers make a successful transition from being in care to living independently by:

- ensuring that each young person is well prepared for independent living and supported for a period after they have left foster home

- utilising foster carers to both prepare young people for independence and to support them after they leave care

- operating a partnership approach between the young person and their family, the foster carer(s) and their family, the local authority with the legal responsibility, the Peabody Housing Trust, and the NFCA.

The conditions for entry to My Place (NFCA and Peabody Housing Trust, 1995) are:

- from 16 onwards the young person agrees to undertake with the foster carer(s) a programme/process of preparation for independent living

- at 17 the young person is interviewed by the Housing Trust and housing options explored and support services discussed

- the young person's foster carers will contract to provide support prior, during and after the move to their own tenancy

- the local authority contracts to provide support to the foster carers which formally recognises their expertise and role, with detailed financial entitlements specified

- the local authority will provide access to relevant training for foster carers and young people

- the local authority will nominate the young person for housing by the named housing trust (i.e. Peabody).

This then is an innovative scheme to provide supported housing to young people leaving care with a particular emphasis on foster carers being supported to offer planned additional support to young people in their care. As of 1996 this scheme was working in six London boroughs in different ways. For example, in the London Borough of Brent there is a particular emphasis on those young people leaving care in further/higher education, and in the London Borough of Croydon 'My Place' takes the form of a self-help foster carers group. In the other four London boroughs the scheme is also developing in different ways, for example by working specifically with young parents or more with teenage teams which link in with foster carers.

2. A second innovatory practice development called 'Preparation for Adult Living' (or PAL), funded by the National Lottery, also involving the NFCA, helps young people to leave care in a planned way. This help consists of a self-help pack for foster carers, residential workers and others to emphasise the importance of preparation and to provide

information and training for foster carers. These then are two further important housing developments from the NFCA after the Children Act 1989's introduction in 1991.

Practice pointers: planning for accommodation and support

The Following Should Be Considered:

- it is essential to plan and fund a personal support package for young people leaving care
- preparation for independent living should be addressed in reviews
- it is vital to have a choice of accommodation available which is needs and not finance led
- wherever possible do not rush a young person on to move; emphasise planning
- set out an alternative plan in case the proposed accommodation breaks down
- plan ahead and establish the policies and procedures concerning subsequent accommodation that may be needed
- check on the financial requirements of supported accommodation and the possible grants or benefits available
- the young person must be fully involved and consulted, preferably underpinned by procedures about how this should be done.

A high degree of planning and co-operation between the housing, social services department, and benefit agency is essential for a properly planned supported accommodation upon leaving care.

Supported accommodation: key issues

Whilst there have been considerable achievements in housing, there remain some fundamental outstanding questions which are of both a longer term and immediate nature.

In the longer term, one of the most critical questions remains: 'why *do* young people have to leave care at 17 or 18 to become independent?' This is not expected of other family-based children, and the fact that in one large study quoted earlier some 65 per cent of 19-year-olds are still living at home, and a third of the remainder will also return home from time to time (according to Jones, 1995), serves to re-inforce the point about unrealistic and undesirable expectations for this younger and more vulnerable age group. Local authorities should, at the very least, consider a policy shift away from finding different ways for young people to leave care at 17 or 18 towards a more flexible approach.

Although this could be undertaken in a variety of ways, in general terms, by the latter is meant care provided by the local authority which assumes continuity, not discontinuity, emphasises flexibility and not rigidity about when a young person can leave and return, and overall lends more support than is provided at present (ADSS, 1997) to foster carers to sustain continuity. Perhaps local authorities also need to look harder at the possibilities of placement with the members of the extended family option. It is possible that new approaches complementary to existing ones of providing support care for young people leaving care, which might involve family members, are needed.

In the short term, there are other issues. First, at the practical level about timing, it is also very important that leaving care projects do not engage in a headlong rush into providing accommodation at too early an age. Thus, as Robertson points out, 'encroaching earlier and earlier into a young person's childhood' and institutionalising 'the notion of move on (accommodation) at 16' (Robertson, 1995).

There is also an ongoing debate about what are the most appropriate legal agreements to support young people leaving care, and this point is raised in Smith (1994:49). Suffice it to state here that the questions of centre on issues relating to 'rights' and 'welfare' approaches to social care provision. The housing associations are obliged to promote tenants rights, encouraged by the Housing Corporation, and others, such as some of the voluntary organisations providing support, such as the Royal Philanthropic Society, promote the use of Assured Shorthold Tenancies particularly in relation to shared accommodation because the accommodation is temporary, and the need flexible. Issued by the Housing Corporation in April 1996, the code of practice on tenure in association with the Tenants' Guarantee has as its basic principle that in shared housing, hostels and self contained supported housing wherever possible arrangements should be made which afford the occupant the security of an Assured Periodic Tenancy. The latter does not have a definite date of termination but goes from week to week or month to month. Although as with all these housing codes, it is somewhat complex, the thrust of the April 1996 particular code of practice is to give 'more muscle' to housing associations in its dealings with social services departments or others, to encourage such authorities offering to provide support to people in such accommodation to do just that, as well as to plan their move on accommodation situation more actively. The code also seeks to discourage housing associations from using licences which have minimal security. In a very real way this code provides the housing associations with a bargaining tool to remove tenants more easily after a specific period of time, and is forcefully encouraging a faster turn over of people, including young people leaving care of course, living in such properties, and struggling to find move on accommodation. Together with the changes to housing benefit discussed, in the chapter on financial supports, a picture emerges of a deterioration in the availability of and funding for public housing, regardless of the other vital point, namely of whether or not it is appropriate for vulnerable young people who have left care.

There is also the pressing and complex issue of financial arrangements, especially which agency can or should pick up the bill for housing 'voids' (or empty rooms/flats) which exceed agreed levels, in service agency agreements. This also raises the broader question about who pays for other problems that can occur in the rented housing sector, whether these are property thefts or losses. The changes to housing benefit entitlements and other entitlements described in the chapter on financial supports also reflects a deteriorating financial climate for supported accommodation. Affordability of accommodation is a key issue and the funding regime of a housing corporation which, since 1996, encourages increased private borrowing for new developments has served to increase rents and make them less affordable.

There are additional housing management issues to be faced, ranging from resistance to leaving care projects proposing to setting up accommodation schemes in an area, to serious complaints and even threats from neighbours about schemes that do become established. Good housing management plans and skills should normally deal with all but the most intransigent of situations and circumstances, but the 'nimby' factor can be a powerful one, and should not be underestimated. The problem for young people leaving care of not having a home, and therefore not being able to return there or anywhere else, as a right, compared with the population as a whole being able to do so (see Jones, 1995:66–68) is also another critical point for this group. It is far more difficult to return home if a person leaves because there was a problem forcing the move in the first place, as is usually the case for the young people described in this book, than if they leave home to try out a job or training course elsewhere, and it does not work out.

Not least of all, to return to the comprehensive 'young person centred' list above (Kay, 1994), are the problems for young people of not being given any real choice about the type of accommodation available and desirable (they are not necessarily the same). Where should they live, and with whom? Unless these questions are answered satisfactorily, at least up to the point where the young person values and accepts the supported accommodation that is offered, there is the very real danger that the young people leaving care may feel their leaving care experience, like their in care experience may have been, is being driven by cost and availability concerns, and not deriving from their own preferences.

The final key issue concerns the extent to which local authorities are capable of providing a corporate housing and support strategy which encompasses a breadth of approaches, funding sources and supports for young people leaving care and to what extent can this be done in a stringent financial climate.

Regrettably, it cannot be expected that all of these issues will be addressed in a consistent manner across all local authorities. Nevertheless, by any reasonable measure many of the leaving care projects in the survey have made great strides with local authorities to promote the housing needs of young people leaving care. According to the director of Coventry social services department the question is not necessarily a resources one, about how to find ways of obtaining more local authority tenancies, but 'what is it that a young person leaving care needs to help her or him on the path to being a success as an adult?' (Hendley, 1995). This view about the value of tenancies contradicts those held by many of the survey's responding leaving care projects. Further, whilst making sense from a director's local 'finite resources' perspective, it fails to fully recognise it is that type of accommodation, local authority tenancies, which normally provides the most security for young people leaving care, and needs to be retained as one valued option. Without it, another option is removed. The same director was most supportive of the idea of specialist accommodation for those with special needs, whether young people with disabilities, young parents, or other groups, and provided some local examples. This debate about the suitability of accommodation for young people leaving care, and who funds it, is likely to run and run.

The issue about the availability of appropriate housing is related to the question of the ways in which local authorities have introduced and implemented leaving care policies, including those concerning housing. Thus having described the young people leaving care's housing situation in this chapter, and pointed to the need for a corporate approach it is time to examine, in the next chapter, the findings and issues concerning providers' general leaving care policies and procedures.

CHAPTER SEVEN

Local Authority Policies and Procedures

Introduction

As was seen in the last chapter the issue of corporate responsibility is a key one, as was education earlier, in connection with provision of planned and not *ad hoc* leaving care services. One of the key areas, if not the key area governing leaving care work, is the production, comprehensiveness and implementation of local authority leaving care policies and procedures. Concern about their importance, as well as concern about them not being produced by many local authorities, has been raised in many places, including the Short Report in 1984 (DHSS, 1984), by many commentators (see especially First Key, 1992; Stein and Carey, 1986) and, not least of all, in official documents, such as the Children Act 1989 Guidance and Regulations (DoH, 1991c). Policies and procedures are vital in establishing what should happen in local authorities, when and how, and to whom. Therefore it was important that the research asked respondents about the existence, content and implementation of local authority policies. Questions were also asked about whether a local authority's leaving care responsibilities are presented in leaving care guides, and whether leaving care grants are available as of right. Respondents were also asked whether agreements were in existence between social services and housing departments about definitions of 'in need' in order to gauge the progress about agreed definitions across housing and social services departments.

The last section of this chapter concentrates on another Children Act 1989 duty, that relating to local authority's complaints systems, with findings being presented about how they apply to, and are used by, young people leaving care. The general purpose of this chapter then is to explore the degree to which specific policies and procedures have been developed and implemented. Wherever possible, and in order to do this across a wide time scale, findings from the 1992 survey as well as this 1995/6 survey have been included.

Leaving care policies and procedures – survey findings

Context

The guidance states (DoH, 1991c:7.19,7.20, 7.21,7.22.7.23) that:

> Each local authority should take the above principles into account in developing leaving care and aftercare policies and in applying those policies to the needs of individual young people. To help ensure this, each SSD should provide a written statement of its philosophy and practice on the preparation of young people for leaving care and the provision of aftercare support. It is a requirement of paragraph 1(2) of schedule 2 that each local authority must publish information about services provided by them under section 24 and take such steps as are reasonably practicable to ensure that those who might benefit from the services receive the relevant information. The statement should be comprehensive acknowledging the different leaving care and aftercare needs of different young people...it should take into account the special needs... The statement should also cover the role of other agencies...be informed by the views of young people...and foster parents.

> In addition (to providing a written policy statement to care leavers)...each social services department should provide an easy to read guide to its services for young people when they leave care. (DoH, 1991:93)

Earlier, the 1984 Short Report (DHSS,1984: para.307) stated:

> We recommend that the department consider the imposition on local authorities of a general statutory obligation both to prepare those in care for leaving and to support them thereafter, in the manner of a good parent.

Findings

The main finding, as Table 7.1 illustrates, is that 34 or 74 per cent of respondents in 1996 stated that the local authority in which they worked had a written leaving care policy. This compares with the 1992/3 survey figure of 76 per cent of respondents stating they had such a policy. The majority of projects working in areas which had written leaving care policies (see below) were single tier, urban local authorities.

Analysis and discussion

It is encouraging to see that 74 per cent of the 46 leaving care projects are in areas which have leaving care policy and procedures in place, and that in 97 per cent of cases these policies are mostly or sometimes followed. There were just two cases where leaving care policies were always followed, and 18 cases where they were mostly followed. In only one case did respondents consider that the local authorities leaving care policies were 'hardly ever' followed. There was some

Table 7.1 The existence and implementation of local authority policies:
a comparison of 1993 and 1996 survey findings

Local authority policy survey date	Policy in existence?	Policy always/mostly/ sometimes followed?[1]
1992/3 (no. of projects questioned)	21 (76%) (25 projects)	19 (90%) (20 projects)
1995/6 (no. of projects questioned)	34 (74%) (46 projects)	32 (97%) (33 projects)
Percentage change	-2%	+7%

variation in the answers given to the question 'to what extent are leaving care procedures followed in your area?' The survey recorded that 92 per cent of responding local authority projects stated that these were 'always' and 'mostly' followed. This compared with just 50 per cent of voluntary organisations giving this 'always or mostly' answer, and 33 per cent of jointly run projects.

The responses to these questions were not sufficiently detailed to offer explanations about whether this difference could have been because local authority projects were more informed about implementation than the other two project types, or whether these others experienced a different and less organised and coherent reality about local authority policies, by virtue of being more removed and based outside local authority settings. Of more significance in explaining the different implementation responses was the different authority types in which the projects were located. Of the 33 projects which responded to the question about the degree of implementation, 21 were based in single authorities in urban settings, and the remaining 12 were in county settings where considerably more liaison between local authority organisations (i.e. between housing and social services) is required.

In respect of leaving care guides, 36 or 79 per cent of respondents (n=46) stated that the local authority in which they worked had produced a written guide for young people describing the leaving care services it provided. The level of this response represents an improvement on the 1992 survey which produced a 66 per

1 Just one leaving care project in 1992/3 stated that their local authority always followed the leaving care policy and procedures, and there was just two for the 1995/6 survey, with this same reply. There were four 'no' answers to the question in the 1992/3 survey and 12 in the 1996 survey.

cent positive response rate about provision of a leaving care guide. This is a welcome improvement, although it must be acknowledged that the content and quality of these guides was not covered by the research.

The introduction of leaving care policies by local authorities is not only necessary for them to fulfil the requirements placed on them. It is also one way for them to be seen to have responded to an issue, recognising that individual initiatives are insufficient and that co-ordinated actions and procedures are necessary. The introduction of leaving care policies by local authorities is a relatively recent phenomenon, only receiving statutory authority by the introduction of the Children Act 1989 in 1991. As recently as 1990 Bonnerjea (1990:6) discovered in her study of London boroughs that 'the large majority' of these boroughs did not have leaving care policies or programmes. She also found that the most common model for delivering care services to these young people was through the generic field social worker team model. The First Key leaving care policies 1991 survey, with responses from 88 local authorities (DoH, 1993:70–71; First Key, 1992:10) indicated that 44–50 per cent of social services departments had no written policies or procedures in place. Furthermore, and tellingly, the same survey reported that of those that had a policy, over half had not written them before October 1991 (the date the Children Act 1989 was introduced). Alarmingly, another question produced the answer that 11 per cent of those who did have a leaving care policy had no intention of writing one in the future. If the findings of this survey concerning leaving care policies and policy implementation were repeated nationally, then it would point to a considerable improvement, compared with the 1991 position, and as such is to be welcomed as illustrating continued progress. Yet it is also worrying that some local authorities are still considering a draft policy two or three years after a leaving care project has been established.

In line with the 'you get what you get' (and, incidentally, 'be grateful for it') perception of the role of public services, as a residual provider, it is to be regarded as most encouraging that some three-quarters of local authorities have leaving care policies which are mostly or sometimes followed. Yet imagine if you were a young person leaving care in one of those authorities which did not have a policy or had one which was only sometimes followed – what would you do about the help you most needed and were not getting? Furthermore, if you lived in such an authority how would you know to what services, as of right, you were entitled? Is it acceptable that there are still 23 per cent of local authorities from this survey which do not have written policies and procedures? It is also important to understand the content of local authority leaving care policies, as a way of determining the way in which local authorities are interpreting their responsibilities. It is to the content of leaving care policies that attention is now turned.

Leaving care policies: practice/policy pointers from local authorities

A number of leaving care projects sent me the local authority leaving care policies. Although they all varied slightly, they contained similar core sections which are worth listing here, as an illustration of good practice in this area. It is also worth making the point that some local authorities actively involve young people in local policy development work, and the extent of this work, alongside other forms of young people's participation in projects' work, is discussed in the next chapter. The main local authority whose policies are described, the London Borough of Hackney (1994), initially makes reference to the fact that:

- 80 per cent of young people looked after are now with foster parents and this is to increase to 90 per cent
- foster carers' support to them is a central feature of the policy
- carers are at the centre of good practice
- acknowledgement should be given to the different needs and aspirations of young people leaving care
- preparation for leaving care plays a vital part in the care planning process once it becomes clear that a return to home to parents or extended family is not a realistic option
- young people need to be prepared emotionally for independence and fully involved in discussions about their future.

The policy has four sections:

Section 1: a statement of policy objectives and the principle upon which they are based.

Section 2: the legal framework.

Section 3: standards of good practice.

Section 4: local resources available for young people leaving care and responsibility for implementation.

Local Authority Leaving Care Policies: Example

Section 1 specifies the level of service to be delivered to all young people who are being prepared for independence and the support they should be offered subsequently.

- a leaving care grant not exceeding £1000 to be made available, supervised by a social worker
- the decision about entitlement to a leaving care grant to be made following an assessment

- that encouragement to staff to use the DoH's looking after children action and assessment records

- guidance for good practice – on leaving care it is mandatory that contact is maintained by the allocated social worker with the young person at a minimum of every two weeks during the first three months of independence and a minimum of once a month for the following six months

- partnerships with other agencies encouraged

- (abbreviated) under Section 24 Children Act 1989, any financial assistance should not replace state benefits and is 'disregarded for the purpose of calculating entitlement to income support, housing benefit and student maintenance grant [this may have to be revised if certain changes to state benefits are made]

- for black young people: all the issues about partnership are especially crucial 'when working with black young people for whom confusion about their cultural and racial identity may compound already considerable problems of being in care. In devising plans for black young people leaving care the need to address racial and cultural factors must be central.'

POLICY IMPLEMENTATION

The implementation of this policy should be carried out as a partnership between the following key services and individuals:

- the children and families teams (including youth justice and fostering teams)

- designated senior practitioners in each area

- aftercare specialist social worker

- the leaving care project

- foster carers

- the Hackney foster care association

- residential staff

- young people's response

- Off Centre (a centre providing counselling and advice to young people aged 14–25; a designated counsellor has responsibility for assisting care leavers)

- the housing directorate

- specialist services (children and young people with disabilities).

Other policy statements, for example Hammersmith (London Borough of, 1992), have additional comprehensive sections on young women with children or pregnant young women and leaving care policies for young black women and men, and these are included in the later chapter which discusses anti-discriminatory policies and practice. Suffice it to say here that both of these boroughs' policies are regarded as being two of the most comprehensive leaving care policies in England and Wales. There are other complex issues and questions about leaving care policies to which attention is now turned.

Leaving care policies: a critical overview

As with many of the policies seen, although there was some considerable detail concerning which department did what, exactly how leaving care work would be undertaken, co-ordinated and monitored was not apparent. The London Borough of Hammersmith and Fulham's policy, like that of Hackney's, and that of Kent County Council policy (see, for example, N. Roberts 1993), and many others, are comprehensive and face up to reasonable scrutiny. Highlighting the key practice and policy points, especially relating to young black people, women and young people with special needs, will still be instructive for some managers, whilst for others, a confirmation of their current practice. Yet one is still left asking some fundamental questions about these policies, as well as about leaving care work as a whole. As Roberts (1991) observed, when a local authority is drafting a leaving care policy the following factors are of the highest importance:

- that the policy is owned and identified with a particular manager, tier of management or reviewing group
- that the overall policy document or statement links into a system of implementation (guidelines and directives) and in turn to working practice guidelines for 'front-line' staff
- that all staff whose work is somehow shaped by the policy are consulted and informed
- that policy and practice are regularly monitored and reviewed.

Despite the earlier finding here of a high proportion of leaving care policies being in existence, and mostly followed and implemented, there remain outstanding questions about exactly what is being implemented and what is not. These outstanding critical questions focus around the following:

1. What is the funding situation for leaving care work? Who? How much? For how long? On what basis?

2. Have local authorities found any new money to fund the implementation of their leaving care policies post Children Act 1989 and on what basis is this calculated?

3. How is the information gathered about the implementation and monitoring of these policies?

4. What help do local authorities receive, based on 'what works approaches', to draw up or amend or update their policies?

5. To what extent might leaving care policies, more open to monitoring initiatives than before, be guided if not actually driven by the depleting budgets scenario?

6. To what extent can the needs of young people be identified, assessed, and broadly budgeted for?

Biehal *et al.* (1995) concluded that local authorities needed to produce a structured authority-wide leaving care policy and procedure framework which is built on their child care procedures, and which is reinforced by written practice guidance. Again, Roberts's comments are relevant here (Roberts, 1991):

- policies to be an integral part of any local authority's child care policies and procedures

- the potential for organisations to work together be fully recognised and utilised

- for there to be corporate local authority, not simply social services responsibility for the policy and its implementation

- the policy be comprehensive

- there is no blueprint leaving care policy for all local authorities

- the policy must address the needs of all young people leaving care

- provision needs to be substantial, wide ranging and flexible

- the policy will require regular evaluation.

Policies about children and young people leaving care and 'in need'

This section examines two inter-linked issues: the definitions of 'in need' provided by local authorities, and, second, if and whether there are agreements about definitions of 'in need'. The context for this section is Section 20 (3) of the Children Act 1989 which states that the local authority 'has a duty to provide accommodation for any 'child in need' who has reached the age of 16, and whose welfare is likely to be prejudiced without accommodation'. Under Section 27 (1) local authorities have a power to request the help of other authorities, including housing authorities, to enable them to comply with their duties to provide accommodation. Under Section 27 (2) it is the duty of housing authorities to assist so far as is compatible with their own statutory duties.

During the research period and prior to the Housing Act 1996, in the Homelessness Code of Guidance for local authorities covering the Housing Act 1985 (DoE, 1991), young people leaving care were listed as one of the 'groups at risk' and therefore vulnerable by means of being homeless. It is therefore vital at the time this research was conducted (prior to the Housing Act 1996) to understand if and how young people leaving care were seen as in need, and if there was agreement about the terms 'vulnerable' and 'at risk'. The code of guidance to the Children Act 1989 also acknowledges that there could be circumstances where the terms 'vulnerability' and 'in need' might be expected to arise in similar circumstances. This section about definitions of 'in need' and the situation regarding young people who leave care, and become homeless, acknowledges the changes brought about by the Housing Act 1996, described in the opening social context chapter to this book, and goes into further detail here about interagency co-operation, especially between housing and social services pre-dating and making comparisons with that legislation. It is also accepted that the term 'in need' normally applies more to services to young homeless people than to care leavers.

Given the similarity between the terms 'in need' and 'vulnerability', and the importance they placed on the term 'at risk homeless young people leaving care', it was important to explore the possibility that local authorities' social services and housing departments could or would arrive at a joint definition of the two terms. Respondents were first asked, therefore, whether the local authority in which they worked *automatically* regards a young person leaving care as 'a child in need' in the terms of the Children Act 1989.

Findings and Discussion About 'In Need'

The survey found that 19 or 43 per cent of respondents (n=44) considered that the young people leaving care were *usually* seen as a child in need, and 16 or 36 per cent of respondents replied that a person leaving care in their local authority area was *always* regarded in these terms. In those 16 local authorities, in addition to services it provides to young people leaving care under Section 24 of the Children Act 1989, it should be the case that they have an additional duty, under Section 20(3) of the Children Act 1989, to provide accommodation for young people leaving care (indeed for any child 'in need' who has reached 16 and whose welfare is likely to be seriously prejudiced without accommodation). The answers compare slightly unfavourably with those received from the 1992/3 survey where 45 per cent of respondents (n=22) took the view that their local authority *always* regarded young people leaving care as 'in need'.

In Kay's study into local authorities' policies towards homeless 16- and 17-year-olds, it was found that a considerable proportion of local authorities did not accept young people as vulnerable if they had no parents, or had experienced family breakdown, or were living on the streets, or had drug or alcohol problems, *or had left care*. In respect of the latter only 52 per cent of the local authorities surveyed (n=293) reported that they would regard having left care as being vulnerable (Kay, 1994:2–6). Kay's survey also found that nearly 60 per cent of housing authorities had entered into formal negotiations with social services about trying to overcome the problems of jointly defining 'in need' and 'vulnerability' (Kay, 1994:3). Definitions of 'in need' can still be a very important issue for those young people leaving care who leave in an unplanned way.

In respect to the second aspect relating to 'in need', namely the degree of agreement between social services departments and housing departments about definition, these were the findings: 24 or 59 per cent of respondents (n=41) indicated that their social services and housing departments *did* have a joint agreement about the definition of 'in need', while 17 or 41 per cent of respondents either did not have an agreement or did not know.

McCluskey (1993) found that although 18 per cent of local authority housing departments (n = 86) were failing to carry out 'in need' assessments on homeless 16- and 17-year-olds, 48 per cent of housing departments did have a written policy and procedure statement that identified their assessment criteria under section 20(3) of the Children Act 1989. She found that homelessness in itself was not enough to enable 16- or 17-year-olds to be accepted as being entitled to accommodation under the Children Act 1989. Young people leaving care are a priority group but not *the* priority group, as the children in need list below illustrates. These priority groups, adapted from the Leicester University's manual for managers entitled *Children in Need and their Families* (1992:70), consists, in summary form, of:

- children with disabilities
- children at risk of abuse or neglect
- children who are delinquent or who are at risk of becoming delinquent
- children separated from their parents by reason of divorce, hospitalisation, parent in prison, immigration restrictions and so on
- children with caring responsibilities
- children whose home conditions are unsatisfactory (e.g. those who are homeless, in temporary or sub-standard accommodation or accommodation for homeless families)
- children who may be broadly defined as living in poverty and at high risk of family breakdown
- children leaving care.

McCluskey also found that there was a perception, by one in four respondents, that social services departments had sufficient funding for young people leaving care. This compared very favourably with the group which was the focus of her research, namely those young people who are homeless. Colton's work (Colton *et al.*, 1995) examined the Welsh local authorities' definition of the *actual priority* and the *ideal priority* given to 'in need' groups. The research found that the actual priority categories were sexual abuse, other abuse/neglect, delinquency, leaving care, then disabilities, followed by others. This compared favourably with their ideal priority positions except in relation to the higher rating that was given to prevention (Colton *et al.*, 1995:719).

Colton concluded that there were serious operational problems in defining 'in need' groups, and that the decisions about 'in need' prioritisations were being made within a 'social and political reality' framework which contradicted the all embracing spirit of the Children Act 1989. Young people leaving care who become homeless cannot rely on being regarded as a child 'in need', simply on the basis of having left care. The depleting resources scenario and resource focusing and gatekeeping can also result in services being guided by pre-determined levels (first, second, and third or top priority level) of intervention (on this point see McCluskey, 1993:29). Yet all of these approaches and operational decisions must not serve to blur the key point being made here, namely that the legislative links between housing and social services for young people leaving care who become homeless, and who for some reason are not automatically given accommodation under Section 24, are extremely convoluted.

However, in some areas there *is* a policy agreement between the local authority's homelessness department and leaving care teams (young homeless) to offer permanent housing to young people aged 16 or above. This initiative could still operate under the Housing Act 1996 but the duty on the local authority under that legislation is to prove temporary not permanent accommodation, as it did under the housing legislation prior to January 1997. The key point is still that young people leaving care should not have to rely on the homelessness legislation, but some of them have to and will continue to do so, however unsatisfactory this may be. The following is a good example, from Cardiff, of a policy for young homeless.

Housing the Young Homeless: the Cardiff Example

In Cardiff a young person may be eligible for housing in the following circumstances: aged 16+, whose welfare is assessed as 'seriously prejudiced', under the Children Act 1989, and 'vulnerable' under 1985 housing legislation. To be considered further the following guidelines are to be followed:

- the young person must then be identified as being as in proper housing need

- care packages put together by social services must be put in place and presented to housing (homelessness) department

- criteria for vulnerability under housing legislation (e.g. fear of offending or institutional background) to be specified

- the young person's latest addressees (two or three) to be provided with reasons for leaving the accommodation given).

In this particular area if the application and investigation into their housing needs is successful then support continues, a property is offered and tenancy arranged, presumably subject to regular review. If the application is unsuccessful, then reasons are given and the young person would be presented with private sector accommodation. In this example there is a very careful and full assessment of the young person's history, circumstances and capabilities. In Cardiff, as in other areas, a young person in desperate need with a patchy accommodation history might not be deemed capable of holding down a tenancy, even with support, and therefore, in effect, be denied the tenancy and support care package, and instead be offered something less appropriate to their needs and something much less immediately risky, financially at least, in the private sector.

So far this chapter has concentrated on policies about service entitlements and issues about 'in need' and leaving care. Another change brought in by the Children Act 1989 was that relating to systems for making complaints against providers. Given the high and ongoing demands on leaving care projects for services and the pressures on leaving care services, the ways in which complaints system are established, and whether they are working, are most important policy issues, to which attention is now turned.

Formal complaints procedures and leaving care

Context: Under the Legislation the Local Authority has the Following Duties:

- to establish a procedure with an independent element for considering representation and complaints (Children Act 1989, S26:3, 4)

- to give publicity to their complaints procedure (Children Act 1989 S26:8)

- to review the operation of their complaints procedure annually (Representations Procedure Regulations, 1990)

- voluntary organisations are required to appoint an officer to co-ordinate all aspects of their consideration of representations and complaints (The Children Act Representations Procedures Regulations, 1992).

There has been a great interest in developing complaints procedures in the 1980s, in part as a result of the attempt to re-classify 'dependent-passive clients' as 'thinking choice-led consumers', regarding them as if they had the financial capacity to make real choices from a range of different suppliers. Nevertheless, the introduction of the very idea that clients or users could and indeed should have a right to complain if they are dissatisfied with the services offered or not offered strikes a chord with those promoting greater 'downward' accountability *of* providers *to* users and carers. In addition to offering opportunities to users for redress, a complaints system should also act as a management check on whether organisational systems are functioning properly, as well as act as a check for identifying problems.

The Social Services Inspectorate produced practice guidance about complaints procedures (Social Services Inspectorate, 1991) and within the voluntary child care sector there were a number of initiatives emerging from the National Council for Voluntary Child Care Organisations (see, for example, Hodgson, 1994). In respect of complaints about housing, where a young people is living in a housing association property there will be a separate complaints procedure produced by that organisation, to which any complaint about matters within the property can be routed. There remain a number of issues in relation to leaving care work. First is the issue of whether voluntary organisations are legally required to produce a complaints procedure where the young people are not being accommodated. If, for example, the young people are being helped by a non-residential project, which is often the case, then the voluntary organisation is not officially accommodating the young people and therefore technically a complaints system is not necessary. Also it is not necessarily the case, bewilderingly in this author's opinion, that local authorities automatically define young people leaving care as children 'in need', which could act as another legal means for requiring complaints procedures to be prepared. Young people leaving care should be automatically entitled to invoke the local authorities own complaints procedures if they are accommodated. The author's earlier survey (Broad, 1994c) did not include an analysis of the use made of complaints procedures, because so little information was provided by respondents. There was much more information provided in the current survey, and this is analysed as far as is possible to do so.

Survey Findings About Leaving Care Complaints Procedures

In this survey all of the leaving care projects which responded to the question (n=45) about whether their project had a formal complaint system answered 'yes.' In the 1993 survey the figures were 19 or 85 per cent. Unlike the 1993 questionnaire, the 1996 questionnaire also asked respondents to state for what sort of complaint(s) had the formal complaints system actually been used. There were a total of 34 complaints listed by the 33 projects[1] which responded to the question, 'For what sort of complaint(s) has it [the project's formal complaint procedure] actually been used?' (Q20). (Eleven other projects stated that the few complaints they had received had been resolved locally and at an informal level.) The few projects which expressed an opinion on systems for reporting complaints gave a preference to the local and informal resolution of them. Three leaving care projects stated that there had been complaints but did not provide any further information.

The 34 complaints fell into five categories, the first two categories, services and funding, being by far the most commonly listed, namely[2]:

1. Those who were dissatisfied with the level and quality of service provided: 17 examples given including:

   ° service not meeting expectations

   ° staff not completing tasks with young people

   ° wanting the service to extend beyond 21

   ° young person stating that insufficient support given when needed

   ° young person felt aggrieved at the level of service provided.

2. Those who sought to challenge decisions made about funding: 12 examples given including:

   ° lack of money to fund support for young people for higher education travel expenses and book purchases

   ° request for funding expenses necessary for legal training

   ° finance under Section 24, usually during the transition period from care to independence – particularly when a private arrangement has been made between a foster carer and previous client

   ° Section 24 funding decisions

   ° the amount of the setting up home allowance.

---

1   Not all the projects provided information about age breakdown at the time of the move to independence and so exact age breakdowns can not be provided.

2   There were just two examples of complaints provided for the third category 'those dissatisfied with an individual worker about their way of doing something.' There was just one example given from each of the remaining fourth and fifth categories 'dissatisfied with the behaviour of other young people,' and 'those with a complaint from carers and professionals, ('complaints about the project's confidentiality policy to them and proactive open access policy to young people'). One other complaint example given about 'disputes about access to social activities' fell outside all of the five categories.

There were just two examples of complaints provided for the third category, 'those dissatisfied with an individual worker about their way of doing something'. There was just one example given from each of the remaining fourth and fifth categories, 'dissatisfied with the behaviour of other young people', and 'those with a complaint from carers and professionals' ('complaints about the project's confidentiality policy to them and proactive open access policy to young people'). One other complaint example given about 'disputes about access to social activities' fell outside all of the five categories.

There was no difference about complaints between the voluntary organisations and local authorities leaving care projects. It also must be acknowledged that for a young person leaving care at a very vulnerable and, most likely, scary time in their life, they would be dependent to some extent on the support of a leaving care team or something similar, for whatever support is being provided. As with other dependent service users with little chance of there being 'alternative suppliers', to complain at all, and thus possibly place at risk one of the few official supports and resources available, can be seen as a relatively bold act. From another point of view the young people may consider that they have nothing much to lose if they complain and everything to gain. Despite a perceived risk of being penalised if they complain, it is important that young people are not simply 'grateful' for whatever they receive, and perhaps suffer quietly. Instead, if they feel they are able and it is a valid complaint which falls within the procedure, they should make a complaint. These caveats need to be made because each local authority or voluntary organisation complaints policy will vary as to its coverage, comprehensiveness, implementation, and effectiveness. All of these complaints issues merit further research in their own right. In the absence of such, however, a model 13 step checklist is included as a policy/practice pointer.

Hodgson's model complaints checklist (1994) for the development of complaints procedures in voluntary child care organisations is also relevant to local authorities, to underpin the importance of the 'complaints message' which is that it is essential to produce *an easily accessible, clear, public and user-centred complaints procedure which assists and does not hinder the complaints process.*

A 13 Step Checklist for Developing a Complaints Procedures for Leaving Care Work (Adapted from Hodgson, 1994)

1. Develop the procedure through consultation and with proper resourcing.

2. Define the scope of the procedure: who is it for?

3. Establish a designated complaints officer to co-ordinate all aspects of representation and complaints.

4. Provide staff training and support.

5. Produce a written procedure which clarifies terms (such as complainant) and roles (such as independent person).

6. Provide written information about rights and responsibilities, and the complaints system.

7. Introduce a mechanism for problem solving and monitoring problems so that a young people can receive advice, but not inappropriately as a poor substitute for using the complaints procedure. This is Hodgson's way of seeking to secure confidential advice. Although I see his point, I am unsure whether this concern should be placed within a complaints checklist.

8. Establish a clear way of registering a complaint.

9. Establish a clear way of investigating a complaint (much more difficult).

10. Establish who can act as independent persons during investigation/provide training and support.

11. Decide who will adjudicate (i.e. make the decision arising from the complaint).

12. Make decisions about the composition of the review panel, which comes into effect if a complainant is dissatisfied with the outcome of the investigation.

13. If a voluntary organisation, then it should establish proper links with local authorities.

There is also the issue for young people attending voluntary organisations' leaving care projects whether technically they can access *two* complaints systems, the local authority's and the voluntary organisation's, and whether accessing one route denies one access to the other. In turn, this can bring to the surface issues of justice done or justice denied, for staff as well as young people's rights in such circumstances. Is also apparent that a number of voluntary organisations receive complaints about the local authority with whom they are in partnership, and in these instances it is often the case that the voluntary organisation acts as an advocate on behalf of the young people. This direct advocacy can be especially helpful on a case by base basis, though not often more widely, by, for example, settling the principle which may be behind the issues in question. An example of this would be where the local authority's policy on leaving care grants is unclear and, discussed at an individual level, assessed on individual need.

By contrast with voluntary organisations, local authority leaving care teams do not have to write their own policies, although they may do, and they can use the local authority complaints system instead. The leaving care team based in the

London Borough of Sutton is an example of one such team. The complaints policy includes an acknowledgement being given to the complainant within five days, different stages of appeal, and an independent review. The procedure also allows for complaints to be made by phone 24 hours a day, in person or in writing. Departmental procedures set out clearly the way investigations will be handled. Information about how to make complaints is widely disseminated throughout the borough in a user friendly information leaflet which includes a freepost tear off card. They also specifically inform users of the procedure through their brochure, the Leaving Care Pack and copies of leaflets displayed in their offices. In the four years the team has been in existence there has been one formal complaint, which was investigated independently. The investigation recommended that the team extend its support to the complainant beyond her 21st birthday – the point at which leaving care services usually cease. The team also seek to actively promote other ways for users to make complaints and comments through volunteers who can take on an advocacy role, our suggestions box and comments book, drop in sessions and group discussions, and meetings with young people such as review meetings (London Borough of Sutton, 1996:6).

Key Points About Complaints Systems

Finally in this section some key points about the important issue of complaints are summarised:

- in some cases the essence of the complaint may be about the way something was done or not done, and not a complaint about the service as such. It is therefore important that the nature of the initial complaint is fully explored to establish exactly what is the complaint? What was its origins? Why has it become a complaint? Is it a formal or informal complaint and, crucially, at what level will/should the complaint be resolved?

- unless users are informed about their service entitlements, set within a legal framework and most probably expressed as written standards, it is difficult to see how users can effectively complain and improve services

- users need to have confidence in complaints systems to use them – and although more research would be necessary to explore the detail and outcomes, there is a measure of confidence in such systems by young people leaving care, according to the survey

- making full information readily accessible to users is a vital and necessary first step for users to redress, inevitably only in part, the power imbalance that exists between providers and users

- self-advocacy and advocacy organisations and service users should become part of a panel with elected members to monitor how complaints procedures are working, or not

- the raising of expectations about service entitlements for all, as a right, to help minimise or eradicate the 'be grateful for what you are getting' approach, is a vital step to take if service organisations are to open things out, not close them up, to users

- groups of users, here those young people with learning difficulties, young women, young people with physical disabilities, and black users, although all different, also share a history of being at the receiving end of a range of institutional discriminations. It is especially important therefore for these groups of users that what for many has previously been a negative experience of receiving services, often from white able bodied suppliers, is transformed to positive service experience, delivered by a diversity of people, who if it comes to the point of there being a complaint, are prepared to respond positively, promptly and properly. For this to happen a strong culture of organisational trust and responsiveness is necessary

- keep procedures as simple as possible, otherwise they will deter users

- it is far harder to introduce a complaints system which strikes the right balance between the organisation's needs and the young person's needs than it is to produce one which will crush, exclude or make impotent the young person

- in the event of a complaint being made against a member of staff the majority of people will find the invoking of a formal complaint against them a painful event meriting sensitive as well as clear handling

- offer support, whether through an independent person, as advocate, written into the complaints procedure, or through a separate advocacy service. The organisation Voice for the Child provides this sort of service, providing organisations are willing to purchase it

- in the child care field there will be lessons that can be learnt from the use of complaints systems in other areas, possibly from the child abuse field, but there are also likely to be other, more appropriate areas involving young people where complaints systems have developed, and which could be applicable to leaving care work.

Conclusions

There has been steady progress concerning the introduction of leaving care policies, leaving care guides, and the introduction of complaints systems. This progress needs to be seen in the legislative, financial, resource and professional contexts within which leaving care projects work. On the other hand, and this point needs emphasising, what has been recorded in the survey as reported in this chapter is continued activity at the leaving care policy development level amongst the leaving care projects committed to replying to the questionnaire. The real 'test' would be to enquire, with all leaving care work, which policies are being implemented and which are not and, in each case, why? This research has made a start, building on the 1993 survey, in establishing which, in general terms, leaving care policies are being followed, and to what degree. In relation to the 'in need' issue, and young people who leave care and become homeless, the Housing Act 1996's duty on local authorities to provide temporary not permanent accommodation for certain groups will make an already discretionary situation more so. In relation to complaints, what can be said here is that there seems to have been steady policy progress, and that young people have made some use of complaints systems, although the project responses to these are unknown. It remains a matter of interpretation, as with complaints to the National Health Service perhaps, as to whether increases in the number of complaints made is a 'good thing' (i.e. more confidence by young people in themselves as well as about the system they are complaining), or a 'bad' thing (i.e. the service is getting worse!), or something of a mixed blessing. The issue of complaints is not only directly related to issues about service entitlement and expectations, but also about young people's involvement and rights, issues which the next chapter addresses.

CHAPTER EIGHT

Young People's Participation, Project Achievements and Problems

Introduction

This chapter records the concerns and actions of leaving care projects and provides insights into day to day and longer term operational issues. Projects responded well and creatively to the invitation to record the extent and nature of young people's participation in the projects, as well as to prioritise their main achievements and problems between 1994 and 1996. The rationale for exploring these areas was simply that it was seen as essential and very important for projects to be given every opportunity to provide their views about local practice. Particular questions in the questionnaire (questions 8 and 9) were provided around the area of young people's participation in the work of projects, because of the increased importance of that and associated topics. There has, for example, been increasing emphasis in the 1980s given to issues concerning greater public accountability of services, fuller citizen involvement and users' participation (amongst many, see, for example, Croft and Beresford, 1993) and the associated issue of users' rights, and trends towards partnerships in social care. There was, however, no such focus in respect of the very generalised 'achievements and problems' questions given to respondents (questions 28a and 28b).

The chapter is in two parts. The first part focuses on the context for, and then the extent and nature of, young people's participation in leaving care projects, and the second part focuses on analysing projects' considerable achievements as well as problems. Where possible comparisons with the 1993 leaving care survey have been made.

Young people's participation and rights

Context

The issue of young people's 'participation' in leaving care work, sometimes presented as a straight forward issue, is in fact a complex one in which a number of concerns and ideologies derived from different agendas all converge. The first item to consider is what, if anything, the Children Act 1989 states about this issue. One of the five basic principles of part 3 of the Children Act 1989 (the others being to safeguard the well being of the child, the promotion of partnerships with parents, the restating of the importance of families, corporate responsibilities) is of local authorities having a duty placed on them to ascertain and take due account, if they are deemed to be sufficiently mature, of young people's, as well as parents', wishes and feelings (Children Act 1989, S22:5). The Children Act 1989 then places a clear statutory duty on social services and the courts to ascertain the wishes and feelings of the child and to take these into account when making decisions. In addition, the guidance (para. 7.18) states that:

> young people should be fully involved in discussions and plans for their future. Well before a young person leaves care, a continuing care plan should be formulated with him. This should specify the type of help the young person will be receiving and from whom.

Although the guidance does not carry the force of the statute or the regulations (such as the Children's Homes regulations 1991), it is issued under Section 7 of the 1970 Local Government Social Services Act so that local authorities are required to seek to achieve these standards.

Parents and foster parents should be involved in devising the plan. Local authorities are also advised to ensure that the written statements on their policies and practices, and their leaving care guides, should be informed by the views of young people who are or have been in care, and those of parents and foster parents (para. 7.22). It is suggested that one way of obtaining the views of young people is to encourage groups of young people to meet and discuss such matters. The idea of establishing a newsletter was also presented in the guidance (para. 7.22).

A detailed reading of the primary legislation and the guidance about young people's participation suggests that it means young people being involved in discussions about what has already happened regarding the existing services they are receiving, *as well as* involvement in producing, or at the very least, modifying, leaving care policies. Underpinning these statements about greater participation by young people in the services they receive is the assumption that, prior to the legislation, such listening to children and young people about these matters was *not* everyday practice and could *not* be taken for granted (on this point in respect of residential care for children see Berridge in Hill and Aldgate, 1996). Other wider changes in local government also produced a move away from the 'old ethos' of passive clients simply receiving what the local authority provided, like the old bulk purchasing policies in residential child care. In the new world of 'customer care' the shifts from procedures to outcomes, from provider to consumer orientation, from quantity to quality, from uniformity to diversity, and not least of all, from hierarchy to delegation and personal responsibility are heralded as the new currencies in care.

The notions of a citizens charter from central government in the late 1980s, whilst sometimes mocked and criticised (in respect of probation work see, for example, Broad and Denney, 1996), nevertheless denote a symbolic shift in policy towards users being given a say about services, and in some cases, such as the rail services, being given a right to financial compensation if there is a certain service shortfall. In addition there is the user impetus-user choice arising from community care, one of whose aims is to promote the opportunity for users and carers to have a voice. Payne also points to the development of advocacy movements as strengthening user participation (Payne, 1995: 20–21), although how these services, which usually criticise and call for more flexible services, are to be paid for remains unclear.

The Children Act 1989's support for greater participation by users about the style and substance of service delivery can be seen as being complemented and reinforced by the children's rights movements, with the United Nations Convention on the Rights of the Child being its flag bearer. This Convention was adopted by the United Nations in 1989 and ratified by the United Kingdom government in 1991 (subject to some important reservations). The Convention sets out in a number of statements, called articles, the rights which all children and young people up to the age of 18 should have. The Convention covers three main sets of rights: the child's right to protection from abuse and exploitation, the right to the provision of services, and the right to participate in decision making.

United Nations Convention on the Rights of the Child: Summary of the Relevant Sections that Apply to Young People Leaving Care up to 18 Years of Age

- Any child being looked after away from home in a boarding school, long stay institution or hospital must also receive proper care (Article 3)

- children should be separated against their will only if it is in the child's best interests. If this has to happen, the child, their parents and anyone else entitled to have an interest has the right to go to court and ask to have their case heard (Article 9)

- the right to privacy (Article 16) and to freedom from exploitation (Article 36)

- the child to be provided with the opportunity to be heard at any judicial or administrative hearing affecting the child, confirming the *child's right to participate in decision making affecting them* (Article 12) [emphasis added]

- if separated from their parents, the child has the right to keep in touch regularly with the parents, unless this would be harmful to the child (Article 9)

- children have the right to be as healthy as possible (Article 24)

- disabled children must be helped to be as independent as possible (Article 24)
- children have the right to live in a safe, healthy environment (Article 24)
- every child has the right to an adequate standard of living. This is, in the main, for parents to provide, but in cases of need the government should help parents reach this standard (Article 27)
- State parties recognise the right of every child to a standard of living adequate for the child's physical, mental, spiritual, moral and social development (Article 27)
- the parents or others responsible for the child have a primary responsibility to secure, within their abilities and financial capacities, the conditions of living necessary for the child's development (Article 27)
- every child has the right to benefit from social security taking account of the circumstances of the child and those responsible for the child (Article 26)
- children should be cared for properly. This is mainly for the child's parents to do but the government is expected to give suitable help to parents (Article 18)
- if children cannot live with their family, they must be properly looked after by another family or in a children's home. The child's race, religion, culture and language must all be considered when a new home is being chosen (Article 20)
- a child temporarily or permanently deprived of his or her family environment, or in whose best interests cannot be allowed to remain in that environment, shall be entitled to special protection and assistance provided by the state (Article 20)
- different kinds of secondary school should be available for children. In addition, for those with the ability, higher education should also be provided (Article 28)
- the government must protect children from: doing work which could be dangerous or which could harm their health or interfere with their education (Article 32), dangerous drugs (Article 33), being abducted or sold (Article 35) and sexual abuse (Article 34).

However, according to the Children's Rights Development Unit report (CRDU, 1994), the government has still not fully carried out its responsibilities under the

Convention in respect of young people leaving care. It concluded (CRDU, 1994:39):

> Unless policies are developed at local authority level, backed up with the necessary resources these obligations under the Convention are being breached. There are models of good aftercare provision which have been developed and which, if disseminated, could be widely adopted.

Subsequent to the UN Convention of the Rights of the Child (1991), the Association of Metropolitan Authorities (AMA) produced a checklist for supporting care leavers up to 18 years under Articles 1 and Article 3.2. After posing the question about how authorities can ensure there are sufficient resources available and make 'real' choices possible, the AMA makes a comprehensive statement about leaving care (1995:47).

A Checklist for Supporting Care Leavers up to 18 Years: The Association of Metropolitan Authorities (1995)

Local authorities could consider the following for young people leaving care:

- conducting an assessment with the young person about whether or not they feel ready for independent living
- support, information and training over an extended period to ensure that the young care leaver is confident and ready for independent living
- material assistance and housing to young people leaving care to ensure they are able to achieve an adequate standard of living and to protect them from drug abuse and sexual exploitation
- reviewing policies and practice on early preparation for independence and making sure theses reviews are carries out with young people
- allowing flexibility in the system which allows for the varying needs of different children and young people to be met
- allowing young people to experiment with independence and with the option of returning to accommodation or care, or getting different levels of support if they wish to do so
- that planning is done at corporate level so that all services on which young people depend are provided in a co-ordinated and consistent manner including, for example, social services, housing, education and welfare rights services.

Nationally, young people leaving care have called for a charter of rights on at least two occasions in the 1990s. In 1992 the London and South East Leaving Care Support Group produced its leaving care charter, which was published by the Royal Philanthropic Society in 1992. In the same year another charter with aspirations for national implementation was launched by young people in the North West of England, and handed into Downing Street and the Department of Health in London (Community Care, 1992). What both these charters have in common is their commitment to clearly specified and legally enforceable rights associated with leaving care, which goes some way to explaining their non-implementation to date.

By contrast the Leaving Care Checklist (Community Care, 1995) seems especially weak in the young people's rights section, adding just four 'rights'. Under the heading of young people's rights, as social rather than legal rights, it was stated somewhat weakly that 'young people should be encouraged to think about the following' (Community Care, 1995):

1. Have they been given a copy of the local authority complaints procedure and been shown how it works?

2. Do they know where they can get careers advice?

3. Ask for a list of emergency accommodation.

4. Ask the social worker whether a leaving care grant is available.

These statements do not constitute legally specified and enforceable rights but rather a good practice checklist of what should/could happen regarding young people leaving care. At the leaving care 'practice end' the emphasis about rights and services, throughout this debate, is on developing and building on good practice, however uneven and local this may be. This approach is in considerable contrast with the 'rights and charters' policy approach, although the two should be complementary. Locally it seems to be a question of 'there is good practice in leaving care work out there, you just have to find it' – and try to introduce it in your area against a background of a discretionary legislative base, political inertia about reviewing the Children Act 1989, and dwindling local resources. One area that has taken off and developed in the last few years, according to the findings from the survey, is not in the area of rights, but in the area of young people's participation in developing and contributing to projects. The extent of this participation may come as no surprise to some, although more research would be necessary to establish the extent to which this level of participation is being sustained, and to what effect. It is to those findings in response to the specific question about young people's participation that attention is now turned.

It should also be noted that 'participation by young people' was also the fourth highest achievement category by projects, and a much smaller number of the examples provided are presented later in the chapter under the achievements section.

Main findings about young people's participation

There were a total of 96 examples of participation by young people in local leaving care work, as provided by the 28 projects which stated that young people participated in their leaving care project other than as clients (n=44). Of those 28 projects which answered 'yes' to participation by young people, by far the majority, 19, were from voluntary organisations and the remaining 9 were local authority or joint teams. This general category, 'young people's participation', was then divided into five main categories constituting 88 of the 96 responses: participation as quality control on the project, participation as influencing local policy development, participation as support, participation as project development, and participation as a voice on national policies.

Five types of young people's participation in leaving care work: examples

Participation as Quality Control or Checkers of Service Delivery: 24 Examples Given Including

- contributed to setting/achieving charter mark for the project
- working on staff selection/interview panels (there were several examples given)
- users survey for service feedback
- participation in evaluation of services
- regular evaluation questionnaire.

Participation as Influencing Local Policy Development Work: 23 Examples Given Including

- member of projects' committees (virtually all voluntary organisations or joint projects)
- helped with production of local policies
- young people provide representation /consultation to local authority social services policy working group (forum of councillors and officers from different agencies)
- group feeds into area community care planning forum
- asked to contribute in QA statement
- contribute to social services leaving care policies
- consultation and interviews in the development of new ideas and initiatives
- involvement in development of policies

- to monitor and influence policies around work with young people
- joint consultative group.

Participation as Support for Young People: 16 Examples Given Including

- young people invited to return to project to talk to others
- offer a support service to young people using scheme/tenant support and consultation group
- helping to run our active drop-in group
- furniture for project
- acting as volunteers
- helping with the drop-in
- members of peer education group
- help produce policy guidelines for/with the local authority.

Participation in Shaping the Project's Identity and Administration: 15 Examples Given Including

- member of project committee
- serving as committee members
- young people help to contribute to project leaflets/administration feedback forms for the project.
- some clients took part in competition to design team logo (two cash prizes awarded)
- contribute to the writing of the team's leaving care pack
- staff selection
- employment of young people under employment services agency scheme
- helping make an ecology garden
- on interview panel
- contributing to the production of a project brochure
- promotion and publicity work
- help to produce an (irregular) project newsletter.

Participation as Expressing a Voice on Social Policy: 10 Examples Given Including

- helped set up and participate at conferences run by the project's parent voluntary organisation body

- commenting on youth homelessness generally

- contribute to 16+ forum in the area

- helping with women's health day

- consultancy on national and local policy /development

- a young people users' forum

- contribute to local and national forums (in some cases through voluntary organisation's regional and/or national structure).

There was no obvious explanation (i.e. size, type of project, location) as to why some projects, more than others, answered yes to the question about whether young people participated other than as client-users in the project. Although the proportion of projects that indicated participation (64%) was very similar to the 1993 survey (67%), the range of responses is much wider, and the (proportionate) total much greater. Even if one accepts that it is possible that some projects, keen to display their user involvement credibility, may have exaggerated the actual scope of young people's participation, the long and imaginative list of types of user participation suggests otherwise. It is also a testament to what is possible, despite the grim social context, if the project/organisational climate is right, and the will is there. More than that, the survey reveals participation by young people as a growing area, by all types of projects, although a minority also indicated that this participation was not without its problems, not least its time and resource requirements. As White (1994:9) concluded in her study of user involvement in the planning of services within social services departments:

> User involvement in planning services within social services departments is complex, time consuming, needs financing both directly and indirectly, but above all needs commitment and understanding. User involvement needs to begin somewhere. It does not seem to actually matter where, so long as it begins with the above in mind. The aim needs to be that user involvement becomes a part of the culture, not that it is an added on feature, an optional extra which can be included or excluded as is convenient and expedient. If the underpinning philosophy is empowerment of the user, this requires movement on the part of all social services department workers to be successful: not just by the councillors, directors, senior officers, and strategic planners.

Although the depth and permanence of such user involvement would need further exploration, what these young people and projects have achieved is important, desirable and of great worth given the vicissitudes of young people, ever changing staff groups, of shortage of resources, and crisis work. Let me now turn to other more general areas of achievement by the projects.

Achievements and problems

Leaving care projects were provided with two open ended questions, one inviting the projects' six main achievements, the other the six main problems, both to be listed in terms of priority, and for the previous (i.e. 1994 to 1996) period. The specific issue of housing achievements and problems was discussed in detail within the earlier housing chapter, and not here because that topic is so vast, as well as important, to merit it having a separate chapter. In summary, here the research found that the greatest number of project achievements was in the 'housing' category and were concerned with accessing more accommodation. Paradoxically, perhaps, the second highest listed problem area was also in the housing category and was concerned with lack of appropriate housing. These housing findings are discussed in detail in the earlier housing chapter.

Before providing an analysis of the other answers to the achievement and problem questions, beginning with the achievements answers, here are two examples of the ways that projects responded, one from the voluntary sector and one from local authority teams. The answers themselves are not typical of all the priorities given to answers. They are included to provide an indicative illustration of the respondents' practice emphasis and to provide an insight into their particular concerns. Also, whilst there are differences in answers between the two types of projects, about expectations, security and funding, there are also great similarities in terms of both teams' immediate team concerns.

Achievements and Problems Between 1994–96: Response from a Local Authority Project
ACHIEVEMENTS

1. training flats with Housing Association got off the ground

2. development of project/office space to enable drop-in plus groups work

3. further development of 'protocol' with housing re care leavers, especially young homeless

4. better link up with foster carers

5. practical skills courses – rolling programme

6. networking with Youth Service and YMCA locally.

PROBLEMS

1. inadequate resources, money/facilities etc. to meet demand

2. being used by area teams to respond to young homelessness to the detriment of leaving care

3. benefit problems especially re aftercare – young people cannot survive on restricted income

4. private rented sector rarely used for 'move on' but becoming more difficult to obtain

5. a watershed time for leaving care – after initial publicity, there is a danger of loss of priority with ever greater pressure on finances

6. anxiety over loss of posts etc.

Achievements and Problems Between 1994–96: Response from a Voluntary Sector Project

ACHIEVEMENTS

1. achieving budgeted occupancy and staying in business

2. altering staffing structure and practice to work with young people with more complex needs

3. positive feedback from young people

4. positive department report

5. recruitment, induction and support for seven residential support workers all recruited at the same time

6. successful secondment of member of staff to professional training course.

PROBLEMS

1. local authorities with no money

2. local authorities want the service on the cheap

3. local authorities stop funding regardless of young person's needs

4. time limited placements

5. local authorities expect miraculous progress from extremely troubled young people

6. finding appropriate daytime activities/courses for young people.

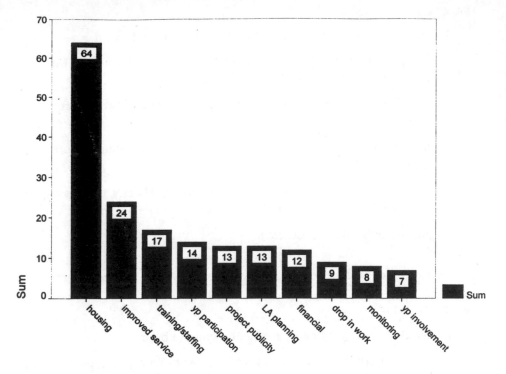

Figure 8.1 The ten main leaving care project achievement areas for the period 1994 to 1996 (n=181)[1]

Achievements of projects

Projects were asked to list their main achievements in order of priority and these are presented in Figure 8.1. The response rate to the question was 98 per cent, much higher than the participation question, with just one of the 46 projects not replying. Everyone had achieved something. Having obtained the responses, these were then grouped and coded. Examples are provided of the six most listed achievement categories after housing, namely, improved service, training and

1   Only those responses which attracted seven or more responses, each representing 3 per cent of the total number of responses, are included in Table 8.1. Thirty-nine other replies are not included in the table because these were made up of lots of smaller items, each constituting less than 3 per cent of the whole. They included a large number (17) attracting just one response, including making links with foster carers, linking with youth service, making care plans, moving to a needs' led service, the project started!, offered family support, started a counselling service, more work in rural areas, and improvements in relationship with the benefits office. Those attracting two responses were work with volunteers, resources, preventive work, networking, community/church support. A number attracted four responses each, again less than the 3 per cent minimum, and these were improvements to the project's workbase, contributing to leaving care forums, and providing help with education.

staffing, young people's participation, project publicity, local authority planing, and finance.

Improving the Quality and Scope of Services

As can be seen from Figure 8.1, after housing the next highest achievement category was the provision of improved services to young people. It was very noticeable that a number of projects had made progress and took considerable pride in the improved quality of their leaving care project's service. All the projects reported that they had extended their work from two years previously and these improvements/additions to services were not necessarily related to enhanced staffing or a higher ratio of staff to young people. Rather, it seemed as if projects were offering a wider range of services, in some cases from a low base the previous year, and in others from a more established level. Another likely explanation is that projects were becoming better at describing and promoting their services, and, in the emerging purchaser/provider climate, at selling their services to others, especially to potential purchasers. This explanation was summed up by one respondent (above) as 'achieving budgeted occupancy and staying in business'. This observation stems from the business-like nature of the housing contract with housing associations/voluntary organisations in which voids are discouraged to the point of carrying financial penalties. In one exceptional case a leaving care project's achievement (London Borough of Sutton) was such that it had been awarded the widely acclaimed National Charter Mark. Let me first list some of the projects' achievements, as given on the questionnaire, and then categorised.

Service Provision Achievements

EXAMPLES OF ACHIEVEMENTS FROM 24 PROVIDED ABOUT EXTENDING THE QUALITY AND SCOPE OF SERVICES TO YOUNG PEOPLE:

- the team is in contact with a large number of young people. We are their team. If we did not shape up to what they want, they would not stay in touch!
- written standards produced and agreed
- integrating housing benefit and careers advisors to regularly attend and provide individual help to the care leavers at their drop in
- planned extensions to the service implemented
- reaching a wider number of young people as a result of increased staff levels (additional staff member)
- development of floating support scheme, advice centre and aftercare service

- ongoing support service – young people have confidence to come back to us

- provided support for several young people with special needs not able to be looked after elsewhere

- provided service to clients of mixed abilities and racial origins, and housing needs closely together

- accessing funds for furniture, furnishings and to support personal developments through Section 17 monies, trust funds and donations.

Services to young unemployed people: example

There were also a number of projects which provided additional information about their services. Although these are too numerous to mention, given the exceedingly high level of unemployment amongst young people leaving care, the recorded approach of one leaving care project in this field, amongst many who recorded similar approaches, is both instructive and impressive.

The London Borough of Lewisham's established leaving care team conducted a survey of its young people in 1993 which revealed that a very high percentage, 65 per cent of young people over 16, had no job or occupation of any kind during the day. Just 6 or 3 per cent of the total were in full time employment. A report and action plan followed involving extensive revisions and developments were undertaken. This consisted of the production of a questionnaire on employment which was sent out to all young people, the production of a special edition of the news letter specifically for careers/employment; the setting aside of one day for employment, forming a partnership with specialist agency bringing in a specialist worker, and an increasing emphasis on employment and careers issues. There was thus a raising of expectations amongst the staff and the young people. Subsequently a specialist service with additional staffing was introduced late in 1993 with a focus on careers and employment services. This service consisted of a wide range of services including vocational guidance, career profiling and planning, help with interviews and curriculum vitaes and educational grants. Resources were also made available in the form of computer training and support, access to training material, literacy and numerical sessions, business and enterprise advice, and access to administrative support. None of this analysis or action plan seems particularly radical or new, and there are many projects doing similar work. Yet in this case the reported result of this initiative is a considerable improvement to the unemployment figures, down from 46 per cent in 1993 to 26 per cent in 1996, and higher rates of 'occupation' of all types during the same period. For example, 15 per cent are in full time employment as of 1996, compared with 3 per cent for the year 1993, despite an increase in overall numbers of young people attending the project, from 198 in 1993 to 325 in 1996. Although more work would need to be done to investigate why these improvements took place, whether they have been sustained and the reliability of the figures, nevertheless this achievement by the team and the young people working in partnership with another agency seems to vividly demonstrate what is possible in the traditionally difficult world of high unemployment by and low esteem of young people leaving care. A connected point is that there have also been achievements in training and staffing, generally, which projects reported.

Training and Staffing Improvements

The third highest achievement rated by projects was that related to staffing and training issues. As a category this did not exist in the 1992 survey and it is probably significant that with the emerging picture of more leaving care projects undertaking more work with more young people, these issues have become more pressing. Of the 15 responses in this combined category, 11 of the responses were from voluntary organisations or jointly funded projects, and the remaining four were local authority projects. The examples given of achievements in terms of staffing were the listings of appointments of an additional staff member during the prior year.

The listed training achievements consisted of projects staff training and training for (other) providers.

TRAINING AND STAFFING: 6 EXAMPLES OF 14 PROVIDED:

- provision of a training package for support workers
- team building exercises
- training for other leaving care workers in the area
- change to the staffing structure
- developed leaving care training for multi agency audience (this has taken some two years to establish)
- training for foster parents and social workers.

TRAINING AND STAFFING: QUALITY STANDARDS

In some instances leaving care projects service level agreements included staff competencies as forming one part of projects' quality indicators and the following provides one example of staff skills and expertise to be demonstrated (Dudley Social Services Department, 1994):

- to work in a professional and sensitive way with young people taking account of their individual needs and issues connected with their gender, race, cultural background, first language, religion, sexual orientation and disability

- use of appropriate advocacy skills
- groupwork skills for staff involved in groupwork activities
- an appreciation of the professional balances between care and control
- the ability to work with a number of different social and bureaucratic and community systems
- the ability to work with young people in crisis, assessing immediate needs, intervening appropriately, and taking actions which complement care plans
- having up to date records of work activity with individual young people
- a profile of training courses and events of the leaving care scheme have attended will be included in their project's annual report.

It is of critical importance for quality staff from a variety of professional backgrounds to work in this area, and staff selection and training, remuneration, retention and motivation are key features. They may even be critical ones to successful outcomes. In the above case from Dudley Social Services Department, these quality expectations could readily be integrated into annual staff appraisals, and encouraged and rewarded. Once this happens then a quality learning culture can be further developed and sustained within projects. Indeed, it should be expected that staff are properly supported if leaving care projects are to avoid some of the appalling problems that residential care produced as a direct consequence of unchecked, under valued, over stretched, and underpaid staff, and uncaring management systems more concerned with 'order and control' issues than quality issues.

Participation by Young People

Of the 11 projects which listed 'participation by young people' as a main achievement, the majority – eight – were from either the voluntary sector or joint projects, with just three from local authority projects. Unsurprisingly perhaps, this same trend, of greater voluntary organisations' involvement in participation, was also true for those listing greater participation by young people as one of the main achievements during 1994–96. However, whether this was because the local authority leaving care teams had already developed ways for the young people to become more involved in the running of projects, or whether the voluntary organisations had been slower to start their participation initiatives, or whether certain projects gave a higher priority to participation by young people, is not known for sure. However, it seems plausible to suggest that local authority teams did not rate the participation of young people as highly as the other project types, or, alternatively, had not pursed or succeeded with it to the same extent. It must also be recognised that voluntary organisations usually have a greater flexibility in terms of management committees and structures than local authorities, and therefore greater scope for young people's participation in them if they so choose.

The following two examples provided by projects, all voluntary or joint projects, were amongst the more creative of the examples that were provided:

- increased participation of young people in the running and day to day life of the project (young people involved in joint consultative group and staff selection)

- enabling and empowering young people to have a greater voice in service delivery (young people form an established consumer group, representatives at local and national voluntary organisation's leaving care committees).

Other sorts of young people's participation listed included the development of a vocal young people's group who share in the decision making in the project (committee members), members of peer education group, consultancy regarding local and national policy, and development.

Higher Community Profile/Publicity Achievements

In addition to overall improvements to services being recorded as a major achievement, it was also noticeable that, unlike the 1992 survey, the category 'obtaining a higher profile for the project' was needed to record this development. This can be regarded as an associated development to the previous 'extended services' category in the sense of it representing the importance leaving care projects attributed to establishing a higher profile and publicity to fulfil project support functions. The examples given by respondents about this area simply stated that the project concerned had increased its profile locally (e.g. 'as a result of our work leaving care work now has a higher profile in the area which is especially good for interagency and community relations work'). Some of the publicity was also in written form and constituted 'information' at least as much as 'publicity'. A number of leaving care projects produce quite comprehensive booklets describing their aims, objectives and methods, and in some instances it was most encouraging to see that the projects took the production of this booklet as an opportunity to provide considerable detail about their services, including telephone contact numbers, contact names, and, in the case of those booklets produced for young people, in a user friendly and not patronising language and style.

For example, the acclaimed Dudley leaving care team had two informative booklets about its services, one for social workers and one for young people, and both covered very similar areas. The one for social workers specified service eligibility issues and services on offer, and the one for young people sought to address and answer directly what it described as the four big issues, namely, work or education? money and how to get it? Where to live? And what help and support have I got? The booklet provided a balanced view of leaving care, including 'the good news' about being free at last and the 'bad news' about loneliness and the difficulties of living on ones own. The leaflet was also honest in not promising what it could not deliver (e.g. not being allowed on the council housing waiting list until one is 17.5 years old, rent guarantees not guaranteed). The booklet also indicated new ways that the projects were developing to meet old problems, in one case accommodation, by looking at supported accommodation and a shared house (Dudley Metropolitan Borough Council, 1996).

The London Borough of Brent's booklet covered similar areas, and was also honest in stating that in those instances where other housing was not made available to young people leaving care, then the housing department made one offer only. It appeared that these offers for single people were mainly in the large housing estates areas within the borough. The booklet also describes the local authority's policy for providing housing for young people, either through the leaving care housing quota or its children in need quota. For those young people who become single parents the booklet stated that the leaving care team liaised with other specialist housing providers within the borough. There was clarity of information about the type of tenancy (i.e. assured shorthold) that would be offered to single parents if a mother and baby unit was inappropriate, and of young people 'under 18 who are offered a tenancy receiving a rent guarantee signed by social services before that take up the tenancy' (London Borough of Brent, 1996).

Local Authority Co-operation/Planning

Thirteen projects reported that local authority co-operation was a main achievement for them, and this represented 5.5 per cent of all answers, compared with 7 per cent for the 1992 survey. If there has been one area of policy that has consistently been experienced as a problem in leaving care work, it has been the lack of, gross inconsistencies in, or just confusion about local authority planning in connection with leaving care services. Thus, any progress in this area is most welcome. Having said that, the 1992 survey did also report some progress in this area, under the heading of 'liaison'. If, as seems to be the case, progress has further slowed down then this is much to be regretted. Although tempting to the person who puts optimism before evidence, to conclude that progress in this 'local authority planning and co-operation' area has reached a sufficient peak so as to make any further progress unnecessary is a gross exaggeration.

IMPROVED CO-OPERATION WITH LOCAL AUTHORITIES/BETTER CORPORATE PLANNING: 7 EXAMPLES OF 13 PROVIDED:

- involvement of the local authority leaving care team in future planning while still 'consumers' at the project rather than waiting for a crisis to occur
- setting up a panel of care leavers whose brief it is to identify gaps in services provided by the local authority and advise on how they could or should be filled
- the team actively participated in drafting the borough's leaving care policy
- some dialogue achieved between young people looked after (not leaving care) and social services
- maintaining a high profile and good working relationship with the local authority and the ability to review standards and implement the necessary change
- relationships with housing and probation and others much improved
- developed policy for young people to attend reviews of young people over 14.

It is significant to record that ten of the responses highlighting this topic were from voluntary organisations, and this observation can be linked to the findings under the later section headed 'problems', about project's feeling excluded from policy decision making forums, which follows this achievements section.

Financial Achievements

Along with increased local authority co-operation, and given the limits on public expenditure, it is a matter of some significance that respondents included a range of financial achievements within their achievements list.

Financial achievements: 11 examples of 12 provided:

- agreement by social services to fund full time employment worker
- achieving budgeted occupancy/stayed within budget
- accessing funds for furniture, furnishings through Section 17 monies, trust funds and donations
- financing found for private accommodation
- the development of a financial policy for Section 24 expenditure
- securing funding to stay alive!

- developed a policy for financial support for care leavers (this is now under threat)
- maintaining financial support in current climate
- securing the funding for a traineeship for a young person, as a project worker
- funding for life skills preparation course
- just agreed new contract with the local authority.

Upon closer scrutiny of these achievements it can be seen that the majority are concerned with simply maintaining the current position, or in making modest gains, either for the project or the young people attending the project. There was just one example given of a team extending its size through local authority funding, and that one example was, in fact, funded through a relatively short term successful single regeneration budget bid.

Discussion of Achievements

Especially at a time of financial pressures and increased caseloads, and of working with even more young people than the previous year, it is important to record any and all main practice achievements by leaving care projects for the period 1994–96. The seven most recorded categories – housing, quality and scope of service, staff and training, young people's participation, higher project profile, better local authority planning, and finances – amounted to some 65 per cent of all responses, the remaining being widely spread amongst many other smaller categories. It is also not easy to gauge the significance of achievements, because it may well be that in some cases the leaving care projects are so well developed that the period of considerable advance is past, and consolidation is appropriate and the order of the day. Yet for others the observation that the production of a leaving care guide, as a main achievement some five years after the Children Act 1989 was introduced, gives some indication of what more needs to be done and how slow and inconsistent progress has been in this leaving care field.

Problems faced by projects

'There is so much to do and so little time or resources to do it': the response of one project summed up the sentiments of many! Just as projects were asked to list their achievements in priority order, so they were asked to list their problem areas and provide examples for the two year period from 1994 to 1996. A total of 176 problems provided by 46 projects, producing seven key categories, were listed as the main problems constituting more than 3 per cent of all problem categories listed. Problems about lack of local authority planning, appropriate housing, insufficient resources, and staffing were the four most common problem areas listed. There were several other problems for projects, the main ones including the benefits system (20 replies), the financing of projects and young people (12 replies), the organisation of the service offered to young people (11 replies) and the feelings of the projects about other service providers (8 replies). Examples of these other problems are not provided here because they all amounted to slightly different versions of the 'lack of money and other resources', in the case of benefits from the social security system, and for the remainder from the local authority, to provide the services needed.

As with achievements, housing again emerged as a key category, and although again this is discussed within the separate housing chapter it is relevant to record here that all the housing answers were concerned with lack of suitable, sufficient, and affordable accommodation.

Local Authority Policy and Planning Problems

The importance of local authority planing in the field of leaving care is critical given the corporate parenting responsibilities laid out in the Children Act 1989. Arguably, local authority planning underpins leaving care work. Without it, or with poor planning, services are likely to be provided on the pre-Children Act 1989 basis which promoted corporate planned services: namely, on an individual *ad hoc* basis, with social workers making new and individual links for each young person with whom they are working. It is then especially worrying that the single biggest problem category listed was local authority planning. The following examples provide an illustration of the nature of some of the problems faced by local authority as well as voluntary organisation leaving care teams.

LOCAL AUTHORITY POLICY AND PLANNING PROBLEMS: 12 OF 39 EXAMPLES GIVEN:

- leaving care work seen as the end of the line (e.g. if a young person is 16+ then must be the responsibility of the leaving care service), and the age group is not always given consideration by area teams

- retaining social work support for families and for that support to be proactive rather than crisis management. Social workers tend to withdraw when other support is available and local reorganisation has compounded this problem

- working in partnership with district social work teams to ensure they understand the service offered

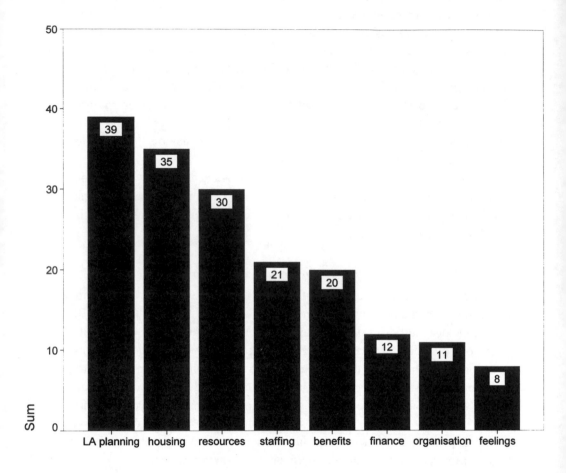

Figure 8.2 The eight main leaving care project problem areas for the period 1994 to 1996 (n=176)[1]

1   There were five further categories of problems, with six responses each, and not included in the table. These were young people, unemployment, special needs, others' perception of what the project had to offer, and education. Twenty-seven additional problems were listed and these included, with four responses each, the state of the project's office or workbase; referrals from social services (both too many and not enough); the lack of preparation given to the young people prior to their leaving care; philosophical/pragmatic (e.g. 'helping young people to stay in poverty'); the health of young people; and project funding (insecure and/or inadequate). The category 'youth training', referring both to its availability and quality, attracted three responses. Remaining problems of the 27 were only listed once.

- co-ordinating payments to providers when housing benefit and social services make cut backs
- ever changing social services department – exclusion of project in strategic development of services
- more bureaucracy regarding setting up home grants
- the culture within social services, stemming from a lack of policy, is that leaving care work is not the responsibility of social workers
- lack of agreement between local authority departments over interpretation of the Children Act 1989
- lack of finance from local authority
- discrepancies in respect of children in need and vulnerability criterion-ongoing problems regarding definition of these terms and therefore of eligibility for assessments etc.
- getting local authority to honour commitment to young people beyond 18
- culture within local authority stemming from lack of policy or provision.

Other Problems

RESOURCES PROBLEMS: 12 OF 30 EXAMPLES GIVEN:

- need for 24 hour support for young people leaving care
- lack of dedicated time for casework
- squeeze on resources including our own staff, social services and housing
- less staff becoming more stretched (many answers such as this)
- insufficient services available for young people (e.g. unless they are prepared to be 'medicalised' and go through a psychiatric referral, we cannot access counselling services or anger management courses)
- inadequate resources in the form of money and facilities etc. to meet continuing demands
- not having our own building or, until recently, a team leader; we also have staff shortages (local authority team)
- project underfunded and local authority wanting more for less!
- lack of emergency provision in the event of young people becoming homeless, especially if out of hours when the local authority housing department is closed

- the number of young people needing support is increasing
- fragmentation of resources available to young people due to competition for funding and lack of cohesion
- can no longer offer a long term service for young people due to insufficient resourcing.

STAFFING PROBLEMS: 7 OF 21 EXAMPLES GIVEN:

- lack of qualified staff or opportunity for workers on team to qualify (voluntary organisation)
- maintaining staffing levels through illness due to stressful/demanding nature of the work
- staff turnover and sickness has meant that the team has not operated at its full potential
- reducing number of workers leading to unassigned cases
- for a long time we had to use agency staff and staff group had little training offered
- staff cut-back has resulted in the staff group becoming less stable
- the service is limited because of lack of any administrative help.

Against this background of the overall problems of inadequate accommodation for young people leaving care, poor local authority planning and lack of resources, it is hardly surprising that there are also staffing and training problems. Also, the fact that so many more projects in the survey, 21 in fact, listed staffing as a major problem, compared with the 17 projects which listed it as an achievement, indicates that this is, and is seen as, a major problem area. An audit of staffing levels, staff training, support mechanisms, and remuneration levels might be a good starting point. Any further detailed analysis would require more research (of course) or local action as already outlined. There was a strength of feeling in many cases about what was seen as inadequate local authority provision and interest in leaving care work. There was no significant difference about the overall number or type of problem responses, although voluntary organisation projects and the joint projects tended to be more critical of the local authority's provisions, policies and planning arrangements. The difference in terms of these responses is mentioned here only to highlight the point that it was those projects (other than local authority leaving care teams) which were experiencing modest expansion which were the same ones experiencing the most problems in relation to the local authority's planning. There may be some significance attached to this point. There were also comments made by these projects about the unacceptable level of discretionary local authority decisions. These were made in connection with:

- service provision in terms of leaving care grants and packages – decisions based more on individual social worker's own power, experience, and workload

- whether social workers became involved, or not – for example, social workers were criticised for withdrawing prematurely from cases when other support became available. Although this can be justified, in terms of preventing duplication, relationships with young people became broken and new relationships had to be formed. It was also considered that local government reorganisation had compounded this problem

- retaining social worker support for families, and for that support to be proactive and willingly given, and not to be crisis driven

- working in partnership between leaving care projects and district social work teams to ensure that they understood the services offered by the team. This co-ordination was seen as vital and essential by teams but reported as being viewed as optional by social services teams

- at its extreme, in some cases, a perception by social workers that they have no responsibility towards young people leaving care.

Conclusion

Despite the United Nations Convention and the Children Act 1989, the issue of legally enforceable and not just social rights for children, including those leaving care, remains deeply complex and unsatisfactory so far as leaving care practice is concerned. Rights have to be given to children by adults, governments or institutions, and as we saw in earlier chapters about the legal and social context, and the terms of local authority policies (and as we will also see in the chapter on that most critical of subjects, financial supports), the dominant terms of the debate in those contexts concerns discretionary powers, actions and governance. There remain vast areas, at a general level, of duties and obligations, about local authorities providing support and advice to care leavers, but again dependent on eligibility and couched in wide terms. Within those prescribed formal limits to defining legal rights there were vast waves of involvement and participation by young people across many areas of leaving care work.

There were also a considerable number and range of major achievements and problems listed by the leaving care projects. If projects had spent even further time on the questionnaire it is likely that there would probably have been many more of both listed. Against, and possibly offsetting these positive findings, especially of housing being the biggest single achievement category, is the key finding that local authority planning and housing are the two biggest problem areas. This latter finding once again makes the point that seven years after the Children Act 1989 was introduced there remain substantial planning and implementation problems emanating mostly from committed and fairly established, and not new, leaving care teams. It would be especially valuable to track project achievements in the future, and involve young people in defining them, perhaps through some of the user monitoring types discussed in Chapter Eleven as well as in other ways.

CHAPTER NINE

Leaving Care Work
and Anti-Discrimination

Introduction

In this chapter the findings from the 1996 survey about anti-discriminatory work by leaving care projects will be presented, and placed within a practice and policy framework. Anti-discriminatory practice examples in leaving care work will be described and analysed, alongside anti-discriminatory local authority and voluntary organisation policies. Whilst anti-discriminatory issues are discussed throughout this book as an integral part of good practice, the view was taken that distinct elements to this work did exist and could be identified separately. This is another important topic in leaving care work. The *Patterns and Outcomes* report concluded, in respect of ethnic minority children in public care:

> The future challenge for social workers and managers will be to move from rhetoric or lip service to action. Racial and ethnic issues must be raised to their proper place alongside those of culture, class and gender without ignoring, exaggerating or distorting any of these essential elements in each child's individuality and personal history. (DoH, 1991c:17)

Context

> The Children Act 1989 recognises that Britain is a multi-cultural society and that cultural back-ground and beliefs are important. For each child and young person the importance of culture, language, racial origin and religion must be considered with other factors relating to their welfare. (S22:5).

In that this section of the Children Act 1989 represents, to my knowledge, the first reference in child care legislation incorporating the recognition that Britain is a multi-cultural society, that legislation represents something of a symbolic milestone. Yet it seems to me, as has been already discussed in connection with the leaving care sections of the Children Act 1989, that this section and the guidance in this anti-discrimination area (see the guidance, DoH, para. 7.52 on enabling certain groups to develop their self esteem) is also very limited. Essentially, the above section is placing a duty on local authorities to adopt an approach which is sensitive to different groups' needs. This approach in relation to ethnicity is often described as an 'ethnically sensitive' approach, and is a most important one to emphasise for individual practice. Yet this approach contrasts with an anti-discriminatory approach, which emphasises the structural and institutional, as well as the individual, nature of staff–client interaction and discrimination. Such an approach, then, calls for institutional responses, and not simply a case-by-case and individual response. It requires not simply practice changes by workers to be more sensitive to clients' needs but requires institutional changes as well. Based on experiences from the criminal justice world (Broad, 1991), it is also recognised that such changes are complex and demanding on all institutions, especially those consisting mostly of white staff.

In seeking to discover the ways in which leaving care projects approached this area, at both the practice and institutional levels, two basic questions were asked:

- Does your project/organisation take into account anti-discrimination issues in its work? (Possible responses 'yes', 'no', 'don't know').

- If 'yes' please highlight how these issues are operationalised.

Detailed practice answers were neither sought nor expected. Instead, the point was to establish levels of awareness, and levels of activity about the subject. It is the answers to those two questions which form the basis of this chapter.

Also in the discussion that follows, the term anti-discrimination is used, rather than equal opportunities, for a very important reason which requires explanation. It seems that in terms of its popular usage, rather than its intention perhaps, the term equal opportunities has come to mean all things to all people. If indeed it now has any clear meaning, it has become a sort of umbrella term, mostly as written aims which cover a range of passive and active phenomena. In short, it has lost the punch it had, or strove to have, in the 1980s. By contrast, the term anti-discriminatory, meaning against discrimination (like anti-apartheid or anti-vivisectionist), indicates *actively* working for change, here against all forms of discrimination and oppression. It is its active ingredient and messages which are crucial. The main themes of anti-discriminatory practice (adapted from Thompson, 1993) are:

- a recognition that discrimination occurs, usually systematically and structurally, within organisations, as well as at the practice level, for a range of groups

- the recognition that social work is a political activity in terms of legislative powers but also sets of power relations

- traditional social work relates primarily to the level of the 'case' and not wider issues, or the three levels of the personal, the structural and cultural

- a recognition that work with young people needs to take place at the personal, cultural and structural levels to be fully integrated and anti-discriminatory

- at the personal level the emphasis will be on personal empowerment and political and social education

- if they do not already do so, staff require anti-discriminatory training to fully understand what constitutes discrimination and anti-discriminatory practice and policies

- the actions of staff, project teams and organisations will either challenge or support discrimination

In drawing up the questionnaire the view was taken that anti-discriminatory work and policies apply to a number of discriminated against groups, which can be listed separately, including women, black people, disabled people, people who are gay or lesbian, or those discussed together. Because of the number of groups discriminated against, the view was eventually taken that the two specific questions about anti-discrimination should be expressed in general terms, and not be presented as representing any one particular group, because this would exclude other groups. It was also necessary to emphasise the point to all projects, even those with nil or few black young people (often voluntary organisation projects based in counties), that anti-discrimination also, perhaps especially, applied to their work. Whilst there were, admittedly, other pragmatic concerns (for example about questionnaire length), it was this aim of obtaining as wide a range of anti-discriminatory practice examples as possible that underpinned the approach that was taken. Despite this aim of encouraging wide ranging responses about different groups, by not stating, for example, 'please describe your work with black young people,' the answers did tend to focus largely on work with black young people. Anti-discriminatory is also often regarded as synonymous with special needs work with single parents.

Young people attending the leaving care projects: ethnic origin

As we saw earlier in the book, of the total number of 3319 young people categorised under the ethnic origin question, 78 per cent (or 2579) were described as white, 13 per cent (or 449) as black, 3 per cent (or 100) as Asian, and 5 per cent (or 191) as 'other', with projects not specifying 'other' in any detail. The term 'mixed race' was not one used by respondents, although it is acknowledged that previous research (for example Biehal et al., 1995) has used this or a similar term for further levels of analysis. It is interesting to see how the ethnic breakdown for this survey compares with Britain as a whole for a comparable age group. For the population in Britain as a whole, according to the

1991 census, in the 16–24 age group (the closest age grouping to the survey group) the national ethnicity breakdown is quite different. Thus, in percentage terms in that age group, there are 93 per cent white, 2 per cent black, 3.5 per cent South Asian and 1.5 per cent Chinese and other (OPCS, 1996:117). Overall, the average caseload for the 14 local authority leaving care projects was 118 young people; for the 15 voluntary organisation projects the average figure was 50, and for the 17 jointly run projects the average figure was 59. There was a further significant difference between the project types in terms of ethnic composition. Overall, the average number of black and Asian young people attending each project, of whatever type, was 22. This compared with the average figures of 26 black and Asian young people attending local authority projects, 3 black and Asian young people attending voluntary organisation projects, and 8 attending jointly run projects. The differences seem directly connected with county/small town location of most non-local authority projects but could also be connected with referral/selection procedures. The potential practice implications arising from this important finding are summarised at the end of this chapter.

The survey figures about the *gender* of the young people attending projects was 1623 women (or 51%) and 1572 men (or 49%), making a total of 3195 for male/female figures provided. In terms of the *age range* of the young people attending leaving care projects, previous research indicates the majority to be in the age range of 16–21. When previously working in a voluntary organisation, for example, the age breakdown for 411 young people leaving care in 1994/5, 82 per cent of the so called 'active cases' (i.e. when new or referrals became active cases for the leaving care projects) became so at between 15–18 years of age, with 72 per cent of that group being either 16 or 17 years of age. The Biehal *et al.* research (1995:30–31), albeit using a slightly different counting point, reported that 85 per cent moved onto independent accommodation at the age of 16 and before 18. Much of the leaving care literature has also pointed to the early age at which young people in care are expected and required to leave care and become established independent of the local authority, wherever possible (see, for example, Garnett,1992).

Moving onto *learning difficulties and physical disabilities* the survey revealed that of the 3100 young people described there were 245 young people with learning difficulties (or 8% of the total number of young people reported in the survey), and 44 (or 1.4% of the total) with physical disabilities. Biehal *et al.*'s study (1995:150) also highlighted the considerable support need of young people described as having special needs, and the considerable amount of inter-agency support that is necessary but often unavailable. In the light of this initial information gathered from the questionnaire, let me now consider the ways in which the projects answered the questions about whether, and if so how, they operationalised ant-discrimination issues in their work.

Anti-discriminatory work by leaving care projects

Of the 44 responses to the question 'Does your project/organisation take into account anti-discrimination issues in its work?' (Q21a), 38 projects stated that they did take into account anti-discrimination issues in undertaking their work. Three projects stated they did not do so (all based in county areas). A further three answered 'don't know'. Of those projects which did provide the 151 answers about how they operationalised anti-discriminatory policies, there were no differences, at first sight, in terms of project type, about these answers. Upon closer examination of responses, of all of those that either answered 'do not know' to the anti-discriminatory implementation question (Q21b) or gave a one line answer indicating intention, such as 'policies being developed' or 'action is being taken', all of these (n=11) were voluntary organisations' leaving care projects. Although the questionnaire did not define anti-discriminatory work as being work with black young people, this finding about under-developed or non-existent anti-discriminatory policies in a number of leaving care projects run by voluntary organisations is likely to relate directly to the earlier finding about the different average numbers of black and Asian young people attending the three different project types.

Operationalising Anti-Discriminatory Ideas

The 38 projects which stated that they took anti-discriminatory issues into account provided a total of 151 answers. Table 9.1 indicates the different headings under which projects' answers were framed. Different departmental, team, practice and policy levels are identified at which anti-discriminatory work can take place. In some instances the topics were being tackled at both practice and policy levels simultaneously, and therefore it was not possible to separate them. It was not possible to obtain more detailed information from leaving care projects about this important area of work. Had it been possible, further questions would have been raised about how these policies were discussed and absorbed into practice, often a most difficult matter. Nevertheless, there was a considerable amount of material collected, and this is presented first in Table 9.1 and then as exemplars, to illustrate anti-discriminatory policies and practices in leaving care work.

Table 9.1 Ways in which anti-discrimination work is operationalised by leaving care teams

Anti-discriminatory topic being tackled	Level at which anti-discriminatory work described[1]	Number (n=151) of answers
Team policy level		
General issues		29
Monitoring		4
Office culture		4
Disability		3
Written materials		3
HIV/AIDS team policy		2
Single parents		2
Campaigning		1
Practice level		
General issues		64
Behaviour and language		3
Advocacy work		3
Monitoring		2
Single parents		1
Special needs		1
Practice and Policy levels		
Accomodation	practice and policy	10
Gender issues	practice and policy	8
Recruitment and selection	practice and policy	6

Anti-discriminatory work at team policy level

General (14 Of 29 Examples Given)

- ensuring a balance of race and sex when young people are placed with the project
- everyone is treated equally and we have an equal opportunity policy
- we have an action plan
- anti-discriminatory issues on the agenda at every team meeting

---

1   The responses about recruitment, equal opportunity and monitoring issues were identified by four projects and directed at departmental level. The examples given abut those issues were simply references that policies about them were in existence within the organisation. There were also four responses concerned with issues external to the team.

- ensuring a balance of race and sex when young people are placed with the project
- translation of leaving care standards
- documentation from parent voluntary organisation about anti-discrimination
- written into policy level agreement
- support for the area's anti-racist group
- targets regarding quality assurance
- the project has a black cases forum to discuss work with black young people
- local project training
- a standing agenda item at team meetings
- identified a need to develop contacts with the ethnic minority groups in the area and see this as a target for the next year.

Office Culture (4 of 4 Examples Given)

- we challenge discriminatory comments and behaviour
- positive images in office
- we challenge discriminatory comments and behaviour at the office
- positive images in the office/mixed culture team.

Monitoring (4 of 4 Examples Given)

- gender and ethnicity monitored on both social services and housing department forms
- targets + action plan + policy
- equal opportunities monitoring group feedback to the team monthly
- developed quality assurance targets for users.

Written Material (1 of 3 Examples Given)

- ensure that promotional literature reflects positive images re anti-discriminatory issues.

Single Parents (1 of 2 Examples Given)

- establishment of group for young female parents

Disability (3 of 3 Examples Given)

- meetings with disability team (a team representative attends)
- weekly visits to young people with disability/learning difficulties
- successfully negotiated for additional funding for placements for young people with special needs.

HIV Issues (2 of 3 Examples Given)

- HIV issues contained in the project's operational policy statement
- project statement on HIV.

Anti-discriminatory work at practice level

General (13 of 64 Examples Given)

- allocate workers according to needs taking into account race, gender, culture, sexuality and disability
- recognising that anti-discriminatory work is different from direct work
- involvement of young people
- young people's wishes are usually adhered to
- anti-discriminatory work at forefront of all work, including group work
- complaints procedure displayed for all to see
- project has a black cases forum to discuss work with black young people
- charters/agreements with users, and education work on their behaviour and language
- allocate workers taking into account young people's race, gender, culture, sexuality, disability
- we work alongside young people in an honest manner, showing them respect, and always seeking to work in partnership with them
- anti-discriminatory care plans
- in our group work we explore issues of discrimination
- education work with young people.

Behaviour and Language (1 of 3 Examples Given)

- challenging comments and behaviour.

Practice Monitoring (2 of 2 Examples Given)

- anti-discriminatory practice is monitored in supervision
- monitoring of quarterly reviews.

Advocacy Work (1 of 3 Examples Given)

- advocacy on behalf of clients re access to services.

Anti-discriminatory work at combined practice and policy levels

Accommodation (10 of 10 Examples Given)

- work with housing anti-discriminatory policies, to the point where contractors need to be 'approved'
- young black people supported in choosing housing in boroughs where they feel safer
- requests to housing panels for transfers based on harassment of and violence towards young black people and gay young people
- monitoring housing work re placements
- grant aid to housing project
- matching of young people with supported lodging providers
- training accommodation providers to recognise power dynamics
- information pack given when moving to supported accommodation
- training for supporting accommodation providers
- matching of young people with lodging providers for services to young people.

Recruitment and Selection (6 of 6 Examples Given)

- mandatory anti-oppressive staff training
- mixed culture team
- ensure that employment/recruitment issues, especially adverts/interviewing procedures, reflect the borough's policy
- exempted posts for black workers
- Section 52d of the Race Equality Act 1976 has been used
- interviewing procedures to reflect anti-discriminatory guidelines.

Gender Issues (8 of 8 Examples Given)

- gender issues are very alive in a project which supports young parents
- male parents are actively involved in all areas of work, particularly group work
- consider of gender issues re accommodation
- women's committee
- address gender issues in placement
- women's only day
- in placements
- women's workers group

In addition to the questionnaire returns, the written material that was sent to me made two direct references to anti-discriminatory work which included the Children Act 1989 'base lines', namely, 'due consideration will be given to the young person's religious persuasion, racial origin and cultural and linguistic background, as well as the needs of a young person with special needs', and 'to always treat people without discrimination'.

The three main findings here about anti-discriminatory policies and practice are that:

1. Many examples of anti-discriminatory leaving care work were provided by projects.

2. There has been a steady increase in the extent and scope of anti-discriminatory work by leaving care projects since the time the 1993 survey was conducted. This is especially the case regarding anti-discriminatory practice, as compared with anti-discriminatory policies, which are less developed.

3. Projects largely interpreted 'anti-discriminatory work' as equal opportunity work with women or black young people, and perhaps this should not come as a surprise given the popular usage of the term anti-discrimination.

Such an extensive listing of examples from this field illustrates a commitment to the issues and a creative approach to tackling anti-discriminatory issues at policy and practice levels. Although the extent of the commitment and the resultant outcomes are not known (i.e. what difference do these anti-discriminatory practices and intentions actually make?), it is especially important that so many projects demonstrated a keen awareness of the issues. The reason for this is because of the changing climate, of people mischievously and deliberately misrepresenting anti-discriminatory work. This is done by claiming to represent anti-discriminatory work as 'political correctness', thus disregarding structural inequalities. Also, the body central to social work values for so long, the Central Council of Social Work, diluted its anti-discriminatory requirements for qualifying social work students in the early 1990s.

Nevertheless, there remains a need to promote more organisationally led policies, which promote systematic work across these areas, in order to further focus the work of practitioners. A greater number of leaving care projects and the young people with whom they work could still adopt an expanded education role towards others in their local areas concerning anti-discriminatory practice, if this is seen as a productive way forward. It is important to place anti-discriminatory practice within a system as well as a context.

In system terms what is needed is a systematic anti-discriminatory policy, planning, action, review, cycle in place in which anti-discriminatory practice is systematically regarded as good practice, and where its absence is regarded as the opposite, namely bad practice, and critically reviewed.

Anti-discriminatory work and local authority policies

The London Borough of Hammersmith and Fulham's leaving care policy contains comprehensive examples of, and guidance for, conducting anti-discriminatory leaving care work with several different groups. It is based on the assumption that members of these groups have been, or are likely to be, the subject of oppressive attitudes and practice unless these are countered, challenged and, above all, changed. The excerpts presented here from policies about young women with children and pregnant young women, black young women and men, and young people with special needs are all taken from that local authority policy.

'Young Women with Children or Pregnant Young Women' Section of One Local Authority's Leaving Care Policy

- work with young black and white women with children needs to create space in which women can develop their own awareness and confidence
- workers within the borough have to develop their understanding of what young women's needs are, what resources are relevant to them, and develop plans that work
- time and energy and discussion must be given to the position of young women within society, how young women relate to other young women and to young men
- attention must be given to developing and supporting young women's confidence in articulating their own needs

- the workers' initial response to pregnancy: to be understanding, responsive, unbiased and informative

- placement response: where possible, the care plan for the young women should not be interrupted

- education and training: to be sensitively and carefully planned, to examine the full breadth of possible career areas, and substitute care issues must be considered if education and training is to be pursued and no other sources of help available

- maternity grants: the state's maternity grant of £100 is limited to those in receipt of income support. Preparation for a forthcoming birth is very expensive; as most young people will not be eligible for income support, a clear method of support, including the contribution towards some costs, should exist.

'Young Black Women and Men' Section of One Local Authority's Leaving Care Policy

- young black people's lives should be seen within the broader context of their being members of a racially disadvantaged group in Britain subject to specific social pressures over and above those experienced by young white people

- racism is real and young black people need support and reinforcement to be able to cope with both the institutional and individual racism they will face. Being equipped to fight racism is just as important as any other aspect of preparation

- direct work with young black people should address the issues of racism

- the main aim should be to give them the strength and confidence to challenge racism

- discussions should take place with young black people and young white people so that both groups can begin to question the basis of stereotypes and the way black people are misrepresented in the media

- racism to be challenged by workers

- racism to be tackled by challenging racist assumptions commonly held

- young black people should never be placed in placements with all white staff

- young black persons' review should address racism and ways for going forward

- time should be made available to identify and develop black people's networks

- independent visitors should come from the same cultural background as the young black person

- at reviews and planning meetings it is important that either the social worker or the chair is black so that a powerful black figure has and is seen to have influence on the young black person's life and is involved in the monitoring of plans

- issues of differences should be respected

- young black people should be given positive reinforcement about their differences of food, and specialist information about skin care and hair care etc. should be made available

- white foster carers and workers would benefit from more information and education about the 'black community'

- young black people need to be helped to cope with, understand and challenge racism

- young black people presently placed with white foster carers will need special help to cope with identity issues

- black and white workers and carers need to work together to achieve these aims.

'Young People with Special Needs' Section of One Local Authority's Leaving Care Policy: Policy and Practice Examples

POLICY

1. With young people with special needs it is important to note that their needs will not suddenly change when they leave care.

2. Co-operation between the various agencies is crucial in providing services to young people with special needs.

3. The primary focus of work should be to achieve the greatest level of autonomy as possible.

4. The transition from 'childcare' services to 'community care' services must recognise the right of these young people to be *adults*.

5. This work will mean a shift of power from 'us' to 'them'. Adulthood is when people control and have power to influence their environment and their life style.

6. Planning for inter-dependence and adulthood for young people with special needs must take place as soon as possible. Planning takes a great deal of time and care packages are likely to be scarce and expensive.

7. Planning must begin as soon as the original placements happen.

PRACTICE

1. Planning must start five years before a young person reaches 18, as soon as possible after being accommodated or in care.

2. The young person's strengths and weaknesses should be fully assessed and made explicit to the young person.

3. The young person must have access to information about resources and facilities.

4. Support should be proactive.

5. Aftercare and preparation support should be part of the mainstream provision.

6. A named person should be responsible for the care to community plan for young people with special needs.

7. There should be facilities to enable a young people with special needs either to stay in the borough or to live out of it.

8. Young people with special needs should have housing which is appropriate to meet their requirements.

These, then, are examples of one local authority's policies (London Borough of Hammersmith and Fulham, 1995) about anti-discriminatory aspects of leaving care policies. There are also relevant policies to record and place here from an important national body, as well as the voluntary child care sector, about equality policies.

General anti-discriminatory practice and policy developments

The Commission for Racial Equality's (CRE) Young and Equal publication (CRE, 1995) provides sets of comprehensive standards in terms of staffing, organisation and services, and provides five standard levels. For example, in relation to services to young people it states that for level 1:

- develop and deliver a curriculum that enables young people to explore issues of relevance to racial equality and

- review the services provided to ensure that they exclude unlawful racial discrimination and review the ways in which they take account of the needs of all ethnic groups.

There are further services provided at level 1, and then for levels 2, 3, 4 and 5. The more advanced level 4 services to young people include:

- use regular consultation with young people from all ethnic groups to develop new curriculum programmes

- review ethnic data on young people and adults regularly to guide targets

- review records of racial harassment regularly and use this to guide policy development and practice.

For the much more advanced level 5, services include:

- hold programmes of visits and exchanges with young people from all parts of the world

- share curriculum development for racial equality with other service providers.

This CRE publication provides an excellent guide to anti-discriminatory practice with young people. The National Council for Voluntary Child Care Organisations (NCVCCO) guidelines offer a comprehensive action checklist for what are described as 'race equality policies', and these are reproduced here as a summary checklist to highlight again the importance of policy and its organisational and service dimensions.

Race Equality Policies: an Example from a Voluntary Child Care Organisation
A POLICY CHECKLIST

- *documentation*: formal written policies relating to recruitment procedures, promotions and internal appointments, staff training, harassment, and service delivery

- *awareness and understanding*: staff understanding and owning of the policy, equal opportunity training for all staff, enhancement of quality of service, written literature in the organisation for all to see

- *signs of commitment*: senior management must be seen to support the policy in their actions, words and written form

- *recruitment and appointment procedures*: including all posts being advertised, with written job descriptions, with balanced interview panels, and specialist staff training

- *positive action in training and staff development*: to include special training for ethnic minority staff, training to be monitored with appropriate venues for training events

- *monitoring and responsibility*: the systematic collection and monitoring of information should be a nominated person's responsibility

- *the working environment*: to include grievance procedures relating to harassment and discrimination allegations, which are clearly known to be disciplinary offences.

AN ACTION CHECKLIST

- *take up of services provided* to be routinely monitored on an ethnic basis, and the data to be analysed and considered in all decision making

- *cultural and religious commitments* and preferences amongst members of the public to be respected, and mainstream services monitored as appropriate

- *effective consultative procedures* for gaining perceptions of the organisation's services from ethnic minority members of the public (but why is this necessary if the staff group is diverse?)

- improvements in service delivery from an equal opportunity perspective are included as *targets in staff appraisal and performance review schemes*

- the organisation's *equality commitments to be listed in public statements* about quality criteria

- *information* about services to be available in *appropriate different languages*

- the visual environment (i.e. premises) to reflect and *respect ethnic diversity*

- *front line staff to be diverse* and be fluent in relevant community languages. (adapted from NCVCCO,1991)

Leaving care with learning difficulties and physical disabilities

In terms of learning difficulties or physical disabilities the research found that young people in these two categories constituted 299 or 9 per cent of the sample. Biehal *et al.* reported that 13 per cent of that research's small sample also fell into these two categories, and subsequently were over-represented in the homeless and unemployed figures, and that the group received very little, often nil, support or contact from the local authority (Biehal *et al.*, 1992:41). It is in these two areas where more work needs to be done, more resources found, and where strategy needs developing. This is to be done in co-operation with a range of agencies as will be necessary. There was only *one example* given by projects of actual work done with either of these groups, that of 'weekly visits' to the young person concerned. Although it is possible that respondents mostly equated anti-discriminatory work as work with black young people, and not work with any other groups, it is also likely that had there been work with young people with learning difficulties or physical disabilities, this would have been recorded by projects under the achievements/problems section, for instance. Thus, whilst not ruling out the view that work with these young people was going on, as part of the team's ongoing work with all young people, what seemed absent was a broader awareness that such work could or should also be considered as meriting a broader anti-discriminatory approach. Of course it is also the case that the day to day responsibility for such support work is and should be with day centre or supported accommodation staff, or other floating support staff. Nevertheless, staff from leaving care teams will also likely have, dependent upon the planning structures for each area, a key co-ordinating and support role.

In the discussion of young people with learning difficulties and physical disabilities Biehal et al.'s key finding that 'over a third of those considered homeless were those considered likely to have special needs for support' (1992:40) is especially significant here, given the numbers of young people falling within those categories. There are, then, a distinct, sizeable and needy group of young people with particular needs which require further support, according to Biehal et al.'s research, they are not receiving consistently from social services or elsewhere.

Anti-discriminatory work: challenges facing leaving care work

According to Whyte (1994) anti-discriminatory practice in leaving care work could be taken forward by restructuring the anti-discriminatory debate to one about differences, and not pathologising it so that it becomes one about 'problems'. Furthermore, she argues that 'real consultation', not tokenism, with black young people is the best way to inform practice, and that action must be taken now by a 'fast track' approach. She concludes by saying that 'managers and planners need to acknowledge the reality, that indicators of need will discriminate if "difference" is not included' (Whyte, 1994:19). According to Biehal et al.'s research (1995:129) 'the majority of the black, Asian and mixed heritage young people [leaving care] had experienced racist harassment and abuse.' As Garnett has observed:

> ... in addition to the many difficulties experienced by young people leaving care, young people from Black and minority ethnic groups may be further dis-advantaged as a result of being cared for within a predominantly White, ethno-centric care system. They may often have been cared for in a way which, at best, ignores their racial, religious and cultural heritage, or at worst, is overtly racist. (Garnett, 1992:34)

It was argued earlier that anti-discriminatory work is vital and needs to go on constantly to act as a check against racist practices, or, more obviously, as a check against assumptions that everyone's needs are similar. It has also been shown earlier that at a national level, where information about ethnic origin is available concerning children in care, it is not drawn from a consistent definition about ethnic origins. Based on the difficulties experienced here in obtaining data about the ethnic origin of young people leaving care (although this had improved compared with 1993), and the research of others, it appears that there is considerable room for improvement and greater consistency in recording this information. Another area of concern has been that relating to services for black homeless young people, and the inadequacy of existing services in this area (CHAR, 1995).

Building on the findings here from this 1996 survey about work with black young people, in addition to Biehal et al.'s 1995 findings, what follows is a summary of the key challenges facing local authorities and leaving care projects working with black and other minority ethnic young people.

Key Challenges Concerning Leaving Care Work with Black Young People

- to collect accurate and consistent information about the ethnic composition of children in/leaving care. Without this information it is impossible to gauge who is receiving what services and why, and record appropriate services, care patterns and support systems. It is also the case that this absence of information prevents a coherent national view being produced, which is both baffling and inexcusable, and an excuse for inaction

- the very low numbers of black and Asian young people leaving care attending voluntary organisations may lead to the erroneous view by voluntary organisations that anti-racism is not an issue for them, compared with local authority project types. At these voluntary organisation projects the low number of black young people requiring services demands an even higher level of awareness by informed staff to ensure that anti-discriminatory practice takes place.

- at the national and local policy level it is necessary to seek explanations for what appear to be slightly different patterns for black and white children entering and leaving care

- to understand the explanations for and practical consequences of black and white young people leaving care having different educational experiences and the implications for leaving care projects

- to explore whether there are perceived differences about patterns of family contact and therefore different practices that have been put into place
- to acknowledge the experiences by black young people of racism and further operationalise anti-discriminatory work at practice and policy levels by projects
- for institutions to counter the view held, rightly or wrongly by black young people, that institutions are racist, when the leaving care projects' staff and other agencies consists of all white personnel with no anti-discriminatory action plans
- to establish closer links between local authorities and leaving care projects with black and other minority ethnic groups.

None of these challenges are beyond the scope of social services departments and voluntary organisations, given the numerous examples of good practice and policies demonstrated here, providing they develop the will and commitment, not evident from the research findings to date, to a systematic anti-discriminatory policy, planning, action, review cycle.

It is especially important that anti-discriminatory social work practices and policies are accessed and recorded through anti-discriminatory research. Anti-discriminatory research is research which, like anti-discriminatory practice, is actively working for change against all forms of discrimination and oppression. Like anti-discriminatory practice it should permeate all social research and is component, not a separate model, of social research. It is described at greater length in 'Anti-discriminatory practitioner social work research' by this author (1994b). At the very least anti-discriminatory research requires different ethnic groups to be identified (preferably self-identified) and knowledge on the researcher's part, if not already present, about anti-discriminatory issues, especially experiences of racism and sexism, but also other forms of oppression. If the researcher does not already have such knowledge it is essential that such information is accessed, and the involvement of an informed research steering group, also acting as a gatekeeping group, is essential for that purpose.

CHAPTER TEN

Financial Support for Young People Leaving Care

Introduction

This chapter will examine the position regarding financial supports for young people leaving care. It will do this by reference to this survey and the 1993 survey's findings, and by examining other research and relevant social legislation. The Children Act 1989 empowers local authorities to provide 'financial assistance in kind or in exceptional circumstances, in cash' (Children Act 1989, S24:6, 7). There is evidence presented here that in the light of continuing changes to the social security system, the financial burdens are increasingly falling on, but not being taken up by, social services departments. Indeed, Biehal *et al.*'s study concluded that '...local authorities are increasingly having to take some responsibility for ensuring that young people leaving their care have a basic minimum income to enable them to manage independently' (1992:29). The social policies which have been introduced since the mid 1980s are increasingly based on the assumption that young people remain their parents' responsibility until they leave home and receive an independent income, and that non-householders have dependent status. According to Jones, these various policies have effectively extended dependency to the age of 18 and semi-dependency to the age of 25 (Jones, 1995:12). If this is the case, then the situation of young people leaving care is an especially bleak one. What immediately follows is a summary of the main changes concerning financial support for young people living away from their parental home. These are summarised here and presented as contextual material, having been discussed in detail both within specific subject chapters, for example housing, or in the earlier general social context chapter.

Key changes concerning financial support to young people living away from home 1988–1997

- 1988: the withdrawal of Income Support for under 18s (with the replacement of the 'training guarantee').

- 1988: the introduction of lower than adult rate of Income Support for 18–24 year olds.

- 1988: the withdrawal of Unemployment Benefits for under 18s.

- 1988: the abolition of the distinction between householders and non-householders in social security payments.

- 1989: the abolition of Exceptional Needs payments which met minimal furniture and equipment needs of those setting up home on social security.

- 1989: the introduction of Severe Hardship payments for under 18s proving an exceptional case.

- 1989: the introduction of the Social Fund loans for exceptional needs.

- 1990–1: removal of full time students' entitlement to Income Support and Housing Benefit.

- 1996: Job Seekers Allowance replaced Income Support and Unemployment Benefit.

- 1996–7: Housing Benefit and housing changes.

The Job Seekers Allowance (JSA) was not in place at the time the survey was conducted. It replaced Income Support and Unemployment Benefit from October 1996 and places obligations on the unemployed to satisfy more rigorous 'availability for work' criteria, and produce detailed 'seeking work' plans. Under the Jobseekers Direction employment staff issue a direction to improve employability. Claimants refusing to complete a Jobseekers Agreement or to act on a Jobseekers Direction are disqualified from benefits until they do so. Under the JSA, entitlement to contributory benefit is cut from one year to six months, after which Income Support is payable.

This change is likely to impact most significantly on 18–24-year-olds, who already receive a lower rate than those over 24, as a result of social security changes introduced in 1988. These changes to the way contributory benefits are calculated meant that the entitlement of 18–24-year-olds after six months of contributory JSA is reduced by 20 per cent from £46.50 to £36.80 a week (according to 1996 benefit rates). Further changes about education, namely reducing the amount of time for claimants to study, from 21 to 16 'guided learning hours', and being eligible for benefit entitlements, were also introduced in 1996. Automatic hardship payments for those eligible for Income Support were also stopped under the JSA.

Again, all these policies are informed by the assumption that after a child is born it is the sole responsibility of the parent or parents, and not the state, to support them. This involves paying for their accommodation, meeting their day to day expenditure, and further and higher education expenses – unless there are extraordinary and exceptional circumstances. The position of young people leaving care receiving parental support is especially galling because they have been placed in the care of the local authority to be, quite literally, *looked after*. As such, there are certain moral and legal responsibilities for the local authority towards young people leaving care. The issue of financial support for the 88 per cent of young people in the survey leaving care who are not financially self sufficient is critical to their making the transition from care to more independent living.

Potential financial support comes from local authority and central government sources including:

- funding for accommodation in the form of help with deposits (social services)
- leaving care grant for setting up home (social services)
- Housing Benefit for rent (department of social security)
- top up financial support for various things including housing (social services)
- Income Support, if entitled, for under 18s (local benefit office)
- Income Support for over 18s (local benefit office)
- social fund in the form of loans (local benefit office)
- Community Care Grants (local benefit office).

Having established the general position regarding young people and financial supports, the sources for the same, and outlined the nature and direction of the changes being introduced, it is to the particular findings of the research concerning finances that attention is now turned.

The occupational situation of young people leaving care

As was revealed earlier, the occupational breakdown of the young people leaving care in the sample revealed that, of the young people whose occupation was recorded (n=2905), 88 per cent were not financially self supporting but required other state funding sources to live on. The group of young people leaving care being discussed fall within the broad 15 to 21 age range with the majority attending leaving care projects in the 16 to 19 age group, with the average age estimated as 18. The fact that this group is young, vulnerable and over-represented in the unemployment and poverty figures is not new. Also, it is young people generally who are over-represented in the unemployment figures. For example, the employment rate amongst all 16–24 year olds in 1995 was 15.4 per cent, nearly double that of the 8.5 per cent national average of whom, of those under 20, 19.5 per cent are unemployed. The difference between youth unemployment and the national average has risen from 67 per cent higher in 1992 to 81 per cent higher in 1995. Under 25s account for more than 1 in 4 of all those unemployed and claiming benefit and 1 in 6 of all long term unemployed claimants (Trades Union Congress, 1996; Central Statistical Office, 1995/6).

What this research reveals is the harrowing extent of the poverty faced by this group, as well as the disturbing finding that the situation is further worsening. This means that the young people's situation is descending to depths of financial desperation hitherto unknown. Having identified through the survey the inadequate financial support position of young people leaving care, particularly the under 18s, the projects' perceptions of financial support will now be examined, in order to establish whether the position is changing. This information was obtained by asking questionnaire respondents to record their views on a five point scale, ranging from 'improved significantly' to 'worsened significantly', across 10 social policy areas. The responses of the leaving care projects in the survey are contained in Table 10.1.

Key Findings

Across all 10 main areas of potential financial support for young people leaving care, *88 per cent of the responses indicated that the position had either remained the same or worsened.* If one also takes into account the earlier key finding that 88 per cent of the sample (n=2905) were not working in full time jobs, the situation looks especially bleak. It will be recalled that 10 per cent of the young people in the housing sample (n=2096) were living in supported lodging accommodation. As Table 10.1 shows, the projects' perceptions about supported lodgings affordability were that only 10 per cent considered the position had improved whereas 17 per cent considered that the position had worsened. A majority of 54 per cent of respondents believed that the affordability position, an already precarious one, had remained the same.

By far the worst of these areas was the position concerning Housing Benefit, which 67 per cent of respondents considered had worsened 'a little' or 'significantly' between 1994–96. The situation regarding Income Support for the over and under 18s, recorded as having worsened significantly or a little, by 17 or 37 per cent, and 29 or 62 per cent of respondents respectively, also points to a grim and deteriorating situation regarding that benefit.

By combining the 'improved significantly' responses with the 'improved a little' ones, we get 12 per cent of the total (n=427), but by combining the 'worsened a little/significantly' we get 42 per cent of the total responses. Thus, overall there was exactly three and a half times the percentage of responses indicating a worsening of, rather than improvement to, the situation concerning financial supports. In addition to these findings, there are three critical changes to

Table 10.1 Financial supports for young people leaving care: perceptions by leaving care projects (n=44) for the period 1994–6

Topic	Significantly improved	Improved a little	Remained the same	Worsened a little	Significantly worsened	Total[1] %
Housing Benefit	2 (4%)	2 (4%)	10 (22%)	17 (37%)	14 (30%)	97%
Income Support for 18+ yrs	1(2%)	2 (4%)	25 (54%)	9 (20%)	8 (17%)	97%
Income Support under 18s	1 (2%)	5 (11%)	9 (20%)	15 (32%)	14 (30%)	96%
Community Care Grants	1 (2%)	6 (13%)	13 (28%)	16 (35%)	7 (15%)	94%
Social Fund (loans)	0 (0%)	3 (6%)	26 (56%)	8 (17%)	6 (13%)	94%
Leaving Care Grant	2 (4%)	7 (15%)	24 (52%)	8 (17%)	3 (6%)	91%
Funding for accommodation (e.g. deposits)	4 (9%)	4 (9%)	22 (48%)	11 (24%)	2 (4%)	94%
bed and breakfast affordability	0 (0%)	1 (2%)	21 (46%)	10 (22%)	3 (6%)	76%
Supported lodgings affordability	3 (6%)	2 (4%)	25 (54%)	5 (11%)	8 (6%)	81%
Top up financial support	4 (9%)	1(2%)	21(46%)	14 (30%)	2 (4%)	91%
TOTALS	18 or 4% of total	33 or 8% of total	196 or 46% of total	113or 26% of total	67 or 16% of total	427 (100%) answers

[1] The percentages in the last column do not add up to 100 per cent because the missing responses are excluded from the calculations across the preceding rows. Nevertheless, the high percentages in the last column illustrate the high overall level of response.

housing finances that warrant recording. They are primarily in relation to homeless young people but will also include some young people leaving care not receiving accommodation, or returning to local authorities for help.

Three Further Critical Changes to Finances (Housing)
1. INTRODUCTION OF TEMPORARY HOUSING STATUS FOR THE HOMELESS

Amongst other changes the Housing Act 1996 removed the previous duty on local authorities to provide permanent housing that was affordable to those people deemed homeless under the 1985 housing legislation. Instead, homeless people are offered temporary accommodation of up to two years maximum. Suffice it here to state that there is no specific reference in the legislation to young people leaving care (for example as an exception group), although the guidance makes references to the needs of young people leaving care. According to Community Care (1996:19), 'without a legal requirement, housing departments are unlikely to nominate voluntarily the tenancies needs for care leavers'. The point being made is that a tougher, not softer, legal responsibility needs to be placed on housing authorities than exists in the Children Act 1989 (S27:1, 2), for young people leaving care to receive a good chance of obtaining appropriate housing. Shelter, the national housing charity, noting the increased role for the private sector, comments, 'the private rented sector tends to have the most expensive housing, in the worst condition, and with the least security' (*Education Guardian*, 1996a).

2. REDUCTION IN HOUSING BENEFIT

In January 1996 the government changed Housing Benefit payments throughout the United Kingdom. This was as a result of the rising Housing Benefit bill, which has been estimated as doubling in real terms since 1998 to over £10 billion in 1996 (Kirk, 1996:11). Benefit is now paid according to a 'local reference rent' based on the site and location of a property, and if the rent is higher, housing benefit will only cover half the difference. This measure further removes basic protections for the vulnerable homeless. Also as a result of these changes, with Housing Benefit being paid in arrears, this will have a negative impact on landlady/lord schemes, with the net effect on young people being to put them in arrears from the start.

The 1996 Housing Benefit regulations allow payments in excess of eligible Housing Benefit to be made to prevent exceptional hardship, yet it is also unlawful for local authorities to exceed the set amount, even if a person is in exceptional hardship. These changes have introduced an incentive *not* to make discretionary payments because local authorities are under no duty to spend the whole amount permitted, and are entitled to put any surplus towards other Housing Benefit expenditure (Kirk,1996).

3. 1996 REDUCED HOUSING BENEFIT ENTITLEMENT

An important housing circular effecting this group (DoE, 1996) states that young people under a care order or where a social services department is providing accommodation under Section 20 (Children Act 1989) are not normally entitled to Housing Benefit as the legal responsibility for accommodation costs lies with the social services department. The legal position is that young people entitled to Section 24 services are entitled to Housing Benefit provided they are not subject to any other order under the Children Act 1989 which places liability back on the social services department. First Key's response (First Key,1996b:9) to this circular was as follows:

- ° young people may experience early discharge of care orders or accommodation under Section 20, regardless of need, due to resource implications

- ° partnership schemes (between social services and voluntary organisations) financed by a combination of housing benefit and social services funding will be under threat

- ° there will be a disincentive to accommodate 16/17-year-olds in need if financial responsibility lies totally with social services departments

As was noted earlier, this increased pressure on social services departments, not social security, to pay support costs is part of an overall trend, and is one taking place at a time of severe reductions to local authority budgets. This will likely mean that these support costs to young people living in hostels and lodgings especially will simply not be met by local authorities. The other emerging issue is that with the increased withdrawal of support funding for self-contained accommodation for young people there are increased dangers of exploitation of young people living in cheap and unsuitable shared accommodation.

As well as housing, another key area of financial support concerns the provision of leaving care grants, and the first findings presented here concern the proportion of local authorities in which young people were entitled to receive a leaving care grant.

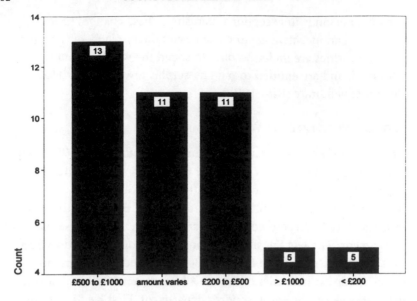

Figure 10.1 Average sizes of leaving care grants from local authorities (n=45) for 1995–96

Leaving care grants

The question of financial support to young people leaving care is at the heart of any move away from public care, as is ongoing personal support. The financial demands on a young person leaving care, as with any young person leaving home, can be predicted as likely to be considerable and ongoing. Assuming that the young person moves to unfurnished rented accommodation, s/he would need money for a wide range of things, including a deposit, ongoing rental payments, plus heating and lighting expenses, plus finances for furniture and other basic goods including food. As was revealed through the survey, at the point of leaving care the young person is most likely to be either attending further education, a Youth Training Scheme, or unoccupied and not receiving any state financial support. A good parent is required to help support the young person during what will likely be a long transitional stage to full financial independence. Let us now examine what young people leaving care actually receive from the local authority, as they make this major transition.

Entitlement and Amount

Thirty-four respondents, or 75 per cent of those answering the question (n = 45) stated that young people in their area received a leaving care grant as of right. In the 1992 study the same question produced a 83 per cent 'yes' response. Ten respondents (or 22% of the sample) stated that young people did not receive a leaving care grant as of right. In respect of the size of leaving care grant the research found that this varies from less than £200 (in three instances) to 13 respondents indicating that their local authority's leaving care grant was normally in the £500 to £1000 range, as Table 10.2 shows in more detail.

A situation whereby young people may or may not receive a leaving care grant at all, and where the amount varies from less than £200 to £1000 or more, is not acceptable seen from the perspective of young people's needs and service users' rights. Yet viewed from the twin pinnacles of budgetary constraints and inadequate discretionary legislative powers, it is difficult to see the attraction to local authorities of paying any more than they have to! Yet it is especially critical for young people leaving care to have proper support, including financial support, to meet their planned needs. The leaving care grant has traditionally been used for help with the first transition from care to more independent living. Garnett's study recorded that none of the three authorities in her study paid a leaving care grant as such, and although financial assistance could be made available to young people moving into their own accommodation 'the administration of these monies, and the sums involved, varies considerably' (1992:91). She also found that the decision as to whether there was any entitlement was discretionary, and authorised at a high level, and that young people placed at home or in foster families were least likely to get any financial support. This was a practice which she questioned. The more generous of the three authorities she researched paid a maximum allowance, in 1992, of £590. The study concluded that this discretionary, 'almost secret' system was inadequate and unfair. Biehal et al. (1992) found that some 78 young people, or 42.5 per cent of the sample from that study, received a leaving care grant, the amount varying enormously between £50 and £1000. Slightly less than half received more than £500 and further help in the form of weekly top up monies was also provided in a number of cases. The 1992 First Key survey revealed that all but one of the 88 local authorities responding stated that they make leaving care grants available to young people with, again, the amount varying considerably, between £62 and £2000. That survey did not ask the question, raised here, about whether these grants were made available as of right.

Perhaps the point has now been reached when it should be more openly acknowledged that it is simply unrealistic to think that young people's multiple financial needs upon leaving care can or should be met simply by the mechanism of a widely variable leaving care grant provided by social services.

Financial policies and national finance standards concerning leaving care

All of these findings beg the question that for the majority, 88 per cent, of all young people leaving care in this survey who are not in full time employment, where do they receive financial support from for their supported accommodation or other needs? Leaving care projects are in a very difficult position because they are the mediators between the resource holders and the young people. In addition to their role the projects and the local authorities in which they are based are usually facing such a level of internal financial constraints that they are not in a position to provide financial support themselves, as a general right, but rather to individuals in particular need, as a limited one off payment. It seems to be the case that local authorities are continually tightening and not widening their guidelines concerning financial payments to young people leaving care, whether single payments or ongoing support. The leaving care service agency agreements usually include financial support issues about young people leaving care in somewhat cautious terms. The following is an excerpt concerning finances from one service agency agreement in use in 1996:

> The leaving care team will provide advice and guidance to young people ena-bling them to claim all appropriate benefits and grants to which they are enti-tled. Funds are available within the purchasing of the scheme to cover a range of costs. The following payments may be administered where appropriate:
>
> ° departmental leaving care grants
>
> ° assistance with payment of rent
>
> ° assistance with surety of rent
>
> ° subsidising of rents
>
> ° assistance with travel and subsistence
>
> ° emergency cash aid for food and essential clothing
>
> ° assistance in purchasing equipment to assist young people taking up employment
>
> ° financial support to young people to pursue activities as part of their individual agreement. (Dudley Metropolitan Borough, 1994)

Another leaving care team's service agency agreement referred back to the local authority policy regarding financial assistance, and stated that as a minimum it shall include:

> assistance connected with the customer's expenses on their education, employ-ment or training, e.g. purchase of travel cards, text books, materials, college fees etc.

Charitable assistance

> The service provided shall also link the customer with a variety of charitable and benevolent organisations that may be able to offer financial assistance to needy customers including projects that can assist customers to furnish their ac-commodation at a reasonable price. (London Borough of Brent, 1996)

In Leicester, generally regarded as 'a good provider' of leaving care services, further guidelines were introduced some years ago, as elsewhere, to remove internal discretionary arrangements. Thus in 1993 financial guidelines were issued for all young people for whom the department had responsibility by virtue of Sections 17, 20, 24 and 31 of the Children Act 1989, to be treated similarly, namely in this authority to receive an income equivalent to the age appropriate Income Support level (this was £34.80 per week in 1992). It was recognised that 'the income maintenance figures are significantly lower in comparison with those paid in the past which puts more emphasis on the preparation and work that is carried out prior to the young person leaving a care placement' (Leicester County Council, 1992). It was also stated that support from that local authority social services department should only be used to *top up income* from other sources. One of the main implications of these consistent practice guidelines towards young people looked after, especially concerning single payments, is that the local authority needs to consider the financial implications of early revocation of care orders or ending of arrangements for accommodation.

The Social Services Inspectorate's draft leaving care standards concerning finance (Social Services Inspectorate, 1996: Standard 7) take this crucial matter of financial support no further. They simply confirm the existing, unsatisfactory, and sub-standard minimum, stating that the department's policy on financial support to address:

1. eligibility and entitlement to financial assistance for care leavers up to the age of 21

2. eligibility and entitlement to support for care leavers with employment, education and training programmes up to the age of 21 and the circumstances in which it may be extended beyond the age of 21

3. the amount of the leaving care grant or the criteria to determine payment for furnishing and equipment for a care leaver to establish an independent home to an agreed minimum standard

4. confirmation of the local agreement between the Housing Benefits Agency and social services regarding liability for rent/eligibility for housing benefit

5. ensuring that the amount of financial support to a young person, taking account of all sources of income from employment, training or benefits agencies does not fall below a stated minimum level

6. local agreements between the social services department and the benefits agency are in place which recognise that local authority financial assistance to young people is designed to supplement their needs, not to duplicate or replace social security payments

7. the agreements emphasise that financial assistance provided under Section 24 of the Children Act 1989 is disregarded for the purpose of

    calculating entitlement to Income Support, Housing Benefit, council tax
    benefit and student maintenance grants

8. the agreements encompass entitlements to benefits for young people
     with disabilities

9. a named 'liaison' officer is identified within the benefits agency who is
     available to discuss problems should they arise and who participates in
     the formal agency/inter-departmental planning structures

10. an element of this financial support is provided at the point where the
     young person moves to independent accommodation for the purpose of
     establishing themselves in such accommodation. (Social Services
     Inspectorate, 1995)

With regard to point 5 it is unclear what is meant by 'a stated minimum level' and, even if such a figure is published somewhere, a national standard, however desirable, must be undeliverable because of the wide and local variations, and delivery systems, concerning payments. Points 6 and 7 are extremely important and have major repercussions for young people because some local authorities may be tempted not to make any monies payable to young people leaving care via Section 24 Children Act 1989 because, they say, their financial obligations are being met through social security payments. Not only are the levels of financial supports from local authorities insufficient – they are often not even universally publicised or forthcoming.

By contrast, the draft national standards about finances produced by the First Key group (1995:11) called for publicised entitlements which address:

- eligibility and entitlement to financial assistance for care leavers with
  employment, education and training up to the age of 21

- eligibility and entitlement to support care leavers with employment,
  education and training up to the age of 21 and the circumstances in
  which it may be extended beyond the age of 21

- the amount of the leaving care grant or the criteria to determine
  payment for furnishing and equipment for a care leaver to establish an
  independent home

- confirmation of the local arrangements between the housing benefits
  agency and social services regarding liability for rent/eligibility for
  housing benefit/supplement action.

Yet even here the difficulty of specifying legally binding entitlements is apparent, both in terms of legally binding criteria for single agencies, and criteria which are binding on other agencies, especially the housing and benefits agencies.

What seems to be happening is that individuals negotiate what are, in effect, local rates or grants or support for their individual situation. For the next person this may be different. Yet is this discretionary approach so bad? The answer is 'it depends'. If what is offered is next to nothing and more of the same (and no complaints either), then the answer must be 'no'. If, on the other hand, discretionary funds and powers are creatively and generously interpreted, for example to help a young person who is disabled and has considerable needs which are as fully met as any agencies can, then of course the answer could be 'yes'. However, what far too many young people leaving care receive is something akin to the 'the parent in crisis' scenario described at the end of this chapter. Having examined financial supports for young people leaving care in some detail, it is time to examine the financial situation outside social services departments as it relates to youth training for young people leaving care.

Youth training finances

It will be recalled that 289 or 10 per cent of the young people whose occupation was recorded (n=2095) were attending youth training courses. When projects were further questioned about both the availability and appropriateness of this youth training for the young people with whom they work these were rated the worst, namely as *additional areas of significant deterioration* on the five point scale provided. Given the similar findings from the 1993 survey, the conclusion can be reached that from 1992 up to 1996 there was a consistent and marked deterioration in the level of financial supports available to young people attending youth training. A proportion, probably a majority, of young people leaving care attending youth training need skilled, intensive and individual input because of their lack of self-esteem, as well as the lack of financial incentives to attend. At the time of writing (1997), allowances paid to Youth Training trainees had remained frozen, at £29. 50 per week since 1988 for 16-year-olds, and at £35.00 per week since 1986 for 17-year-olds. These allowances are lower than the Income Support payment of £36.15 for 16- and 17-year-olds living independently from their family. Although this Youth Training allowance once meant that trainees could also access 'top up' payments, this disappeared with the introduction of the Job Seekers Allowance in 1996 for training allowances above Income Support/Job Seekers Allowance level.

Training is not just youth training, and without solely focusing on youth training the following case study illustrates the holistic nature of the 'training solution' for young people, and the need for agencies to work closely together, since one agency alone cannot normally provide all the elements of a holistic solution.

Training Case Study:
'Pete' aged 20

Pete and his sister came into care aged three and four respectively when their mother died and their father was unable to cope. He subsequently experienced a number of placement breakdowns, emotional rejection and neglect. At 16 he returned to his home town as a foster child and took up a Youth Traineeship at a local garage for two years. At 18 his foster placement ended and through a voluntary organisation working with young people leaving care he was found shared accommodation elsewhere, supported by a resident volunteer. He found the move very difficult and needed a considerable amount of support. Above all he needed something to occupy himself with during the daytime, preferably work. He spent the next five months drawing up a CV, attending interviews and writing to potential employers, all with no success. He then found himself voluntary work at a local stables, and this was converted into an Employment Traineeship (ET) with another employer undertaking farm work, for £30 per week for a five days a week 10 hours a day job. After some time Pete wanted to gain a qualification and he obtained a place at a college of agriculture for a BTEC First Diploma in Agriculture. Eight weeks before he took up his place he was informed that his maintenance grant of £1500 would be cut to £850. With four weeks to go, the local education authority reinstated the grant and Pete took up his place on the course.

In addition to his own considerable efforts there were many people who supported him in his endeavours including the college, voluntary organisation, social services and education.

Youth training was not the answer for this young person. Research elsewhere confirms that youth training is not necessarily seen as worthwhile and desirable (Payne,1995) and that it is regarded as the least favourable option for 24-year-olds, and that it leads to lower qualifications, worse pay, and increased risk of unemployment. Also, as the Coalition on Young People and Social Security (COYPS, 1995:5) report about the transition to adulthood revealed:

> ...a continuing picture of lack of choice, a lack of opportunity and financial poverty for young people attempting to enter the labour market. The transition from school remains difficult, obstacle ridden, uncoordinated and inadequately funded. Support and help for young people through the period of transition are lacking. In addition to these general difficulties, some young people face further obstacles because of their ethnic origin, class, economic disadvantage or disability... Motivation and commitment to achieving skills and employment is

repeatedly blocked and discouraged by an unnecessarily difficult, complicated and uncoordinated obstacle course.

The report recommended that a coherent policy be developed for young people post school leaving age, that young people attending further education automatically be entitled to a subsistence allowance, that benefits should be reinstated for 16- and 17-year-olds, and that the Youth Training Allowance be increased to £50 per week (COYPS, 1995:52–3). All of this begs the question what else can be done to improve the situation concerning training? What follows are suggestions, based on discussions with practitioners and projects, for making the existing training systems, including youth training, work much better.

Improving Training for Young People – Practical Suggestions

- youth training and preparation for employment programmes for seriously disadvantaged young people need to employ sufficient skilled staff and be flexible enough to access and sustain young people
- youth training should be focused, for seriously disadvantaged young people, on meeting their holistic needs, including care and support and confidence building, as well as skill training
- young people need to be helped and advised to sustain training and employment
- more clarity about what is available from the Training and Enterprise Councils (TEC) is required, especially about the degree of funding flexibility
- more flexible funding for training courses for seriously disadvantaged young people are required
- special needs funds allocated to TECs should be ring fenced
- tax benefits for potential and/or actual employers to train/employ a young person
- creativity in the funding regimes needed to support training and employment initiatives
- more training providers needed or an agreement that a wider range of people can be regarded as training providers
- young people leaving care often have a wide range of emotional, financial and skill needs which require considerable understanding, and support, to sustain a place on a training scheme.

Underpinning these suggestions are sets of values about the desirability to expand and improve existing training for vulnerable young people. This requires either additional funding, a re-appraisal of how existing funds are allocated, a restructuring of existing services or a combination of all three. Yet these suggestions are underpinned by a set of values and expectations about the role of the state which are mostly at odds with those promoted since the Children Act 1989. To end this chapter the following two financial scenarios represent contrasting ways of interpreting the issues, problems, and recommendations about financial supports for young people leaving care.

Contrasting financial scenarios and solutions for young people leaving care

Scenario 1: Crisis and Cost Driven Services – The Motto of this Parent in Crisis is 'You Get What You Get'

Here the state and local authorities are acting as the struggling parents under emotional and financial pressures from other family members, and sometimes presenting as bullying and not caring by their attitudes and actions. In this scenario young people leaving home, including those leaving care because the state acts as the parent, are regarded as a financial liability with their parents being responsible for their situation and liable for their financial support. Having framed the problem in such terms the solutions become:

- try to prevent the 'problem' in the first place by placing less children into care

- try to identify such parents and deter them from having 'too many' children in the first place

- provide less children's homes and foster placements, and no family support services

- ignore the situation until it reaches crisis point, and then refer them to special crisis teams, in criminal justice, homeless families or mental health fields, invoking short term institutional solutions (i.e. bed and breakfast, or child protection procedures)

- emphasise parental responsibility to the exclusion of all other people/state agencies

- introduce tough deterrent social policies for all young people leaving home

- all polices to be cost driven

- the state acts as a broker for less, and not a provider for all – this means it does not provide or fund other than minimum services required by law

- use all resources including family members, especially older siblings (especially if female, reinforcing stereotypes), to help out, and make do, and put off

- there may be an interest in caring and an agreement that there are minimum legal levels of support

- all the key institutions of the state become smaller self-managing agencies with reduced budgets and downsizing as the key quality indicators

- financial decisions are presented as professional decisions rationally accounted for.

In this scenario levels of support that are presented are presented within the context of having other mouths to feed, simultaneously, and in the full knowledge that 'make do parenting' may have occasional tragic consequences including neglect, abuse or death.

Scenario 2: Preventive Needs Led Services – the Motto of this Good Parent is 'We Are Here to Help All'

This scenario assumes that the state is interested in young people and the problems they face and present, and wish to help to resolve them. In this scenario it is assumed that partnerships between the state, children, young people and parents require nurturing, otherwise they will break down if they have not already done so. Sustained nurturing requires professional and fully funded partnerships to be established. The solutions to the problems then become:

- an emphasis on preventive child care

- provision of fully funded nursery places

- provision of parental and family support services

- provision of a properly funded benefit system for those families without employment

- provision of guaranteed funding for all children in need

- provide professional services to explore/encourage partnerships between young people, their parents and families

- provision of properly funded and supported foster care

- provision of a range of skilled family support services

- provision of employment.

In this scenario services are provided according to a set of moral and pragmatic principles that children and families should be supported through a partnership involving the state, parents, family, professionals, and children and young people. It seems as if a slightly watered down version of the first scenario is the one that has applied to children and families since the Children Act 1989 and during the research period.

Whichever of the scenarios applies, the overriding conclusion that can be drawn from the findings in this chapter is that it is impossible for local agencies to deliver on national financial standards in leaving care work, however desirable this may be, because there is no single state agency which plans, funds, co-ordinates and delivers financial benefits or grants for young people, and because budgets are locally decided in an *ad hoc* way. The implication arising from this finding is that the delivery of financial supports is yet another discretionary area with the opportunities for providers being creative, and on occasions possibly 'generous' for the few, being outweighed by the detrimental effect this approach has on the majority. Given that implication, local authority leaving care projects and local authorities probably have little choice than to examine their budgets and produce financial support policies for young people leaving care very carefully, as was evident from those policies described above, and then prioritise accordingly, in consultation with those affected.

CHAPTER ELEVEN

Monitoring and Evaluation Issues

Introduction

The purpose of this chapter is to examine what is meant by the monitoring and evaluation of leaving care work, and what progress has been made in the field, according to the 1996 survey. The chapter provides an analysis of different types of research and evaluation drawing on examples from the field. The chapter begins by examining the context within which such work takes place, before moving on to describe the different types of monitoring and evaluation, and, finally, the survey's limited findings and examples from the field.

Context

The guidance to the Children Act 1989 states that 'it is desirable to *monitor* aftercare schemes and to *evaluate* them, *to establish how effective they are*' (*DoH, 1991c:107; my emphasis*). *Like so many aspects of the Children Act 1989 concerning leaving care work, the wording is advisory, making the tasks discretionary. The guidance also states that a leaving care co-ordinator is necessary to undertake key monitoring responsibility for young people leaving care to inform service planning, the most relevant areas of responsibility concerning:*

- the monitoring of all those aged 15+ being looked after by the local authority, including all those who became looked after aged 16 and 17 and who qualify for aftercare services

- the monitoring of service provision to all young people to ensure proper planning and co-ordination, within the framework of identified needs.

It is also significant to note that 'leaving care monitoring' is something not only the Community Care publication's 1994 campaign was centred around, but also something which the late Baroness Faithful (the government's health spokesperson in the House of Lords, as of 1994) publicly commented on during a 1995 Community Care/First Key parliamentary lobbying event held at the House of Commons. In particular she recalled how during the passage of the then Children's Bill 1989 through parliament she and others lobbied unsuccessfully to try to make leaving care monitoring a *duty* to be placed on local authorities in what was to become the Children Act 1989. Once again it can be seen, as has already been demonstrated in respect of other dimensions of leaving care work, that legislation and guidance is lacking regarding monitoring. There remains lack of clarity about what is or should be monitored, by whom, and for what purpose. This uncertainty makes a national description of leaving care work rest on individual studies like this one, and not on agreed and nationally collected information.

The other critical monitoring dimension, the one called for above by Baroness Faithful and others, concerns the monitoring of the whereabouts and circumstances of young people leaving care moving on, as well as after they have moved away from one social services area to another. Yet the absence of a national duty and a working guide to monitoring has not prevented leaving care projects developing a range of research and evaluation approaches, some of which are included here, in the form of summary examples. The different types of research monitoring and evaluation are also described here in order to more fully understand their direct application to leaving care work.[1]

The first task is to summarise what leaving care research has reported about leaving care monitoring. There have only been two substantial references to leaving care monitoring in research writings, and the second source suggests that it is the contract culture which has made monitoring a more pressing matter. Bonnerjea commented in her extensive London survey:

> There is as yet no department which has effective systems for planning for the young people in advance, and for monitoring their progress after leaving care. And perhaps most importantly there is no local authority that rigorously evaluates what it provides, to ensure that it is effective as well as value for money. It is hoped that this report will enable all authorities to move towards these aims. (1990: 44)

1   It is especially important that anti-discriminatory social work practices and policies are accessed and recorded through anti-discriminatory research. Anti-discriminatory research is research which, like anti-discriminatory practice, is actively working for change against all forms of discrimination and oppression. Like anti-discriminatory practice it should permeate all social research, and is a component, not a separate model of social research. It is described at greater length than is appropriate here by this author as 'Anti-discriminatory practitioner social work research' in Humphries and Truman (1994). At the very least anti-discriminatory research requires different ethnic groups to be identified (preferably self-identified), knowledge on the researcher's part, if not already present, about anti-discriminatory issues, especially experiences of racism and sexism, but also other forms of oppression. If the researcher does not already have such knowledge it is essential that such information is accessed, and the involvement of an informed research steering group, also acting as a gatekeeping group, is essential for that purpose.

Biehal *et al.* (1995) spent the last page of their large leaving care study on monitoring. They identified the monitoring of outcomes in leaving care work as needing to take place at two levels: local authority level to develop procedures to monitor the progress of all care leavers, and monitoring as the evaluation of outcomes of young people attending leaving care projects. Whilst stressing its importance the researchers make no references to any monitoring systems identified at the four leaving care projects they researched. They emphasised the importance of involving young people in the setting, meeting and monitoring of leaving care services. Indeed according to Ward (1996:242) it is often the researchers, and not the agencies, which systematically collect information and undertake monitoring activities, and she cites leaving care as one such example where this is the case. The Audit Commission's report *Seen but Not Heard* (Audit Commission, 1994) was based on evidence concerned with co-ordinating social services and community child health work with children in need, rather than young people leaving care as such. Nevertheless its comments, especially regarding monitoring in the emergent purchaser/provider world, are relevant to leaving care work. It reported that information, both to evaluate effectiveness of activities purchased and to monitor progress of the contract, is lacking at present, and that providers, although without much information themselves, are still in control and setting the agenda for contracts (Audit Commission, 1994:51). It could be assumed that the findings from this research's 1996 survey might confirm this unsatisfactory picture. Yet the findings suggest the situation is not that clear. First let us turn to general definitions and issues concerned with monitoring and evaluation, before examining the case of leaving care in particular. These are presented in Table 11.1.

Monitoring: purpose and examples

In leaving care work monitoring is important in order:

- to inform and influence policy
- to monitor policies in action (i.e. implementation)
- to provide basic information so that service needs can be identified
- to record whether service needs are being met or whether service gaps remain
- for young people's benefit at practice and policy levels
- to evaluate service and delivery (i.e. effectiveness and efficiency)
- to ensure that local authorities know the whereabouts of young people leaving care when they move

Table 11.1 Leaving care project monitoring and evaluation types (author's preferences marked ***)

Type of monitoring and evaluation	Likelihood of it taking place? Who involved?	What is it?	Typical questions	Key features
Inspection	most likely: managers less likely: practitioners/ users unlikely: above three groups in a partnership	usually a way of monitoring minimum standards	set over period of time, how many social work visits were there? how many reports during the period	can be externally imposed frame work predetermined
Evaluation ***	most likely: managers less likely: practitioners/ users unlikely: all three groups together	a means of making a judgement about the extent to which objectives are met	what do you think of the service offered to you? objectives met how and by whom?	identifies what has gone 'well'/'badly' and why; findings can be used to introduce changes
Monitoring	most likely: managers less likely: practitioners /users unlikely: all three groups	a systematic analysis of routinely gathered information	who are the users? who is working with whom? services needed?	raises as many questions as it answers
Action research ***	most likely to involve teams; least likely to be initiated at agency level	an approach to finding out whether and how a project is working	what parts of a programme are going well which are not?	action research takes successive readings of situation at pre-specified points in a programme

Table 11.1 Leaving care project monitoring and evaluation types (author's preferences marked ***) (continued)

Type of monitoring and evaluation	Likelihood of it taking place? Who involved?	What is it?	Typical questions	Key features
Performance review	most likely: managers less likely: practitioners/ users unlikely: above three groups in partnership	a systematic periodic review of project performance set against peformance standards/ targets	what have been the occupancy levels throughout the year, set against specified performance	answers largely determined by target setters explains what happens but not why
Quality assurance/ standard setting ***	most likely: managers less likely: practitioners users/unlikely: above three groups in partnership	different systems which can work through people, systems, standards or all three	what are you guaranteeing to do? what is the (minimum) standard here?	should involve all key players; tends to be complex and costly

It can also be used for reasons other than its prime reason. One example of how monitoring was developed to serve wider purposes relates to Place of Safety Orders (POSO) and is taken from Leicester social services department's research section (quoted in Sinclair, 1990:63):

> Following the use of a POSO the social worker completes a monitoring form which asks questions about the case and the actions of the social worker. This serves three purposes: it provides detailed information about the circumstances of each POSO case, it ensures adherence to procedures, and it acts as an aide-memoire to the social worker in terms of good practice.

When working at a voluntary organisation providing leaving care services a considerable amount of management and project time was spent on this monitoring subject. After much discussion four monitoring levels were identified in relation to leaving care:

- project level: internal project monitoring (i.e. by the project and of the project)

- agency/provider level: external monitoring of the projects (by the partnership local authorities)
- user level: individual monitoring of each young person's progress
- agency/purchaser level: monitoring the local authority's work and its leaving care population.

Yet the issues that arise time and again, as Biehal *et al.* (1995) mentioned above, and this author has raised (in Broad and Fletcher, 1993), amongst many others, is who drives the research agenda? Who will benefit from the research? Who does it belong to? For what purpose? And to what end? In other words, whose research is it?

These questions need to be born in mind when reading through the application of research methods to leaving care research that are reported in the remaining part of this chapter. Practitioner research can be described as an approach in which practitioners and users are involved as a means of fully participating in the research agenda, whichever of the above six methods are selected. Practitioner research seeks to assert the importance of users and practitioners, as well as others, in order to influence the research, to have practical benefits, for example, as well as producing quality qualitative and quantitative data.

The responding leaving care projects also used the questionnaire to take the opportunity to send in a limited number of examples of the ways in which their projects monitored their work, and the young people leaving care, or the ways their work was monitored by the local authority or voluntary organisation. These are presented as lists of examples, by research type making reference to the above six types where possible, starting with monitoring and the survey's modest findings.

Leaving care project monitoring: survey findings

The survey revealed that 30 or 65 per cent of respondents (n=46) stated that leaving care work is systematically monitored by the local authority (or if relevant by another organisation, e.g. voluntary organisation). Additional questions would be required to ascertain whether in practice this monitoring system was in position and being used, and to identify what *type* and level of monitoring was being listed. Leaving care projects were not asked to identify the type(s) of monitoring involved because of the detailed follow-up such a question would involve. The 1993 survey, using the same question, had virtually the same finding, namely, that 64 per cent (n=22) stated their projects' work was systematically monitored. Monitoring of local authority work is not simply a matter of an individual project's discretion. Housing Associations which have contracts with voluntary organisations to provide accommodation for young people leaving care tend to insist on their being monitored in place, and, incidentally, have most detailed monitoring arrangements, especially about the financial matters arising from occupancy levels and voids (see Smith, 1994:120 for example of housing monitoring).

Service Monitoring: an Example from a Local Authority
NUMERICAL INFORMATION TO INCLUDE:

- number of young people having individual agreements
- number and types of groups set up with attendance figures
- drop in sessions: record of use
- urgent needs service: number of service requests and details of request times and response times
- breakdown of how funds were used
- breakdown of service requests from other local authorities and responses.

QUALITATIVE INFORMATION ABOUT SERVICE TO INCLUDE:

- results of questionnaire filled in by young people using the service
- brief report of the work of the leaving care forum
- observations by other agencies, other local authorities
- submissions by social workers, carers and parents.

(Dudley Metropolitan Borough Council, 1994)

Monitoring Young People's Progress: An Example from a Voluntary Organisation

Another type of monitoring system, ACE, developed at the Royal Philanthropic Society and used there in the mid 1990s and, with Department of Health assistance, developed into a software system with Lancaster University, makes use of individual care plan record sheets. It is a most sophisticated and flexible system, produced in association with a private software company, Social Solutions. It is completed by staff working with young people and updated on a three-month basis, using outcomes data at project level, and entered onto computer with the ACE software. Some input from the young person concerned is also possible. These records contain ten 'dimensions' adapted from the criteria used for the Department of Health's action and assessment records.

The ten dimensions are:

- emotional support/development
- self-image

- practical self-care/parenting skills
- family and community support networks
- social presentation
- accommodation
- health
- finances
- education/training/employment
- leisure.

In its original version these ten elements were listed down the side of the first column of a manual A4 sheet. The second column is headed 'agreed tasks', the third column headed 'lead responsibility?' (whether voluntary organisation, local authority, joint or other), and the last column is headed 'target date'. For subsequent three month periods 'progress' (e.g. 'task completed' or 'task ongoing') and 'inhibitor' (e.g. lack of appropriate resources) codes on the work sheets are put against the various agreed tasks. In paper format this sort of monitoring can be most useful to track progress, or lack of it, by young people, although essentially it is a way of locating worker and agency accountability. The ACE software version takes in many other dimensions, levels of analyses, cross tabulations and search tools and functions, for example to enable data to be readily converted to tables and graphs as required. With a modest development grant, from central government for example, this high quality monitoring system could become widely available to all interested local authorities, which probably do not have the necessary funds or monitoring systems themselves to purchase and utilise it without such support.

Monitoring in a Purchaser/Provider Setting

This description of monitoring clearly illustrates the 'policing' or the 'provider accountability' nature of monitoring in the purchaser/provider world.

- to ensure that the service is provided to the quality and standard required by the service purchaser, the service provider will allow the service purchaser access to all reasonable times to inspect the service provision and any associated documentation
- the service purchaser reserves the right to confidentially canvass the views of customers who receive the service
- the service purchaser shall ascertain the standard of service provided against the published performance standards, taking into account the data submitted by the service provider in accordance with clause 15

- any shortfall in the quality or standard of service provided which is evident as a result of the monitoring process will be notified in writing to the service provided by the service purchaser and must be rectified within a reasonable time period given in the written notice

- the service provider shall be expected to establish adequate self-monitoring systems which will ensure that the service is provided to the standards required in this specification, and those published in the current edition of 'What service? What standards?'

- the service provider shall maintain records as evidence that monitoring has been undertaken together with any corrective action in order to meet the published performance standards and those required in this specification. (London Borough of Brent, 1996b)

Performance indicators and targets

In an increasing number of cases the work of leaving care teams is becoming subject to the culture of the service audit and inspection developments in social services at the expense of fully fledged research departments undertaking exploratory research. It is within such a framework that the monitoring of the leaving care services has developed. Statements within authorities often encompass terms of quite different meaning. Normally 'standards', in terms of quality standards, means what is promised to be done or delivered (within reason), or what is guaranteed to be done (i.e. not what we seek or try to do, or do sometimes). By contrast 'targets' are concerned with what is being 'aimed for' or sought or intended, and are less definite than 'standards'.

Five Key Leaving Care Performance Indicators

1. that the department assess and monitor the resources required to undertake the aftercare functions and inform the planning process accordingly

2. that with the consent of the young person the department will track the accommodation position of each young person who ceases to be looked after for the first three years after cessation

3. that in respect of a young person with special needs the department and a nominated specialist, with the consent of the young person, will review the individual's community care plan on an annual basis, and implement the recommendations for four years after cessation

4. that the department will establish an aftercare record for each young person who ceases to be looked after

5. that with the consent of the young person the department will track the education, training or employment status of young people who cease to be looked after, for the first three years after cessation.

These indicators were used by a social services department within a county local authority. To my knowledge, despite their importance not all of them have been followed up, or if they have, been published, as yet.

Performance Targets from Surrey Social Services Department (1994)

1. That 95 per cent of young people who cease to be looked after will have appropriate accommodation throughout the first three years after ceasing to be looked after. Appropriate accommodation will be under one of the three following headings: rehabilitation with family, supported accommodation, and independent accommodation

2. That 75 per cent of young people who cease to be looked after are enabled to achieve their first choice, from the previous general headings.

3. That 95 per cent of young people who cease to be looked after enter either further education, training/work experience, or employment by or within six months of cessation.

4. That 100 per cent of young people with special needs are tracked by the health service or the social services until the Community Care plan determines that this is no longer necessary.

5. That there will be a 75 per cent correlation between the level of service delivery and the assessment of needs of young people who cease to be looked after.

6. That the remaining 25 per cent are expected to deliver into those who refuse services, and a an ability to deliver. In the latter case a record can be made as to whether the reasons for non-delivery are: through service prioritisation, budgetary or absence of appropriate providers.

Interestingly, in the light of what was outlined above it then fell to the quality assurance section to review, on an annual basis, the performance targets.

Standards and Targets for 1995–96: London Borough of Sutton (1996)

WE WILL:

- offer advice and support to all young people leaving care and give all young people leaving care a Leaving Care Guide.

TO HELP US ACHIEVE THESES THINGS WE WILL:

- attend at least 70 per cent of the statuary case reviews of young people who are aged 14 or over that we are invited to

- offer help to every young person using our services to find and maintain permanent accommodation

- provide at least six sheltered lodgings placements for young people aged 16–21 years who are, or were previously, looked after by the (local) authority

- employ at least ten volunteers to befriend young people aged 14–21 who are, or were previously, looked after by the (local) authority

- invite every young person to attend reviews and planning meetings that we arrange.

Whilst there are important issues, generally, about who specifies service standards and targets, and in addition, in this case, a specific issue about the different statuses of standards and targets, it is important to observe, having had sight of the relevant documentation, that these standards are subject to regular internal review and comment.

For example, in relation to delays concerning referrals being made to the team there was the following observation and comment:

the monitoring of the standard of offering advice and support to all young people leaving care revealed that in 1993/4 60 young people aged 14–18 had not been known to the team. One year later, in September 1994 the figure was 20, in January 1995 it was 19, and in March 1995 it was 19. The latter represents 43 per cent of the total number in care or accommodated aged 14–18.

Detailed analysis of the March 1995 figure showed that 79 per cent of the young people unknown to the London Borough of Sutton team were aged 14–15, indicating referrals tend to be made at 15 or over. As from March 1995 a monthly check on all young people aged 14 or over to make sure that social workers make early referrals was included and the appointment of a temporary worker in 1996 from the Department's 'reserve team' was anticipated to fully resolve the issue (London Borough of Sutton, 1996). Whilst there were several cases where standards appeared to have been kept to and met, there were other examples, as one might expect with setting extended standards, where, when problems with standards had been identified through the monitoring system, they were made subject to action plans to resolve them.

Performance Indicators: London Borough of Wandsworth (1996)

A) ASSESSMENT OF NEED

- numbers of young people eligible for the aftercare service (currently 16–21 year olds) by age on leaving care, year left care
- numbers of young people (under 21) who are homeless, resident in the area (by sample) by age and gender
- percentage of those homeless young people of 13 and over; originating from your area, formally looked after by your local authority
- percentage of young people eligible for aftercare services who are, or are about to be, parents, and are in need of additional support (and for whom the local authority owes a grandparent duty).

B) KEY INDICATORS: INPUT AND OUTPUT

- numbers of full time equivalent staff designated for provision of aftercare service for counselling on housing benefits, education, health, health education, cash payments, and provision of accommodation
- cost of support provision/week for 16+ young people in receipt of aftercare services, including housing provision, cash assistance, support services
- number of family centre/residential beds offering a short term base to which young people could return.

C) MEASURES OF OUTCOME AND IMPACT: AGAINST DEFINED OBJECTIVES

- number of young people who are eligible for aftercare service, but with whom there had not been contact for one year
- number of young people leaving care in previous years for whom there is an agreed aftercare plan (care plan to include discussion of links with family and friends)
- percentage of young people leaving care who have been given an information guide about aftercare provisions
- number of interviews with young people who have leaving care aimed at contributing to the improvement of the service for looking after children, and aftercare provision.

D) PROCESS

- care/aftercare plans reviewed at least four times a year.

These then are just a few of the ways in which leaving care work is being recorded to aid and guide planning, and make staff and projects more aware of their responsibilities and targets. If all local authorities employed a similar leaving care monitoring system, or at least one which allows for core national material to be collected, then at long last a national picture of leaving care could emerge. It is also important that young people as service users are involved in the leaving care monitoring process, if they so wish, and not just occupy the role of rather passive service recipients. For this to happen it is important to find user friendly ways for young people to be made welcome and become a part of this process. Consumer satisfaction questionnaires can make an important contribution here, although usually they seem to occupy a limited role in terms of overall leaving care monitoring.

User satisfaction surveys and action research

User Satisfaction Surveys

User satisfaction surveys can take the form of structured postal or telephone questionnaires or a series of face to face semi-structured interviews. These can be conducted with the young people (as service users), and the purchasing agency, usually a separate department within social services if operating along purchaser/provider lines. It will be especially important to seek the views of staff who refer the young people to the specialist leaving care project in a locality where there are no purchaser/provider arrangements in order that they can feel genuinely involved in services and service delivery.

It is important if deciding on this service satisfaction approach for the independent researcher to work closely with all groups of stake holders if all their views are being sought, to define the issues around which the satisfaction questions will be constructed. It is also inevitable but not unmanageable for there to be differences of opinion about what issues should or should not be included, for example stereotypically purchasers will be concerned with value for money and efficiencies rather more than the service users who are likely to focus on their ability to mange their lives both emotionally and in practical terms. To the service users, for example, the use of a satisfaction scale can be a good starting point. The scale can range from 'much improved' to 'much worse' and questions such as how, if at all, have certain services responded to your needs can be a way of addressing simple but important practice issues. Questions can then be readily adapted for the referring social worker's views to be sought to record their views about specified individual cases. In viewing various types of satisfaction surveys it is apparent that in many cases staff have ensured that young people's views are obtained and their views fully and anonymously (by post using pre-paid forms for example) recorded.

The following are examples of the *user satisfaction questionnaires* used in leaving care work taken from work done in a voluntary organisation.

EXAMPLE 1 – THE BASIC MODEL:

These questions were sent out (with slight amendments) separately to both users and referring staff.

1. What were your expectations when you first started attending the leaving care project?

2. How has the experience matched up to your expectations?

3. Are you satisfied with the aftercare support work we provide? (yes/no/unsure/expand on answer)

4. What are the good things about the project?

5. What are the things that need improvement?

6. To what extent have you been adequately involved with the project in making decisions affecting your life? (four lines provided for answer)

EXAMPLE 2 – THE BASIC PLUS MODEL:

This provides scales for the young people's answers (involving a six point scale ranging from 'much improved' to 'much worse').

Since attending the project how is your situation concerning [examples provided]:

• feeling more emotionally supported?

• your feelings about yourself and self worth?

• your practical self care skills?

• your relationships with your family?

• your relationships with your friends and community networks?

• the way you present yourself to others?

• your 'other' needs? [this could include the young persons accommodation, education, health, financial management, and leisure needs, or others as required]

As always a balance will need to be struck between practical considerations (e.g. what time people are willing give to participate and 'fill in more forms') with what is desirable, which might amount to a considerable amount more. In example 1 above the response rate was very high, around the 80 per cent mark, from both young people and social workers, but the information produced was minimal, and, frustratingly for those concerned, not published. In example 2, whose categories were drawn from earlier interviews, the response rate was also high, better quality information was produced, and the results were published, initially internally, with the hope of broader publication in due course. For other leaving care projects and organisations interested in conducting some research into the work of a leaving care team another research method, which avoids some of the publication problems, might be suitable and more responsive is action research.

Action Research: Summary and Examples

If the key question is 'How can I find out, while a programme is going on, whether and how it is working, and how if at all ought I to modify my approach?', then an action research project could well be most suitable. Action research takes successive readings of a situation at pre-specified points in a programme and uses what is found to re-plan some parts of the programme (Stock-Whittaker and Archer, 1989). Sometimes practitioners and managers cannot wait until the end of a project's life, or the end of its service agreement, to know whether it is working. There can be a greater sense of urgency in such cases. Thus they may wish to have information to record what is happening in one part of the programme, a well as shortly after it has happened. This might be one component of a larger programme. Some examples might be:

- which parts of the weekly group work programme are going well and why? And which parts are not going well? and why not? And upon what criteria are 'well' and 'not going well' based?

- in a project which has new working arrangements with other agencies, how are these arrangements working out in terms of users' and agencies' experiences?

- what use has been made of a new open access policy for young people to have direct access to their files?

- what do young people think about the employment advice sessions?

- what are the young people's views of planning meetings?

Action research can also be applied in practice situations where:

- a phased programme has been planned from the beginning with a specified goal in mind

- the workers involved in a programme have a specified goal in mind but only the first step in a programme has been planned; or

- a programme consists of a number of different parts or activities which are going on at the same time and the workers/service users involved have a specified goal in mind

- it is not unusual for the successive event/action cycles of assessment, planning, action specification, re-plan, and reassessments to suggest an explanation or refinement of the goals which were specified at the beginning.

In one leaving care action research project information required included:

- the workings of a one year innovative employment project involving the private sector in partnership with the voluntary organisation

- a 5 point scaled assessment system for gauging young people's independence

- ways of recording users' and purchasers' views about the services received.

This action research work took place over a one year period and the findings formed a major part of an interim report (Broad, 1993). The findings from these three measures were then used to re-examine the project's aims, but it was found that other more formal data such as numbers in employment and in accommodation was also necessary to produce a fuller picture. Eventually, the findings were published internally.

Another action research approach has been used in research into identifying and meeting the health needs of young people leaving care being conducted by De Montfort University in conjunction with East Surrey Health Authority and the Mid Surrey Stepping Out Project. Involvement by young people has been central to that two stage research project (Saundess and Broad, 1997).

Conclusion

The final choice of research, evaluation or monitoring methods will ultimately be determined by pragmatic and political concerns, as well as by finances, more than simply aims and objectives. It is safest to assume that someone is wanting to use the research for their own purposes. The point is to find out what these purposes are. Then, if the purpose being proposed is unacceptable, because for example it ignores the views of practitioners and users, discuss the matter and try to influence this agenda. There may be demands for *both* qualitative and quantitative methods, or for questionnaire surveys (like the one which underpins this book), or for the design of imaginative experiential methods, such as self-completion diaries, or Delphi panels designed to capture different perspectives, or for non-participative observation methods to be employed to collect and record data. *As a general rule of thumb the data that is collected by a combination of qualitative and quantitative methods will produce the richer, more valid and reliable data*, providing the questions asked are the relevant ones to the group or individuals involved. It is often the case that despite the 'good intentions' of all those involved, the final 'results' will be shaped by those with the most power in the research relationship, in this case relating to leaving care work. However, it could equally apply in other settings, especially where equal opportunities, or lack of equal opportunities, is an issue (on this point see Humphreys and Truman 1994). One way forward in the leaving care research field is to involve some of the young people at all stages of the research, up to and including the point of report editing, production and delivery. Research findings can and do contribute to discussions about improvements to services. The risk for the less powerful stakeholders in research is that whilst their views are initially sought, the research findings may not emerge. Findings are not published for a number of possible reasons. It can be as a result of the research revealing some minor operational shortcoming about which the commissioning agency becomes embarrassed. In the emerging purchaser/provider climate it should also be recognised that projects and organisations are increasingly, and understandably, defensive and sensitive about their research endeavours. These feelings need to be acknowledged, and, wherever possible, accommodated.

There would appear to be a preponderance of finance led research initiatives concerned with small scale performance review inspections. Although it is important that research does this 'checking up' task, it can do so much more. It is also at least as important, especially if the research is focused on defining and improving service delivery, that it involves young people and practitioners. The collection of statistical information, unless it is perceived of as useful and relevant, is not normally seen as a priority for practitioners. Therefore it is important to produce an evaluation system which is designed alongside practitioners and, if possible, users as well. Experience reveals that the process of negotiating a monitoring schedule is important, although in the purchaser/provider framework it is difficult to see how inclusive/participatory processes can be accommodated and acted upon. The London Borough of Brent's (1996a) monitoring schedule, described earlier, illustrates the that the purchaser not the user or provider is in the monitoring driving seat. At the more strategic authority wide level it is *absolutely vital that the local authority engages in systematic monitoring of its leaving care population to enable strategic planning to take place*, something which seems haphazard at present. There is now enough local experience and initiatives, (especially that of the Royal Philanthropic Society's /University of Lancaster) to take things forward in a more focused and rigorous way than has previously been the case.

CHAPTER TWELVE

Leaving Care Management
Service Agency Agreements
and Planning

Introduction

This chapter seeks to address issues concerned with the management of leaving care services and this will be done in a variety of ways: by drawing on research findings about purchaser/ provider developments, by providing examples of service agency agreements and by discussion. Because the focus here is also on the planning, not just the management, of child care services, wider national developments, including the requirement on local authorities to produce Children's Plans, are discussed. In the first instance the management context of contracts, service agency agreements, and purchaser/provider developments will be described, especially as they relate to specifying standards.

By management is meant the formal way in which leaving care teams' work is delineated, whether by a service contract, or, more commonly, according to this research for voluntary organisation projects, by a partnership approach involving a service agency agreement. The main differences between the two terms are as follows:

1. The *contracting out of a service* normally involves a particular service (for example children's homes) or part of a wider service (for example a counselling service for young people in custody) being specified and drawn up by a service purchaser (normally a social services departments). Subsequent to the defining of the service required, and in a local authority where there is a purchaser/provider system, a service will be put out to tender, and, if it goes out to compulsory competitive tender or CCT as it is more commonly known, then the provider winning the contract is required to deliver that service according to the terms of the contract. The contract is a legally binding document, often with penalties, and based on a clear agreement that at any time each party can seek legal redress if necessary. A successful contract can be held by a local authority, whose 'in-house bid' proved successful, or a voluntary organisation, or the independent sector. One of the

disadvantages of a contract is that it distances the provider from the purchaser and 'a place at the table' for the provider has to be negotiated. Some of the examples, given later in this chapter, about purchaser/provider developments echo this point.

2. A *partnership approach* involves a less legalistic arrangement between, in this case, local authorities and voluntary organisations in which the consultation between parties is a central feature, as is joint funding, as is consultation about and co-ordination of services. The *service agency agreement* is the mechanism used for specifying the service although, confusingly, they can also be used in drawing up contracts, as opposed to contract specification. According to one voluntary organisation:

> A service agency agreement is a mechanism for enabling voluntary organisations to receive the necessary funding to provide good quality services, and it must always be the provision and development of the *services* which take priority over the *mechanism*... The *process*, as well as the *outcome*, of negotiation is frequently to be valued. To ensure that targets are realistic and within the capability of the voluntary organisation, it is important that they are fully involved in the drafting of agreements. (Smith, 1994:9)

One of the advantages of being subject to a contract or agreement is that it does offer some security to the services and resources involved in delivering care during the said period. It is much more difficult to cut posts or budgets or to graft on other duties to those specified in the agreement than with other less well specified services. There are a range of models of relationships between the local authority and the voluntary sector from open partnership through to competitively tendered contract. Where local authorities have divided the purchasers from the providers, local authorities define the service specification for the service required, and this can and often does apply to the local authority's in-house provider team. Having drawn up a service specification, the local authority can then undertake a 'market testing' exercise to see if such services can be run more efficiently by external voluntary or private providers. The establishment of a *purchaser/provider mechanism* within some local authorities, as discussed later in this chapter in connection with the research, has enabled those authorities to have much better information about costs, standards, and service delivery.

Any of these approaches, but especially the contract, can pose a threat to voluntary organisations, not simply in terms of technical 'how to draw up a contract' questions, but, much more importantly, in terms of organisational and professional survival. There are also opportunities for local authorities and voluntary organisations to expand and develop. In relation to the latter Barnardo's and the NSPCC, for example, have been most successful in expanding the work they do for and with local authorities. Depleting local authority budgets and the absence of national pay scales in some local authorities, voluntary organisations and independent organisations provides the basis for a more competitive market operating according to price pressures as least as much as quality thresholds. According to Gutch, those voluntary organisation 'involved in contracting will find themselves squeezed. Contracts, particularly with voluntary organisations, provide purchasers with a mechanism for reducing costs, while appearing to maintain services' (Gutch, 1993:5). Whilst there will be some potential providers which will offer services at a (lower) price, and be attractive to those local authorities wishing to cut costs, there will be other local authorities and voluntary organisations wishing to develop quality, not low cost, services. The point has been put to me that such are the level of employment costs for maternity, sickness, etc., that this also provides an incentive for getting another organisation to take on the employment risks – and this is called 'enabling'!

Yet in the face of an ever changing, and at times daunting, climate for conducting this work there remain many examples of good practice in terms of service agency agreements from the leaving care field, and indeed elsewhere, and in these more business oriented times some managers have needed to hone up their financial, legal and strategic skills. It is to this changing management world to which attention is now turned, examining service agency agreements and standard setting issues. In the sense that the research did not systematically require information about partnership service agency agreements or contracts, what is presented here are a series of good practice and good policy pointers from those projects that took the trouble to make materials available. Specific questions were asked in the research about purchaser/provider developments and their answers are analysed later in this chapter in a more systematic research oriented way than was possible with the service agency agreements.

The changing management of leaving care work

In the first place, it is worth reminding readers that all the 46 respondent projects offer specialist after/leaving care services to young people who have left local authority care, that none were residential projects and none were local authority children's homes. Virtually all of the projects carried the word 'aftercare', or 'leaving care' or 'independence' in their title. Two small voluntary sector projects carried the word 'accommodation' or 'homelessness' in their project's title, indicating a particular focus, and although they were working predominantly with young people leaving care, they were also working with a very small number, less than 3 per cent, of homeless young people who had not been in care. Service agency agreements were used to describe the leaving care projects' responsibilities, tasks and activities and ways in which they would provide a service. In one case the activities specified included: skilled staff support, advice and guidance, groupwork programme (these were more popular in urban areas where the young people were relatively local compared with sprawling counties), supportive work with parents and carers, urgent need service (i.e. special advice and support), drop-in advice service, provision of financial support, information service, and other advice provided on site at the project. Other projects, as will be shown, such as Dudley social services department, outlined particular aspects of their leaving care service and specified the ways in which they linked in with residential or foster care and local authority assessment systems.

The parties to management agreements can be the relevant local authority area and the voluntary organisation, in the case of a service being delivered by an organisation in the voluntary sector, or in the case of a local authority team working in a purchaser/provider context, between the children and families purchasing (or in some cases purchasing and assessment division) and the provider or provider division. In the case of joint local authority /voluntary organisation projects there is financial and service planning input from both the local authority and the voluntary sector, such as the London Borough of Wandsworth and the Royal Philanthropic Society, whose service agency agreement is also drawn on here. What follows next is a series of the most relevant excerpts from service agency agreements in the leaving care field.

Service agency agreements and service entitlements

In its entitlements to services the Dudley Metropolitan borough leaving care team service definition was typical of those local authority teams providing a leaving care service, with the possible exception of its out of borough entitlements, where responsibility is not always specified. That team (Dudley Social Services, 1996) was described as providing a service for:

- young people in residential homes
- independent carers funded by the council (out of borough placements)
- young people in foster care
- young people living with their parents but subject to a care order
- young people living in the Dudley area who were previously looked after by another local authority and who require an aftercare service
- young people aged 16 and 17 who may be described as being vulnerable due to being actually or potentially homeless
- young people living in accommodation in a neighbouring local authority for whom Dudley continues to hold case responsibility (including young people in custody).

In some cases projects specify their role in considerable detail. For example in Sutton (London Borough of Sutton, 1995) leaving care staff:

- attend care reviews of young people who are preparing to leaving care from their 14th birthday, in an advisory role (its direct work usually begins around their 16th birthday and may continue until they are 21 or in some cases longer)

- work with other staff and agencies including providing information and advice to social work, housing, health care, and educational professionals who are working with young people as well as helping to shape policy and strategy at a department's management level

- help young people to access a range of housing, offering different types and levels of support. These supports are provided in partnership with local housing associations, the housing section of the council and local residents through the team's sheltered lodgings scheme.

In other cases, and increasingly, service agency agreements for young people leaving care also include other groups of young people. In Mid Surrey the 'in need' group as well as care leavers are included. Generally, this can cause difficulties for workers about legal entitlements and eligible services. In the London Borough of Brent (1996a) the leaving care service `is also available to the following customers':

- those detained under the Police and Criminal Evidence Act 1984

- those remanded to local authority accommodation

- those subject to a supervision order with a residence requirement

- those detained following committing a grave crime if looked after in a local authority accommodation.

As with many other local authority leaving care teams, the service specification, in this case for 180 young people per year (London Borough of Brent, 1996b), is set against a background of there already being a greater and rising number of cases, in this case 195 total cases for 1995, and 217 in 1996. As that borough's annual report for 1995/6 states, 'We have seen over the past year that there is a rising demand for our services, reflecting the amount of young people that are going through the care system, but also valuing the support they receive' (London Borough of Brent, 1996). The additional message comes through from this annual report that young people leaving care often come back again and again for support, advice and counselling, thus increasing caseloads. This 'returnees' issues will be returned to later in this chapter because it can play havoc with caseload management.

The wide ranging service agency agreement for the Royal Philanthropic Society's Mid Surrey Stepping Out Project (for 1994–1997) helpfully specifies the social services, the voluntary organisation and the joint social services/voluntary organisation responsibilities in separate sections. Thus:

The Core Functions for the Social Services Are:

- ensuring effective preparation of young people looked after for the transition to adulthood
- ensure that the housing needs of young people under Section 24 are identified and raised
- ensure the project receives last review papers prior to the young person ceasing to be looked after
- to convene and chair a group to meet quarterly to ensure the effective co-ordination of services
- to convene and chair the monitoring group.

The Core Functions for the Voluntary Organisation Are:
THREE CLIENT GROUPS/GENERAL ROLE:

- young people being looked after, aged 15 to 18 years of age; screening role
- young people aged 18+ who have been looked after; tracking
- all young people aged 16/17 years, assessed by social services as 'at risk'; screening role.

FOR ALL THREE GROUPS:

- assessments must be undertaken, prior to any direct work
- groupwork: to be run as required
- to continue the accommodation strategy
- provide training and consultation for staff/carers
- pivotal role in ensuring multi-agency co-ordination
- housing: development role
- co-ordinating a monitoring group.

Core Functions Where There is Joint Responsibility

- planning of direct services to young people leaving care
- enabling staff to have training

- promoting the development of good practice
- seeking a corporate responsibility within the local authority for the provision of leaving care services
- assisting the quality assurance department to develop quality and outcome measures.

The local authority, in this case Surrey, has the major planning responsibility, as one might expect, with the voluntary organisation having the major individual work responsibilities. Yet it can also be seen that the voluntary organisation is given a quite considerable role in planning terms, in respect of housing and multi-agency co-ordination.

Service standards

By contrast some service agency agreements seem to be much more focused on attempting to specify standards, rather than more general tasks, for each of a wide range of 'good practice' areas. The following core agreement (Royal Philanthropic Society/Kent County Council, 1996) provides one such example:

- services are provided regardless of race, gender, disability or sexual orientation [surely this should read '*taking full account* of race etc.' as so many local authorities including the London Borough of Sutton agreement (1996) states]
- services are provided to meet assessed individual need and written in a clearly understood agreement
- young people have access to information and assistance in using it
- the views, wishes and feelings of young people will always be considered when planning individual programmes and the ongoing review of service planning
- stability, flexibility and consistency are recognised as important elements in the lives of young people
- services will be developed within available resources to allow for choice, opportunity and to meet the different needs of young people leaving care
- young people will be helped to participate fully in meaningful activities which include employment, education, training and leisure pursuits
- young people will have access to high standard and affordable accommodation

- young people will have their needs met on an individual basis with respect, integrity and in a non-judgemental way allowing for self determination

- it is acknowledged that young people make mistakes. The emotional needs of young people will be treated with sensitivity and care

- young people have access to adequate levels of financial support to live in a way that allows for self respect, dignity and privacy

- young people are aware of their rights and how to complain.

In some cases the standards which support these areas are easier to specify as standards, for example, the provision of written information to young people, than others, for example about anti-discriminatory work. It is also apparent that the mechanism of service agency agreements can be used either to specify an unrealistic level of service or to severely limit the scope of services expected. What follows is another example of leaving care standards set out in a service agency agreement, again illustrating the point that the setting of written standards at a general, not individual, level is a difficult and demanding exercise. Yet it is also vital to attempt to do so in order to achieve clarity and accountability.

Dudley Metropolitan Borough's (1994) standards regarding leaving care specify:

- staff support to young people including working in a professional and sensitive way, using appropriate advocacy skills, groupwork skills, an appreciation of the professional balance between care and control, the ability to work with a number of different social, bureaucratic, and community systems, the ability to work with young people in crisis, have up to date records, and attend training courses

- develop a groupwork programme as needed

- undertake supportive work with parents and carers (including monitoring their involvement in the scheme)

- provide advice to young people in crisis, first contact to be within 15 hours

- provide a drop-in service to young people on a regular specified basis plus record to be kept of same.

PROVISION OF FINANCIAL ADVICE AND GUIDANCE: THE FOLLOWING PAYMENTS MAY BE ADMINISTERED:

- department leaving care grants

- assistance with paying rent

- assistance with surety of rent

- subsidising of rents
- assistance with travel and subsistence
- emergency cash aid for food and essential clothing
- assistance in purchasing equipment to assist young people taking up employment
- financial support to help young people to pursue activities as part of individual agreement
- monitor use of these funds
- provide an information pack (as set out under Volume 4 of guidelines and regulations)
- liaise with other local authorities
- provide an annual report
- undertake monitoring of leaving care work. (Dudley Metropolitan Borough, 1994)

It is also noted that financial payments to young people leaving care whilst addressed in the agreement nevertheless remain highly discretionary and unspecified. Clarity of standards can also result in tensions between providers and purchasers about what should be included and excluded, and the advocacy role in leaving care work is one which voluntary organisations often argue for, and local authorities might not find attractive or acceptable.

What has been presented so far in this chapter is a series of examples of service agency agreements, and standards and various other forms of documentation used to specify services. What the research also set out to do was to ask the leaving care projects to report on projects' actual experiences of purchaser/ provider developments, probably the most important management initiative in social services work for many years.

Purchaser/provider developments

In the questionnaire respondents were given two questions about purchaser/provider developments; about whether purchaser/provider developments had impacted on leaving care work and, if so, in what ways and whether to the advantage or disadvantage of young people leaving care. In relation to the first question it was found that 19 or 43 per cent of respondents (n=44) considered that purchaser/provider developments were effecting their leaving care work with young people, whereas 25 or 57 per cent considered that they were not. It was apparent that the local authority teams were experiencing the changes more acutely than the other two project types with 57 per cent of local authority (and 50% of joint project) teams stating that purchaser/provider developments were affecting their work, compared with 21 per cent of voluntary organisation projects. The tentative explanation for these differences is that the changes, and therefore the potential threat that purchaser/provider developments pose to local authority providers, are more likely felt by local authority than voluntary organisation teams. It is also possible that respondents were answering the question in terms of the way services are arranged and changing, rather than changes in providers, although the two issues are linked. Where there were much clearer differences between project types overall was in respect of the advantages and disadvantages of purchaser/provider developments.

Advantages and disadvantages of purchaser/provider developments

Advantages: 14 Examples Given

The 19 respondents who considered that purchaser/provider developments had affected their work provided 53 examples of the ways in which these occurred. Of these examples 14 (26%) were those where the effects had been to the advantage of the young people and the majority, 36 (68%), were of those where there had been disadvantageous effects; 3 (6%) responses were categorised as being a 'mixed blessing'.

Advantages of Purchaser/Provider Developments in Leaving Care Work: 9 of 14 General Examples Provided:

- easily able to identify relevant budgets and social work teams
- trying to establish a more effective and co-ordinated service
- clear contract and caseload (5 further examples given on this theme)
- the development of a special leaving care team
- clear reviews and monitoring
- is now producing needs led not resource led services
- it has helped with the setting of budgets and negotiating with housing associations and recognising the size of the task
- through financial changes the project has funds for and more control over the purchase of supported housing for young people leaving care
- it has helped facing the local authority in providing support to young people leaving care.

Disadvantages: 36 Examples Given

The disadvantages centred on two key themes, namely that of overall planning of services (22 responses), and service delivery and financial issues (14 responses). The full list is given below because of the vital importance of service planning and its emphasis in this chapter.

Disadvantages of Purchaser/Provider Developments in Leaving Care Work: All 22 Examples About Service Planning:

- local authority departments working in isolation
- local authority housing work going out to tender
- providers do not see leaving care work as a priority due to pressure of child protection work; thus the project is increasingly key working for the social services department
- leaving care work a very low priority
- what happens after the three year contract finishes?
- what happens under unitary authority? change again?
- problems over shared responsibility
- conflict between providers and case holders
- in some areas difficulties in maintaining commitment to planning meetings
- the team is isolated in the area
- not able to offer service to young people from outside the area unless finance first obtained
- it has made it difficult for providers to challenge the purchaser, making it more difficult to advocate on behalf of young people
- problems with identifying financial responsibility for young people with learning difficulties
- problems in locating accommodation for young people with mild learning difficulties
- after anticipated move to large multi-functional office, a fear that the service will become institutionalised (lack of identity)
- lack of commitment regarding monitoring
- young people's files on different sites
- duplication of roles and responsibilities
- lack of strategic planning between purchasers and providers

- voluntary organisation not consulted regarding child care planning in the area

- this has led to divisive splits between purchasers and providers

- purchasers under tremendous financial pressures to produce resource not needs led services.

The effect of each of these examples is considerable in terms of the implication for the proper planning of children's services to the point, if these findings were repeated round the country, where one might have thought the Department of Health, or its Social Services Inspectorate, might want to intervene beyond conducting a national inspection (Social Services Inspectorate, 1997).

One of the main aims underpinning the purchaser/provider system is to produce greater financial accountability and efficiencies. These seem reasonable aims until one sees the damage that is caused to local authority planning by managers 'guarding budgets' to the point where local priorities, more than local or national policies, determine practice. Purchaser/provider developments further encourage the trend of local services becoming 'mini policy makers' through localised practice with individual cases. The following examples of disadvantages to young people reinforce an earlier point (concerning leaving care finances) about the difficulties for leaving care services to be subject to national standards, whoever sets them, because of local circumstances and budgets.

Disadvantages of Purchaser/Provider Developments In leaving Care Work: All 14 Examples About Service Delivery/Financial Issues:

- inequality of service

- purchasers want a clearly defined service that falls short of young people's needs

- young people's files in another office creates logistical problems in young people accessing files

- sometimes unclear who does what

- purchasers make initial referral and assessments

- having to pick up issues which should have been sorted out earlier such as remedial education and counselling

- we are constantly having to prove we are value for money

- no increase in funding for project for three years

- local authority cannot be seen to pay for a development worker

- shortage of social work staff and allocated social workers

- budget restrictions and cuts
- service is much more resource not needs led
- funding insufficient/ not available for rural work because of cost implications
- potential threat of privatisation.

Some of those disadvantages are concerned more with lack of resources generally than with purchaser/provider as such, but throughout the replies there is a strong sense that decisions are seen as predominantly finance, rather than needs, led.

There were three examples given where purchaser/provider developments were seen as both beneficial and disadvantageous to work with young people leaving care:

- being located within 'providers' more appropriate than being located in care management? (this has an ongoing effect on the team's training)
- the concept of a mixed economy of care has forced us to clarify and monitor what we offer
- Section 24 budget is held on the purchasers side but providers (aftercare workers) need to access it.

It was also possible, from comments made by practitioners, to draw out their concerns about purchaser/provider developments a little more.

Concerns Expressed by Practitioners About Purchaser/Provider Developments

- the lack of qualifications required in some areas of care or case mangers
- tensions between purchaser/provider at meetings as a 'them and us' culture is enforced around loyalty issues (i.e. who is our team?)
- feelings of another group develop a separate identity – this is a bit of a culture shock
- about case responsibility: case managers only seeing the client once every six months or at monthly reviews
- of workers going to court and not knowing and never meeting the case (or care) mangers
- yet more new management tiers (i.e. 'super' case managers) and ever less provider staff
- young people leaving care being in boarding schools for 52 weeks a year, but social services do not know the number of out of county placements – the case mangers less likely to know

- 'a save money at any cost' culture developing which encourages minimum service working to a price approach (i.e. only offering two hours per week advice on one case)

- the absurdity of weekly invoicing then employing ever more staff to monitor all the invoices!

We have seen then that purchaser/provider developments, where they have been introduced, whilst helpful in financial and accountability terms are predominantly regarded as having a largely disadvantageous effect on the young people needing help and leaving care. Together with the observations above about management and service agency agreements, some key trends in the management of leaving care work can now be identified.

Key trends in leaving care management

The first important management issue here about service agency agreement is where each agreement is negotiated locally with each local social services area, as well as centrally. This puts an additional strain on existing resources and makes the consistency and planning of local authority leaving care services even more difficult.

A second key issue that can be drawn out from examining these service agency agreements is the added expectation on projects, as described above, in addition to working with young people leaving care, to work with young people in need, under Section 20(3) of the Children Act 1989. The research only asked projects to record details about their leaving care work, but the numbers of young people who are assessed as 'in need' may not be insignificant, if one project's service agency agreement is typical. The well established Independent Living Scheme in the London Borough of Wandsworth is expected not only to provide a service to some 150 young people leaving care, but 70 additional young people subject to Section 20 (3), which involves 'individual advice and financial assistance' (Royal Philanthropic Society, 1996a).

A third associated trend is that of using the service agency agreements to *limit*, not shape, the quality of service being offered, especially in terms of turnover and throughput. For example in one service agency agreement it stated that target staff caseloads will be between 15 and 20 young people (there were in fact 22 and rising), and that an allowance of 10 per cent (an equivalent of two cases) is made for young people 'returning to the project for support'. In the returned questionnaire from that same project comments were made that it was impossible to limit this figure to the allotted 10 per cent. Furthermore the team concerned were acutely aware that lack of continuity of care was a key issue for young people leaving care, and one which they did not want to continue, but their service agency agreement was acting to promote quick independence with minimal allowance for 'returnees'. In another case the local authority had used the service agency agreement to limit ongoing work with young people returning to the project. Emerging ideas about mentoring or 'buddy' schemes for young people who had graduated from leaving care schemes may be one way forward, as can 'drop in' schemes for returnees.

A fourth development with new service agency agreements is that there is not more but less money being made available for these services. For example in one local authority the leaving care budget for 1994/5 was £139,500, which was some £25,000 less than for the previous financial year. In another local authority the budget for 1994/5 was £149,000, representing a slight decrease on the previous financial year, in real terms, of some £21,000. In another case, that of a joint voluntary organisation /local authority project, the voluntary organisation was putting in just half of the annual £45,000 it had been contributing in the previous agreement with that same local authority.

A fifth trend, as we saw earlier in the book, is of continuing decreases in staffing levels for the responding projects (n=44), from a staff team average of 5.12 for the year 1992/3 to a staff team average of 4.88 for 1995/6. This compares with a 16 per cent increase in caseloads for the same period. All of these management developments do not auger well for leaving care work, and presents leaving care work with tough choices to make.

Six Tough Options Facing Leaving Care Projects
Faced with increasing demands and having the same or less resources leaving care projects of whatever type have to make some very difficult decisions about the ways in which they work if they are to sustain existing standards of service. These are:

1. *work with fewer young people leaving care*: do they have the power or authority to make that decision?

2. *work less with the other categories of young people being referred to the projects* (e.g. S20:3 children in need and young people). Have teams got the authority to do this? Who decides? Should they do this?

3. *work in a more focused and more superficial way with the same number of young people*: this is building on what already happens/easier to introduce/begs questions about effectiveness/the values of caring

4. *carry on as at present, trying to work with the same number of young people*: in the long run this must have impact on staff morale and health and the quality of service being offered to the young people

5. *provide the same or enhanced level of service*: if it is a local authority service, by being restructured and contracted out to a voluntary organisation or

independent sector if it has lower salary and overhead costs or jointly run with a voluntary organisation. This could have a detrimental effect regarding the continuity of care for the young people unless this structure is integral to the local authority's child care policy and practice/this could disrupt local relations between the local authority and voluntary organisations

6. *change the eligibility criteria for service recipients:* this will result in some of the more needy young people, for example those young people from another local authority who have left care who move into another area for help, or those with more demanding (and costly!) needs such as those with learning difficulties, not receiving a proper service.

It is impossible to see, from the research material that has been collected from this study, and others, how the current level and scope of service provisions for young people leaving care can be sustained in a climate of increased demand, and reducing resources. This depressing though realistic conclusion about leaving care service quality and capacity brings me neatly to the question of service planning for children's and young people's services.

Children's services planning

In terms of overall planning the DoH's Looking After Children Assessment and Action records (LAC) provide an important structure for collecting information about children and young people, and then recording subsequent actions taken. There is an emphasis on recording outcomes, and Ward, the manager of this project, has stated that, providing the so called LAC materials genuinely improve the outcomes of children and young people (and research as to whether this is the case has not yet taken place), then they will have proved to be a major enabling force in children's services (Ward, 1996:252). The seven key categories used for the 16+ group – that is, those coming to the attention to leaving care projects, namely: health, education, identity, family and social relationships, social presentation, emotional and behavioural development, and self-care skills – cover all but one of the most pressing areas affecting young people leaving care. The excluded area, identified here, and again and again by researchers in the leaving care field, is that relating to financial circumstances. For those who see the solutions to young people leaving care only in social welfare terms, then the seven category checklist is more or less correct. Yet for those who see the remedy for young people in both social welfare and social justice terms, requiring changes at national social policy and legislative level, then the list is incomplete.

Making an assessment of financial need for a young person of 16 or older is, arguably, at least as important to a young person and their care plan as is a tick on a form, as is the case on the LAC form, indicating whether they can change a fuse or repair a puncture! The point is, of course, that we already know that young people leaving care do not have any or much money, so why ask? And what can be done about it anyway? Yet we also know that the health needs of young people leaving care are wanting, yet the assessment and action records raise many important health questions. Although it is understood why the category of providing financial supports might be not seen as 'appropriate', its inclusion could assist social workers and carers to make an informed and stronger case for more help and resources. This brings us back to the point raised earlier about what are the real problems of and for young people leaving care, and in what terms are the solutions described? None of these comments are intended to criticise these assessment and action records, or any other of the social welfare initiatives, but to point out their limits and impact. These are designed to help professionals, carers and users alike, and should also aid accountability and continuity of service. The argument made here is that leaving care, like leaving home, requires financial as well as placement planning and the provision of financial supports to live independently.

Planning for individual children and young people, which informs service planning, and assessments and action are described by the Social Services Inspectorate (DoH, 1991a:19) as:

1. presenting/putting the child at the centre of all planning systems

2. collecting information

3. making full and comprehensive assessments

4. taking decisions with an action plan

5. reviewing that plan

6.   taking further action, if necessary.

This planning framework describes a period of action which may mean the 'end of the journey', with records being kept and used at every stage. In an ideal world such a framework would be applied to the work with each and every young person leaving care, but the document acknowledges that *the right resources, training support and supervision are required for the plan to offer 'powerful protection'*, something which it cannot be said is the case for leaving care work. This is not to say that such planning is not desirable, but rather to put the case that the availability of sufficient resources must be a pre-requisite for full planning. Despite a climate of grossly inadequate resources, planning for young people leaving care needs to improve significantly.

The planning of services for young people leaving care requires the collecting and monitoring of accurate information about them, and the drawing up of regular plans to set out objectives and targets, and ensure the resources are made available. Or is planning more concerned with budget, not needs led services? That is, are local authorities trying to devise imaginative but nevertheless cost driven (often short term) solutions to long term problems? Whilst acknowledging the difference between individual planning and Children's Services Plans, which are concerned with local authority child care planning, it may well be that such plans could have an increasingly important contribution to make. The scope for joint policies and joint action, for example, across education and health, could make a significant contribution to the corporate parenting required for effective leaving care work.

For example, the London Borough of Wandsworth's Children's Plan 1994–97 contains a specific section on what it describes as 'preparation for independent living and aftercare', describing the joint service agency agreement with its voluntary organisation partner, its targets, its housing plans, and its future plans. The council's 1996/7 targets (1996:38) are:

- to reduce the number of out of borough residential placements

- to further develop the educational profile of children looked after and establish new systems for communication between the social services department and Wandsworth schools

- to develop standards for health care and appropriate monitoring arrangements

- to complete the implementation of the Department's Looked After Children System for placement, review and monitoring of children looked after.

Yet it is also important to acknowledge that such plans, as with any other single approach, have limits as to their capacity to provide an inter-agency or corporate overview, an essential element of leaving care work. The Social Services Inspectorate's review of Children's Services Plans for 1993/4 commented on the following significant issues:

- there is a significant differentiation between the planning process and the published Children's Services Plan

- the complexity of inter-agency co-operation

- technical difficulties related to the measurement of need, implementation of policies, prioritisation of services, deployment of resources and the determination of costs

- the problem of inter-agency understanding and the need for a common vocabulary and terminology.

This point about inter-agency co-operation or lack of it is also picked up on by the Audit Commission report (1994:36) on co-ordinating child health and social services, here mentioned in connection with children in need or looked after:

> At present there is little common understanding, between health and social service authorities on how to interpret the criteria in the Children Act 1989 to suit local circumstances...where co-operation is mandatory or strongly recommended, however, as in child protection, greater progress has been made.

Again, to underline the complexities of planning, in what is a most succinct report Jones and Bilton (1994:56) conclude about the future shape of children's services:

> Commitment...is not enough on its own, without reasonably adequate resources... There can...be no real doubt that services for children are in general seriously under-resourced. In the face of this problem, the first duty at the local level is to ensure that the services of the different agencies are so co-ordinated as to deliver the optimum combined response from the separate budgets available.

The voice of users and the voluntary sector are usually absent from children's services planning. If some ways were devised for these views to be heard and incorporated then this would strengthen them and give them greater authority than can be the case for plans which do not involve full consultation.

Conclusions about service management

This chapter has highlighted a number of issues about the management and planning of leaving care services and the ways in which these impact on the services that the young people receive and local authority planning as a whole. Service agency agreements appear to offer greater flexibility of service definition, and draw in funding from voluntary organisations. They also provide an opportunity for voluntary organisations to contribute to local discussions, help to shape services, and allow a climate of tolerance, and possibly even mutual respect, to be developed in which positive criticisms of one by the other are accepted. On the other hand, cosy relationships can be developed through these partnerships, although this can also be said of contracting, which can be to the disadvantage of certain groups, for example small voluntary organisations and ethnic minority voluntary organisations, who can and do feel excluded. It is also the case that the move away from voluntary organisations being grant aided, where the favouritism factor was potentially even stronger, towards contracts or partnerships costs voluntary organisations more time and money in terms of producing more paper, a point made time and time again by Gutch (1994), drawing on his considerable experience. However, it is difficult to see what the alternatives might be with local authorities not being sole providers of services.

In terms of representativeness and greater user involvement Stone (1990:90–92) makes the point that local authorities and voluntary organisations which are unrepresentative (in terms of race, gender and class) are not well placed to encourage clients to take a more active role in terms of users involvement in service or organisational development. There are also other management questions which Stone, and others, have addressed about the possible freeing up of funding from the closure, streamlining or contracting out of residential child care services. In terms of child care and leaving care planning there are still unsatisfactory monitoring systems, and without proper monitoring it is difficult to see how proper service planning can take place. The issue of corporate planning, across housing, education and health, as well as social services, remains firmly on the 'backburner', although the Children's Services Plans could well take matters forward. It seems to be the case, then, that there has been reasonable progress in the management of leaving care services. Already a lot has been learnt about service agency agreements and standard setting, and in many ways leaving care teams can be described as being at the forefront of management developments, especially those concerning purchaser/provider developments.

PART THREE

Implications for the Future

CHAPTER THIRTEEN

Concluding Comments
Ways of Moving Forward

'A leaving care grant and a tenancy in a hard to let property isn't the answer!'
(The words of a project worker in a leaving care team)

Introduction

In this last chapter it is important to draw together some of the findings and themes from earlier in the book, and look at what more can and should be done to help young people leaving care in the future, taking into account the fact that a new government, a Labour government, was elected in May 1997. This drawing together of material will be done in a variety of ways.

After summarising the key research findings from the study, there will be a presentation and analysis of the suggestions made by the leaving care teams in the study about how to improve matters. Next there is a more reflective theoretical section presenting three different models of leaving care work entitled social welfare, social justice and technical assistance models of leaving care. Then there is a presentation of practitioners concerns, and the ways in which these could be addressed. This is followed by a provisional analysis of the ways in which the government's social policy proposals, if fully and effectively implemented, might help to ameliorate some of the problems facing young people leaving care. This is followed, finally, by concluding comments.

First it is necessary to summarise the research's main findings.

Research findings: summary

The purpose of the book was to record local and national developments in work with young people leaving care, identify campaigning and professional developments, and record the ways in which practice and policy and management have developed since the Children Act 1989 was introduced in 1991.

The survey recorded the work of 46 leaving care projects working with 3308 young people, the vast majority of whom were in the process of leaving care. There was evidence to show that these teams were decreasing in size but had increasing caseloads, of 16 per cent between 1995 and 1996. There was evidence of an over-representation of black young people (14%) in the sample, and for all the young people, very high levels of unemployment, very low levels of training income, and a staggering 83 per cent or 88 per cent (depending how the figures are calculated) of the group being dependent on state support of one type or another. In terms of housing it was found that the four most common accommodation types were local authority tenancies, shared/transitional accommodation, housing association tenancy, and 'other' housing (including hostels/council accommodation). 'Obtaining housing' was an area where there had been most achievements, as well as most problems, for the period 1994–1996. These housing achievements are remarkable in the 'cut-back climate' in which the leaving care teams operate. In terms of education it was found that 508 or 19 per cent of the sample were attending further and higher education, and that the very low levels of (largely discretionary) financial supports from local authorities were further reducing or becoming less available. Students also need encouragement and support to stay in the system, having gone to the trouble to obtain a place. There was some evidence from other research concerning in-care groups to suggest that living in independent accommodation was likely to make it more difficult for a young person to go onto and/or stay in further and higher education than being in foster care.

So far as local authority policies and procedures are concerned, 76 per cent of the local authorities surveyed (n=46) stated they had leaving care policies (i.e. 24% still do not have one in place). Where there are policies in place they tend to be very comprehensive, and provide a good guide for practitioners and young people alike. It is not known the extent to which young people contribute to those policies. Where there seems to be a problem with these policies is simply not knowing whether they work because, an associated point, the monitoring of leaving care work is totally *ad hoc*. The teams found that there were many more disadvantages than advantages to working in a purchaser/provider framework. There was considerable unease expressed by the majority of projects, whether local authority or voluntary organisation or jointly funded, about the ways in which purchaser/provider developments operated. Their main advantage was that they clarified the task, but this usually meant limiting the task, which, whilst a relief to over worked staff, meant that the young people received a less comprehensive service, if they received one at all. This was especially the case for young people, the 'returners' as they were described by one project, returning to projects for more help, who were squeezed out by ever restrictive specifications. It must also be acknowledged that the squeeze on services and costs was by no means limited to those working to contracts, but was equally the case for those working in partnerships using service agency agreements. There is progress in joint policies between housing and social services about definitions of 'in need', in 24 or 59 per cent of the authorities surveyed. This should aid planning, and is of sufficient importance to warrant further development work, perhaps by First Key, about its practical implications. Having made that positive observation, the finding that only 36 per cent of authorities always regard a young person leaving care as 'in need', and therefore accessing services through that route if leaving care services are not being provided, is a low figure, albeit one which comes from a nil starting base.

In respect of participation by young people in services, there appears to be continuing progress in this area, in terms of consultation, but less so in terms of the more intractable areas of service planning (which may be expecting too much too soon). There were a remarkable number of achievements by leaving care projects during the survey's two year period. It is worth reminding ourselves that the main achievements were in the areas of housing, improved service, staff training, young peoples' participation, project publicity, and from a poor position in 1993/4, local authority planning of services. Conversely, the biggest problems were in the areas of local authority planning of services, housing and resources, and staffing. Issues of anti-discrimination were often, but not always, addressed in local authority policies in terms of listing groups for whom services should be sensitively provided. The ways in which the teams answered the question about anti-discriminatory work suggested that the vast majority took on this task, and provided many examples of this work (n=151). This included the provision of written material, recruitment and selection procedures, an HIV/AIDS policy, and a variety of support groups or anti-racist local forums. In terms of financial support to young people leaving care the position is bad and getting worse, whether one is discussing welfare benefits, employment levels, housing benefit (if it still exists at the point this book is published), financial support for students, or youth training finances. The picture is bleak, bleak, bleak, and it affects some 2402 young people in the 44 authorities surveyed, which will multiply up to many thousands nationally each year those in desperate financial need. Further comments are made about this later in this chapter because this is a matter of considerable importance and urgency.

In terms of service monitoring the picture was most unclear and inconsistent. Generally, there is no shortage of ways in which leaving care work can be researched and evaluated, and performance indicators and targets are also in general abundance. User surveys and action research have a strong contribution to make as well. Yet there was little, if any, indication of post leaving care monitoring, to inform local authorities of the numbers and whereabouts of the young people. In connection with the management of leaving care services, findings pointed to the disadvantages, rather than advantages of contracts and partnership arrangements. Questions were raised about the way in which contracts are used to drive down costs whilst pretending, simultaneously, to maintain service levels. From the responses there was some indication that leaving care service agency agreements were increasingly specifying standards and not tasks, albeit sometimes in a quite crude way, to shape and guide policies and practice. The question of child care and leaving care planning is one that remains an outstanding question at this stage, in the absence of information about how such planning may take place.

In considering the key question that flows from these findings, namely, 'What is needed to further improve matters?', this will first be done from the projects' perspective, the answers being subdivided into categories.

Ways forward: suggestions from the leaving care projects

The leaving care projects were invited to make suggestions about how matters could be improved, building on the good practice that already exists, in many areas. These are listed in full below and categorised under either campaigning or political or practical or policy/professional headings.

Campaigning

- there should be a national campaigning group
- there should be a national lobbying body
- they should promote a more positive public image of young people leaving care.

Political

- to develop a political will to properly resource the Children Act 1989 for leaving care
- to encourage politicians to positively promote young people
- changes needed to government legislation which is penalising young people
- to amend the relevant powers contained in the Children Act 1989 to duties
- to amend the changes to housing benefit
- to narrow the gap between those young people without work and those with work, otherwise the two groups remain separate from each other, and reinforce each separate group's identity.

Practical

- find better ways of encouraging young people to stay in education
- find better ways of assessing young people's needs

- find more ways of recording achievements
- develop a systematic approach to young people's education
- more funding for housing required
- the right to a specified leaving care grant
- 'more funding to stop our project closing' (the project concerned closed in 1996).

Policy/Professional

- to use children's plans as a mechanism for change/improvements
- a more positive image of workers in voluntary organisations by statutory workers needs to be developed
- there needs to be developed specialist services for young people leaving care who have disabilities or who are young parents or who have mild learning difficulties
- whether projects participate in child protection work with the emergence of child protection issues/resources (i.e. family centres) for projects working with young parents
- something needs to be done about varying standards across different geographical areas
- something needs to be done about varying standards within the same area, as a result of devolved budgets to areas
- no more organisational restructuring by local authorities
- there remain outstanding questions about those young people who go into custody or psychiatric hospital care
- when services are tendered they should be done so honestly and openly
- further improve the monitoring systems of 16- to 21-year-olds leaving care
- there is a need to find ways of surmounting the problem of 17-year-olds slipping between children's and adult services in the new purchaser/provider world.

It is most important to note that the teams that do the face to face work recommend this four pronged approach to improve things in the political, professional, policy/practice, and campaigning arenas. The projects' views reveal a compassion for the young people, a frustration at the policy/political levels, and genuine concerns about how improvements to practice could or should be achieved. They also reveal something about the terms in which the problems can be solved. They are concerned that the principles of social justice be applied to the many, to counter injustice and inequality, and the language of legal rights and entitlements. They are also concerned, especially in the professional liaison and professional conduct sphere, with making improvements to social welfare systems, to improve the lives of individuals. They are further concerned with technical competence issues, namely improving skills to perform in the workplace and the world of independence. It is now time to examine these social justice and social welfare and technical assistance models of service provision and their terms of reference, and these are initially presented in Figure 13.1. This will be followed by a list and discussion of recommendations which embrace all three models.

Social justice, social welfare and technical assistance models of leaving care

Table 13.1 presents the key elements of the social justice and social welfare and technical assistance models of leaving care work. These elements offer contrasting representations of the relationship between the individual – that is, young people leaving care – and the state, and the subsequent rights and responsibilities that follow.

Social justice is concerned with concepts about the nature and place of 'just principles' in society as it applies to 'the division of benefits and the allocation of burdens' (Harvey, 1973:97). The allocation of burdens can consider conflicts over the locus of power and decision making, the distribution of influence, and the bestowal of social status. Disadvantage defined in structural deficiency terms provides the necessary framework to facilitate progressive (i.e. redistributive and participative) policies, interactions and practices, and not regressive (i.e. non-distributive and elitist) ones. Progressive legal rights, by which is meant watertight legal entitlements, are also included within this model, although enhancement of 'legal rights' alone would be insufficient to improve practice. The social justice model assumes that hardship and difficulties are experienced through no fault of one's own (i.e. the opposite of the 'blame the victim' or pathological view). In this model attempts to begin to resolve problems arise from collective effort. Here, this would be campaigning and lobbying, designed to empower the young people. The importance of linking up different groups, strength through collective action and education, as exemplified by the National Association of Young People In Care (NAYPIC), is another key element of the social justice model. Collective action needs to be undertaken purposefully but sensitively in this model; otherwise, ideas can be discounted and ignored. The term empowerment is used here to describe ways in which the 'disadvantaged and disenfranchised' would seek greater access to decision making, influence, and, ultimately, economic and political power. Thomas's (1983:126) methods of community work are relevant in this context:

Table 13.1 Characteristics of social justice, social welfare and technical assistance models of leaving care work

Contextual themes	Social justice	Social welfare	Technical assistance
Guiding perception of the young people	disadvantaged survivors/victims	clients in need of care	consumers
Dominant nature of problem	poverty, abuse by the systems	unsatisfactory relationships, responses by others, and services	needing work/ unemployed
Expression of the problem	oppressed	individuals in need	training
Goal	empowerment	improvement	independence
Main purpose of response	strengthening of collective legal rights	individual help/ strengthening of social rights regarding services	employability
Nature of relationship between the state and the young person	a strong universal partnership between the state, its institutions and the family	individually negotiated partnership between state and other insitutions, including the family and carers	trainee/ trainer
Methods of intervention	campaigning/ lobbying/ legal challenges	social care self-help	Workfare
Focus	legal and social policy changes	improved professional help and assistance	competencies/ skills
Anti- discriminatory focus	respond to individuals needs and recognise structural origins and solutions	individual and sensitive delivery of anti- discriminatory practice	employer incentives
Collective interventions	social action and social education, lobbying/ advocacy	counselling/ advocacy, social action/research	work experience

- encouragement of the collectivisation of problems, and of attempts to tackle them
- a partnership approach to working with people
- putting emphasis on the structural, not personal aspects of the problems
- putting expressed or felt needs above professional or bureaucratic definitions of need
- an equal emphasis on the pursuit of process goals (promoting political organisation and skill development) as on task goals (resource redistribution).

There are of course limits to this approach, whether applied to community work (Marris and Rein, 1972) or to work with individuals. There is the additional criticism that this social justice model is not relevant to young people leaving care because their problems are at least as much of a personal and emotional nature, therefore requiring professional help, as much as they are concerned with poor or non-existent policies. Interventions with young people leaving care will not succeed if their problems are *only* regarded as being of a material nature. Yet, likewise, can it be the case that a social welfare approach *alone*, emphasising individual professional help, can resolve all their problems?

In the *social welfare* model the emphasis is on the provision of a personal service delivered to people hitherto referred to as clients (Marshall, 1965), but whom we now call users, or here simply young people. In the social welfare model the emphasis is on seeking to resolve problematic behaviours and relationships, usually on an individual or groupwork basis. The remedy to individualised problems is individualised solutions, relationships, and services, delivered in a sensitive, appropriate, and anti-discriminatory manner by trained and committed staff who have the time to listen and act. The involvement of other young people in supporting young people leaving care complements the professional approach. The instruments of standards and inspections, and not resources, will be appropriate to this model. In this model, in the purist sense, the connections would not be made about the overall situation of young people in need, but be based on individual concerns and responded to accordingly. In the tough climate in which social welfare operates, not everyone will receive a service or even be seen. It will also likely be the case that needs will be prioritised according to assumptions about the deserving and non-deserving. Unpalatable though this distinction might seem, in the new social welfare climate in which leaving care work takes place, it is probably already the case that such judgements, presented as priorities, take place daily.

Social action, as applied to leaving care work, is a term which emphasises collective action, and the identification of issues and action by young people. This is an approach which the Lifechance project in Oxford employs with the young people with whom it works (Lifechance, 1996). More generally Mullender and Ward (1991) have produced a fully developed model of empowering practice through groupwork which has social action as its leitmotif. The essence of this work is that users are first encouraged in groupwork to confront oppression by confronting power, and that users engage in actions to promote change. Amongst many, the work of the Derbyshire Coalition of Disabled People is described and the way it fought against ingrained paternalism within the authority, and eventually acquired resources, including financial resources, for them to use and run their own facilities (Mullender and Ward, 1991:124). Advocacy work is work which is done by someone else with and on behalf of young people, for example, in order to access resources, or assist a young person in dealing with a complaints system. The fact that advocacy can be concerned with clarifying and possibly accessing legal entitlements, or services, accounts for it being in both the social justice and social welfare models. Also in some service evaluations of work with young people (see, for example, Fleming, 1996), the manner in which services are delivered is most highly valued by young people, as well as the breadth of 'needs and crisis' services delivered.

In the *technical assistance* model the young person leaving care is primarily expected to behave as a consumer whose needs are primarily of a technical/skills based nature. S/he is not recognised as having distinct emotional needs which require expert, peer or professional help or support. In this model the young person is expected to function in a 'market place'. Therefore the young person needs to work to survive, and the technical nature of the model results in expectations being placed on young people to obtain training, and become independent through improved employability. There is a firm emphasis on the individual's need to become competent, through skills acquisition, in order to compete and perform. It is assumed that with the 'right skills' and competencies the young person will obtain and access training, through training credit schemes for example, and gain employment at some point. 'Workfare' based on assumptions about the poor being required to earn their benefits is ultimately regarded as the necessary method of intervention, if a job is not forthcoming. There is no sense of there being any form of collective rights or action but rather individual obligations. The technical language of competencies and credits, and assumptions about everyone having the same starting point, is central to this model of leaving care work. It is the treatment of young people leaving care as the same as everyone else, simply as another consumers without any additional needs, which characterises this model.

In the light of these characteristics a summary of recommendations building on respondents' views is presented about future leaving care work, as they arose from the research. A large proportion of them are located within the social justice and social welfare models, and only a few can be placed within the technical assistance model of leaving care, one with which young people leaving care are increasingly presented when the supports fall away.

What is needed to improve matters? Recommendations from the research

Table 13.2 A summary of respondents' concerns and changes required

Concerns arising	Type of changes required to improve matters from the research
Basic Assumptions	
Theoretical	re-educate, so that the aim is not to get the young person to become independent at as early an age as possible but instead to see interdependence as the goal, at a time of mutual agreement
Social Policy Issues	
Education	more funding/support/inter-agency planning required
Social security	funding for 16–17 year olds+; higher rates necessary
Accomodation	more appropriate/affordable accomodation/funding for rents
Equal opportunities	offer appropriate support, being sensitive to the needs of ethnic minority, gay and lesbian, and disabled young people, and young parents, and those with learning difficulties
Youth training	higher quality or scrap/ it is probably beyond help/ guarantees to be kept about provision of places/ better funded/ more choice
Employment	a strategy for providing quality management/ work opportunites
Legislation/ implementation/ funding	voice the view that for leaving care work the Children Act 1989 is totally inadequate and and has taken us little further than legislation passed in 1980 and is urgent need of review. Strengthen the relevant sections of the Children Act 1989, especially the powers to become duties, and make ring-fenced funding available

Table 13.2 A summary of respondents' concerns and changes required (continued)

Concerns arising	Type of changes required to improve matters from the research
Policy/Procedures	
Political	continue with campaigning
Support for young people	support, not simply being given a flat, but support itself to be better funded, especially in accomodation and generally
Professional	these are concerned with having a more flexible approach to when young people physically leave care plus an 'open door approach' to young people returning if/when they need to/ better preparation required/ more continuity of carers throughout and when leaving care
Service monitoring	another matter of urgency: build on existing local initiatives but with young people involved as inspectors (as with residential care) and results to be made public
Child care planning	build on existing initiatives (e.g DoH assesment and action records)
Child care planning for children in need and homeless	given the creeping increased demand on leaving care services as well; other ways should be found to help those groups or leaving care teams obtain more resources
Prevention/child care service planning	for local authorities to review the reasons why children/ young people are taken into planning and undertake a cost-benefit analysis of other approaches. The review to involve other young people

Political change and leaving care

After 18 years of conservative administrations a Labour government was elected in May 1997 with an astounding majority of 179 seats in the House of Commons. Whilst fully acknowledging that the solutions for all the problems facing young people leaving care are not only political, but professional and practical, nevertheless a key question remains, namely what, if any, difference might the Labour government make to this group of young people? Although no-one knows for certain what might happen at the time of writing (late 1997), a review of the new government's pre-election manifesto, and its first Queen's speech outlining its first legislative programme, provides some initial, albeit imprecise, pointers to change. The following is a list of relevant policy issues, mostly aimed at tackling employment, training and education (Labour Party Manifesto, 1997):

- to get 250,000 under-25-year-olds off benefit and into work (using money from a windfall levy on the privatised utilities)

- every unemployed young person for more than six months in a job or training (four options available)

- every 16- and 17-year-old 'on the road to a proper qualification by the year 2000'. All young people will be offered part-time or full-time employment after the age of 16

- any under-18-year-old in a job will have the right to study on an approved course for qualifications at college.

- failed Youth Training to be replaced with Target 2000 programme

- tax rebates of £75 a week to employers to encourage employing people who are long-term unemployed

- Labour's national childcare strategy will plan provision and help parents to balance family and working life

- government must assist families to achieve collectively what no family can achieve alone

- a review of educational finance and maintenance for those older than 16 to ensure higher staying on rates at school and college and that resources are used to help those in most need

- support comprehensive enforceable civil rights for disabled people

- place a new duty on local authorities to protect those who are homeless through no fault of their own and are in priority need.

The 1997 Labour government then is proposing policies which, if fully followed, would have a positive impact on young people leaving care, for whom the vast majority the issues of employment, education, accommodation and training continue to be the most pressing. This is encouraging. It is also encouraging to those who advocate effective children's rights that the previous administration, which had promised a review of the Children Act 1989 with a view to moving towards increased family responsibilities and a further lessening of children's rights, was not re-elected in 1997. Nevertheless it is a matter of some concern that there is nothing in the Labour party manifesto, or other Labour party documents so far as is known, about specific plans for children in care, or about children leaving care. None of the 22 bills outlined in the May 1997 Queen's speech to parliament, laying out the government's legislative plans up to the year 2000, concerned social services, but the above welfare reforms were clearly signalled. It is possible, likely even, that if there are any changes to be introduced affecting social services and children in and leaving care, these will not be immediate. If this assessment is correct, then yet again those involved in improving the situation of young people leaving care will need to lobby hard, both professionally and politically, for matters to improve substantially. The expectations on the Labour government elected in 1997 are very high, probably unrealistically so, to deliver a wealth of welfare reforms. The earlier that interested parties, principally the Association of Directors of Social Services, the British Association of Social Workers, First Key, the merged Association of Metropolitan and Local Authorities, the National Foster Care Association, other key voluntary organisations, young people and interested academics begin lobbying, the more likely that positive changes might take place. As we have seen there is a wide range of ways for improving practice and extending the entitlements to care leavers without authorities necessarily incurring additional costs. Perhaps the safest political view to adopt is to assume that only by careful and constant lobbying and campaigning will the issue of young people leaving care, in terms as defined by the young people themselves, and those sharing their concerns, be placed on the political and professional agenda.

Concluding comments

The majority of young people leaving care have multiple and considerable needs which are usually of an immediate emotional, financial, personal and professional nature. It has also been shown here that young people's basic needs would be greatly reduced if additional funding was made available, and restored and increased, across a range of social policy areas. Yet it is also the case that the direction of governments since the early 1980s, and at least up to 1998, has been towards reducing, not increasing, public expenditure. This has applied in particular to young people aiming, or having, to be independent of their parents. The assumptions made by governments about this group of 16–18-year-olds have been that they are and should be the financial responsibility of their parents, and not the state. In the absence of additional funding being made available, one is left with the following choices:

- to accept this is the case and not make any further recommendations which involve any more funding (such an approach could be seen as 'realistic' but would be to ignore and condone poverty)

- not to accept this is the case and to keep questioning it and campaigning against it (this could be seen as 'unrealistic' and may not lead to improvements anyway)

- to define the complex issues as ones which can simply be resolved in terms of more social welfare type of support and advice, and, therefore, ignore social justice issues (this could also be seen to be 'realistic' by locating the problems and the solutions at the individual welfare level).

Perhaps the guiding light is and should be to record the views of practitioners, as has been done here, and elsewhere, as well as users – that is, the young people themselves (see, for example, Save the Children Fund, 1995), and report on them accordingly. Yet these views seem always to involve calls for more resources.

At another level, the professional level, Moseley, Director of Hackney social services (1994), has stated in respect of the state as parent and leaving care work: 'I do not believe the state can become an adequate parent, however well intentioned and however much resources we put into it' (in Henson, 1994:54). She is talking about caring and helping, as well as simply providing financial resources. If she is right, as seems reasonable, to expect that a state institution cannot act, ever, as an adequate parent (like a 'real parent' might claim to be) then this is a statement with staggering consequences for young people leaving care. One way of responding is to accept that this tends to be the case – a sort of 'make do/struggle on regardless' approach with the likely consequence of this inadequate parenting producing inadequate offspring, to be then taken into care for 'not coping'! Another response is to understand, but not accept, that this is the case. It then becomes necessary to assist that failing inadequate parent, to become an emotionally responsive, financially sound, coping, nurturing and sustaining parent.

This links to yet another approach to the problem, often seen as the radical one: prevention, by which the government supports the family *in situ* much more, and pre-crisis and family breakdown. This requires fundamental changes by social services in responding to children and families. It also requires families in need, families who are not coping, being confident to ask for help, a most difficult thing to do in itself, with the knowledge that someone from social services or a voluntary organisation will respond helpfully and appropriately. Crucially, such an approach requires social services to assess the family concerned as needing help, perhaps from other agencies, and not immediately tend to regard that family as either requiring 'full blown' child investigation procedures, or assessed as entitled to nothing. A different balance may need to be struck between these two critical preventive and policing functions. Offering a quality, non-stigmatising, anti-discriminatory approach which celebrates family diversity, and delivers planned skilled services, in partnership with families, is likely to prove the greatest challenge to many social services departments and voluntary organisations. Yet such a shift, for example, by preventing crisis admissions of teenagers into care, by working with, at an earlier stage, the families concerned, is crucial. It would also complement and drive a broader strategy of reducing the numbers of children being received into care. If this scenario were to evolve, and the balance changed between preventive and policing functions, then within five to ten years there could be significantly less young people being taken into, and leaving, care. This would leave specialist leaving care services to work with smaller numbers of young people, probably the more troubled and troublesome young people. This would be preferable to what teams are actually facing, namely carrying an even greater responsibility for working with all manner of young people, who are variously homeless, needy, unemployed, 'in need', leaving care, and any others who are referred to them.

Next, if the ethos of customer care has truly arrived with concomitant shifts – from procedures to outcomes, from provider to consumer orientation, from quantity to quality, from uniformity to diversity, and from hierarchy to personal responsibility – then this research did not find it applying, either at all, or where it did exist, superficially and unevenly across authorities. There were notable exceptions and many individual working relationships were highly valued.

Overall, the research findings here indicate that the availability and quality of services to young people leaving care remains a lottery in terms of entitlements from the state, and local authority policies and implementation. Leaving care work still remains unsafe in the hands of the Children Act 1989. To pretend otherwise, that additional funds and duties are not required, and that the introduction of more standards and inspections is a good enough response, flies in the face of the views of the 46 projects participating in this research and the situation of the 3308 young people leaving care attending those projects. At the rate of an estimated 8000 young people aged 16 and 17 leaving care each year, since the Children Act 1989 was introduced, and as of 1998, an estimated 56,000 of these young people have attempted to fend for themselves, most probably in a state of near poverty and poor prospects for the future, after being placed in and then leaving, public care. A review of the legislation and child care planning, with a move towards more supportive preventive family work, is more vital now than ever. More support for foster carers, and extended family members who support children and young people is also vital. As was shown earlier, the powers concerning local authorities and the education of young people leaving care have remained the same, and possibly even weakened, since as long ago as the Children Act of <u>1948</u>. We should not need to wait a year longer, or another fifty years, or indeed for some dreadful personal and family tragedy to occur concerning a young person leaving care, before we act. We must act now. To do otherwise will be to condemn the future of young people who leave care to the vagaries of the market, and the streets of despair, and prey to those who seek to abuse vulnerable children and young people living in unprotected circumstances. The many examples of good practice and policies presented here provide a valuable platform for further developments, commitments and investments. The vogue of promoting good practice and standards alone, without a wider review of family and youth support work in addition to leaving care work, is a bland, inadequate, and irresponsible response to the continuing, immense and complex problems facing young people leaving care.

References

Abrahams, C. and Mungall, R. (1989) *Housing Vulnerable Homeless People*, London: NCH

Action on Aftercare Consortium (1996) *Too Much Too Young: The Failure of Social Policy in Meeting the Needs of Care Leavers*. London: Barnardo's.

Advisory Centre for Education (1989) *ACE Guide to the Education Reform Act 1988*. London: ACE.

Aldgate, J., Heath, A., Colton, M. and Simm, M. (1993) 'Social work and the education of children in foster care.' *Adoption and Fostering,* 17 (3) 25–34

Association of Directors of Social Services (1997) *The Foster Carer Market: A National Perspective*. Bury St Edmunds: Communique.

Association of Metropolitan Authorities (1995) *Checklist for Children: Local Authorities and the UN Convention on the Rights of the Child*. London: AMA.

Audit Commission (1994) *Seen but Not Heard: Co-ordinating Community Child Health and Social Services for Children in Need*. London: HMSO.

Banks, M. *et al.,* (1993) *Careers and Identities*. Buckingham: Open University Press.

Barn, R. (1990) *Black Children in the Public Care System*. London: Batsford.

Bebbington, A. and Miles, J. (1989) 'The background of children who entered local authority care.' *British Journal of Social Work 19,* 5, 349–68.

Berridge, D. and Brodie, I. (1997) 'An "exclusive education".' *Inside Community Care,* 1156, 4–5. Sutton: Community Care.

Biehal, N., Clayden, J., Stein, M. and Wade, J. (1992) *Prepared for Living? A Survey Of Young People Leaving Care Of Three Local Authorities*. London: NCB

Biehal, N., Clayden, J., Stein, M. and Wade, J. (1995) *Moving On*. London: HMSO.

Bonnerjea, L. (1990) *Leaving Care in London*. London: London Borough's Children's Regional Planning Committee.

British Youth Council, (1996) *Never Had It So Good? The Truth About Being Young In 1990s Britain*, London: BYC

Broad, B. (1991) *Punishment under Pressure: The Probation Service in the Inner City*. London: Jessica Kingsley Publishers.

Broad, B. (ed) (1993) 'Medway and Swale aftercare project: an action research project: preliminary findings.' (unpublished) Kent: Royal Philanthropic Society.

Broad, B. (1994a) 'Aftercare work in the 1990s.' In A. Henson (ed) *op.cit.,* 7–15.

Broad, B (1994b) 'Anti-discriminatory practitioner social work research: some basic problems and possible remedies.' In B. Humphries and C. Truman (eds) *Re-thinking Social Research*. Hampshire: Avebury, 164–184.

Broad. B. (1994c) 'On behalf of the After Care Consortium.' *Leaving Care in the 1990s*. Kent: Royal Philanthropic Society.

Broad, B. and Fletcher, C. (eds) (1993) *Practitioner Social Work Research in Action*. London: Whiting and Birch.

Broad, B. and Denney, D. (1996) 'Users' rights and the probation service: some opportunities and obstacles.' *Howard Journal of Criminal Justice 35*, 1, 61–77.

Broad, B. (1997a) 'Lessons for life.' *Community Care*, (1158), 32–3. Sutton: Community Care.

Broad, B. (1997b) 'The inadequate child care legislation governing work with young people leaving care. A research based view.' Childright, September (1939), 17

Buchanan, A., Wheal, A. *et al.*, (1993) *Answering Back. Report by Young People Being Looked After on the Children Act 1989.* Southampton: University of Southampton.

CAHAG (Children Act Housing Action Group) (1994) Interpretations of the Children Act 1989 by the CAHAG Lawyers Group. London: CHAR.

Cardiff Young Homeless Project (1993), *Annual Report 1993*, Cardiff: CYHP

Central Statistical Office (1995/6) Working Brief, December 1995 and January 1996. London: Central Statistical Office.

Centrepoint (1997) *The Jobseekers Allowance*, London: Centrepoint.

CHAR (1995) *Planning for Action: the Children Act 1989 and Young Homeless People – A Black Perspective.* London: CHAR.

CHAR (1996) *Inquiry into Preventing Youth Homelessness.* London: CHAR.

Childright (1996) *Social Services Inspectorate Standards For Leaving Care Work* (123) 14–15.

Coalition on Young People and Social Security (1995) *Taking Their Chances: Education, Training, and Employment Opportunities for Young People.* London: The Children's Society.

Coleman, J. and Warren-Adamson (eds) (1992) *Youth Policy in the 1990s: The Way Forward.* London: Routledge.

Colton, M., Drury, C. and Williams, M. (1995) 'Children in need: definition, identification and support.' *British Journal of Social Work 25*, 711–28.

Commission for Racial Equality (1995) *Young and Equal.* London: CRE.

Community Care (1992) 'Care Leavers' Charter highlights deficiencies,' 3 December. Sutton: Community Care.

Community Care (1993) Article in *Community Care* about Welsh Social Services Inspectorate Inspection of leaving care work in Wales, 5 August, 1993. London: Reed Publishing

Community Care (1995) *Leaving Care Checklist.* London: Reed Publishing.

Community Care (1996) ' House hunting.' *Community Care*, 9–15 May. Sutton: Community Care.

Craig, G. (1991) *Fit For Nothing: Young People, Benefits and Youth Training.* London: COYPSS.

CRDU (1994) *Children's Rights Development Unit Report.* London: CRDU

Croft, S. and Beresford, P. (1993) *Getting Involved – A Practical Manual.* London: Open Services Project.

Darke, J., Conway, J., Holman, C. and Buckley, K. (1994) *Homes for Our Children.* London: National Housing Forum.

Dartington Social Research Unit (1995) 'Matching needs and services, the audit and planning of provision for children looked after by local authorities.' Prepared by Dartington Social Research Unit in conjunction with the Support Force for Children's Residential Care. Devon: Dartington Social Research Unit.

Department for Education (1994) *Code of Practice on the Identification and Assessment of Special Educational Needs.* London: HMSO.

Department for Education (1994a) *Education of Children Being Looked After By Local Authorities.* Circular 13/94. London: DFE.

Department of Employment (1993) *Employment Gazette, March 1993.* London: Department of Employment.

Department of Health and Social Security (1984) *Report of the House of Commons Social Services Committee (The Short Report).* London: HMSO.

Department of Health and Social Secutiry (1985) *Reviews of Child Care Law.* London: HMSO.

Department of Health and Social Security (1987) *The Law on Child Care and Family Services.* London: HMSO.

Department of Social Security (1996) *The Housing Benefit (general) Amendment Regulations.* London: DSS.

Digby, A. (1989) *British Welfare Policy.* London: Faber and Faber.

DoE (1991) *Homelessness Code of Guidance for Local Authorities (Housing Authorities).* London: HMSO.

DoE (1996) *Housing benefit draft circular: Housing Benefit/CTB AX95.* London: DoE.

DoH (1993) *Children Act 1989,* cm 2144. London: HMSO.

DoH (1991) *The Children Act 1989, Guidance and Regulations.* Volume 4. Residential Care. London: HMSO

DoH (1991a) *Planning for Children and Young People; a Framework for Planning.* London: Social Services Inspectorate.

DoH (1991b) *Patterns and Outcomes in Child Placement.* London: HMSO.

DoH (1991c) *The Children Act: Guidance and Regulations.* London: HMSO.

DoH (1994a) *Children Act Report 1993,* cm2584. London: HMSO.

DoH (1994b) *Raising the Standard, Social Services Inspectorate.* London: DoH.

DoH (1995a) *Children Act Report 1994,* cm 2878. London: HMSO.

DoH (1995b) 'Children looked after by Local Authorities.' 14 October 1991 to 31 March 1993'. London: Department of Health.

DoH (1996a) *Focus on Teenagers.* London: HMSO.

DoH (1996b) 'Children Looked After by Local Authorities': year ending 31 March 1995, England, bulletin 1996/8. London: Government Statistical Service.

Doogan, K. (1988) 'Falling off the treadmill – the causes of youth homelessness.' In G. Bramley *et al.* (eds) *Homelessness and the London Housing Market,* Occasional Paper No. 32, School for Advanced Urban Studies, Bristol: University of Bristol.

Dudley Metropolitan Borough Council (1994) *Service Level Agreement Leaving Care Services.* Metropolitan Borough of Dudley: SSD.

East Midlands Leaving Care Forum (1995) 'Funding and support in further and higher education for young people leaving care, policy and procedures.' Northampton.

Education Guardian (1996a) 'Homelessness.' *The Guardian,* 5 March.

Education Guardian (1996b) 'Purchasing sixth form education: the new big idea.' *The Guardian,* 4 June.

Employment Department (1994) *Developing Good Practice Effective Training Delivery Youth Credits: Learning from Experience.* London:

First Key (1987) *A Study of Black Young People Leaving Care.* Leeds: First Key

First Key (1992) *Survey Of Local Authority Provision For Young People Leaving Care*. Leeds: First Key

First Key (1994) *Practical Housing Solutions*. Leeds: First Key

First Key (1996a) *A National Voice*, mimeo. Leeds: First Key.

First Key (1996b) *Housing Act 1996 Briefing Paper*. Leeds: First Key.

First Key (1996c) 'Housing benefit changes.' *Keynotes*, 13. Leeds: First Key.

First Key (1996d) `Standards in leaving care', report of the national working group. Leeds: First Key.

Fleming, J. (1996) `Birmingham Young Homeless Support Project, Second Year Evaluation Report', De Montfort University. Leicester: Centre for Social Action.

Fletcher, C. (1974) *Beneath the Surface. An Account of Three Styles of Sociological Research*. London: Routledge and Kegan Paul.

Fry, E (1992) *After Care. Making the Most of Fostercare*. London National Foster Care Association

Garnett, L (1992) *Leaving Care And After*. London: NCB

Goldman, R. (1992) *Plans, No Action: The Children Act 1989 and Homeless Young People*. London: Housing Campaign for Single People (CHAR).

Gutch, R. (1993) 'A mission to survive.' *Community Care: Inside*, 28 January. Sutton: Community Care.

Hackney Social Services (1994) *Leaving Care Policy and After Care Policy*. London: Borough of Hackney.

Hampshire County Council (1993) *Listening to Children*. Southampton: Hampshire Social Services Department.

Hampshire County Council (1994) *Young People's Charter. A Users Guide*. Southampton: Hampshire Social Services Department.

Hansard (1992) `Training and Enterprise Councils', House of Lords debate, 9 February, 1255–6.

Hardman, P. (1994) `The contract culture and leaving care', in Henson, A. (ed.) *Improving Practice And Policy In Aftercare Work– A Report On The NCB/Aftercare Consortium Conference*, London, 29 November 1993, Leeds: First Key

Harris, N. (1992) `Youth Citizenship and Welfare.' *Journal of Social, Welfare and Family Law* (3) 87–103.

Harvey, D. (1973) *Social Justice and the City*. London: Edward Arnold.

Hendley, W. (1995) 'Closing address.' In A. Henson (ed) *op.cit.*, 55–9.

Henson, A. (ed) (1994) Improving practice and policy in aftercare work. A report on the NCB/Aftercare Consortium Conference, 29 November 1993. Leeds: First Key.

Henson, A. (ed) (1995) *Practical Housing Solutions for Young People Leaving Care*. Leeds: First Key.

Hill, M. and Aldgate, J. (eds) (1996) *Child Welfare Services*. London: Jessica Kingsley Publishers.

Hodgson, (1994) *Developing a Complaints Procedure for Voluntary Organisations*. London: NCVCCO.

Humberside County Council (1996) *Could do Better? The Educational Attainments and Career Destinations of Care Leavers*. Humberside: Humberside Social Services Department.

Humphreys, B. and Truman, C. (eds) (1994) *Re-thinking Social Research*. Aldershot: Avebury.

Hutson, S. and Liddiard, M. (1994) *Youth Homelessness: The Construction of a Social Issue*. Basingstoke: Macmillan.

Jackson, S. (1995) `Transforming lives: the crucial role of education for young people in the care system.' First Tory Lauchland Lecture. London: Royal Society of Arts.

Jones, A. and Bilton, K. (1994) *The Future Shape of Children's Services*. London: National Children's Bureau.

Jones, G. (1987) 'Leaving the parental home: an analysis of early housing careers.' *Journal of Social Policy 16*, 1, 49–74.

Jones, G. (1995) *Leaving Home*. Buckingham: Open University Press.

Kahan, B. (1994) *Growing Up in Groups*. London: HMSO.

Kay, H. (1994) *Conflicting Priorities*. London: CHAR and Chartered Institute of Housing.

Killeen, D. (1992) 'Housing and income–social policy on leaving home.' In J. Coleman and Warren-Adamson, *op.cit.*, 189–202.

Kirby, P. (1994) *A Word from the Street*. London: Centrepoint.

Kirk, D., Nelson S., Sinfield., A. and Sinfield, D. (1991) Excluding youth: poverty among young people living away from home, Edinburgh, Bridges project/University of University of Edinburgh

Kirk, N. (1996) 'Opportunity, choice and housing benefit: a system in conflict.' A briefing paper. London: CHAR.

Labour Party (1997) *A Manifesto for Britain*. London: Labour Party.

Leeds City Council (1996) *Educational Support Team*, (leaflet). Leeds: Leeds Social Services Department.

Leicester University (1992) *Children in Need and Their Families: Manual for Managers*. Leicester: University of Leicester.

Leicester County Council (1992) `Report to operations group from leaving care team', mimeo. Leicester: Social Services Department.

Lifechance Project (1996) *Annual Report 1995/96*. Oxford: Lifechance.

London Borough of Brent (1996a) *Aftercare Team Annual Report*. London: Brent Children's Resources Team.

London Borough of Brent (1996b) *Service Specification For The Provision Of Aftercare Services For Children/Young People*. London: Borough of Brent SSD.

London Borough of Hammersmith and Fulham (1995) *Leaving Care Policy*. London: Hammersmith and Fulham SSD.

London Borough of Sutton (1995) *Charter Mark Application Leaving Care Team*. London: Borough of Sutton Housing and Social Services Department.

London Borough of Sutton (1996) *Standards, Internal Review And Summary Of Performance*. London: Borough of Sutton.

London Borough of Wandsworth (1995) *The Quality Of Education Provided For Children Looked After By Wandsworth Council*. London: Wandsworth Education Department.

London Borough of Wandsworth (1996a) *Draft Children's Services Plan 1994–1997*. London: Borough of Wandsworth.

London Borough of Wandsworth (1996b) *London Borough Of Wandsworth's Children's Plan 1994–97*. London: Borough of Wandsworth.

Lupton, C. (1985) *Moving Out*. Portsmouth: University of Portsmouth.

Maclagan, I. (1992) *A Broken Promise*. London: Youthaid and the Children's Society.

MTS (1995) *The Manchester Teaching Service.* Manchester: Manchester City Council SSD.

Marris, P. and Rein, M. (1972) *Dilemmas of Social Reform,* 2nd edition. London: Routledge and Kegan Paul.

Marshall, T.H. (1965) *Social Policy.* London: Hutchinson.

McCluskey, J. (1993) *Reassessing Priorities. The Children Act 1989: A New Agenda for Young Homeless People?* London: CHAR.

McCluskey, J. (1994) *Acting in Isolation.* London: Housing Campaign for Single People (CHAR).

McParlin, P. (1996) `Education of children looked after– a series of publications', Leeds: First Key

Mills, D (1994) `A follow-up study of the housing situation of young people leaving care in one local authority', unpublished undergraduate study, London: Roehampton Institute

MORI (1991) `A survey of 16 and 17 year old severe hardship payments', research study conducted for the Department of Social Security, London HMSO

Morris, J. (1995) *Gone Missing? A Research and Policy Review of Disabled Children Living Away from their Families.* London: Who Cares? Trust.

Mullender, A. and Ward. D. (1991) *Self-directed Groupwork. Users take Action for Empowerment.* London: Whiting and Birch.

Murrey, N. (1993) 'Social Services Inspectorate attacks failure to aid care-leavers.' *Community Care,* 5 August. Surrey: Community Care.

National Association of Citizens Advice Bureau (NACAB) (1992) *Severe Hardship–CAB Evidence On Young People And Benefits.* London: NACAB

National Children's Bureau (1992), `Childfacts, 25 June'. London: NCB.

National Council for Voluntary Child Care Organisations (1991) *Race Equality Policies, Membership Briefing.* London: NCVCCO.

National Council for Voluntary Child Care Organisations (1995) *No Fault of their Own: The Plight of Homeless Children and Young People.* London: NCVCCO.

National Foster Care Association and Peabody Trust (1995) `My Place', information leaflet. London: NFCA.

National Foundation for Educational Research (1994) *Discretionary Award Provision in England and Wales.* London: Calouste Gulbenkian Foundation.

OPCS (1996) *Ethnicity In The 1991 Census.* London: Government Statistical Office.

Payne, J. (1995) 'Option at 16 and outcomes at 24: a comparison of academic, vocational, education and training routes.' Youth Cohort Report No. 35. London: Policy Studies Institute.

Payne, M. (1995) *Social Work and Community Care.* Basingstoke: Macmillan.

Pinkerton, J.R. and McCrea, R. (1993) 'Meeting the needs of young people leaving care in Northern Ireland: a leaving care population and leaving care schemes. Second Interim Report.' Belfast: Queens University.

Pople, K. (1993) 'From "special measures" to broken promises: the youth training schemes.' *Social Action 1,* 3, 8–12.

Rickford, F. (1993) 'Why the kids aren't all right.' *The Guardian,* 1 September.

Robertson, P. (1995) 'Introduction.' In A. Henson (ed) *op.cit.,* 4–5.

Roberts, K. (1993) 'Career trajectories and the mirage of social mobility.' In I. Bates and G. Riseborough (eds) *Youth and Inequality.* Buckingham: Oxford University Press.

Roberts, N. (1991) *Leaving Care Policies And The Children Act 1989.* Leeds: First Key.

Roberts, N. (ed) (1993) 'The Children Act 1989: Aftercare One Year On.' A report on the aftercare consortium conference. London, 14 October 1992. Leeds: First Key.

Robertson, P. (1995) Introduction. in Henson, A. Ed., op cit 4–5

Rowe, J., Hundleby, M. and Garnett, L. (1989) *Child Care Now* BAAF Research series 6, London: BAAF

Royal Philanthropic Society (1994) *Mid Surrey Stepping Out Service Agency Agreement.* Kent: Royal Philanthropic Society.

Royal Philanthropic Society (1995) 'Annual Monitoring Report 1994–95,' mimeo. Kent: Royal Philanthropic Society.

Royal Philanthropic Society (1996) *Agreement between Wandsworth Borough Council and the Royal Philanthropic Society for the Provision of an Independent Living Scheme.* Kent: Royal Philanthropic Society.

Royal Philanthropic Society/Trust for the Study of Adolescence (1994) untitled conference speech at *Young People at Risk Conference,* also included in 4 separate publications about the education of children looked after, Leeds: First Key

Royal Philanthropic Society/Kent County Council (1996) *Agreement between the Social Services Department of Kent County Council and the Royal Philanthropic Society on Partnership, Standards and Protocols for Leaving Care Services.* Kent: Royal Philanthropic Society.

Saunders, L. and Broad, B. (1997) *The Health Needs Of Young People Leaving Care.* Leicester: Centre for Social Action, De Montfort University

Save the Children Fund (1995) *You're on Your Own: Young People's Research on Leaving Care.* London: Save the Children.

Scottish Young People's Survey quoted in Jones (1995)

Sinclair, R. (1996) 'Children's and young peoples participation in decision making: the legal framework in social services and education.' In M. Hill and J. Aldgate (eds) *op.cit.,* 90–104.

Sinclair, R. (1990) 'The role of local authority research in changing practice.' In D. Howe (ed) *Research and Changing Services for Children and Adults,* papers from the 6th joint SWEC conference. London: Whiting and Birch.

SITRA (1996) News, *SITRA Bulletin,* February 1996

Smith. C. (ed) (1994) *Partnership in Action. Developing Effective Aftercare Projects.* Brasted: Royal Philanthropic Society.

Social Services Inspectorate (1991) *The Use Of Complaints Systems.* London: DoH.

Social Services Inspectorate (1994a) *Corporate Parents: An Inspection Of Residential Child Care Services In 11 Authorities.* London: Department of Health.

Social Services Inspectorate (1994b) *Agendas For Action Arising From The National Residential Child Care Inspection 1992–1994.* London: Department of Health.

Social Services Inspectorate (1994c) *Raising The Standard: The Second Annual Report Of The Chief Inspector.* London: Department of Health.

Social Services Inspectorate (1995) *Draft Standards For Leaving Care: Mark One.* London: SSI.

Social Services Inspectorate (1996) 'Social Services Inspectorate Standards for leaving care work', in *Childright* (123) 14–15

Social Services Inspectorate (1997a) *Inspection Of Leaving Care Services.* London: Department of Health.

Social Services Inspectorate (1997b) *When Leaving Home is also Leaving Care: An Inspection of Services for Young People Leaving Care.* Wetherby: DoH.

Social Services Inspectorate and the Office for Standards in Education (OFSTED) (1995) *The Education of Children Who Are Looked After by Local Authorities.* London: Department of Health

Social Trends (1995) Central Statistical Office, Number 24. London: HMSO.

Stein, M. (1989) 'Leaving care.' In B. Kahan (ed) *Child Care Research, Policy and Practice.* London: Hodder and Stoughton, 202–13.

Stein, M. (1990) *Living Out Of Care.* London: Barnardo's.

Stein, M. (1991) *Leaving Care And The 1989 Children Act, The Agenda.* Leeds: First Key.

Stein, M. (1997) *What Works in Leaving Care?* London: Barnardo's.

Stein, M. and Carey, K. (1986) *Leaving Care.* Oxford: Basil Blackwel.l

Stock-Whitaker, D. and Archer, L. (1989) *Research by Social Workers.* London: CCETSW.

Stone, M. (1990) *Young People Leaving Care.* Kent: Royal Philanthropic Society.

Strathdee, R. (1993) *Housing Our Children: The Children Act* 1989. London: Centrepoint.

Surrey Socal Services Department (1994) *Performance Targets In Leaving Care Work.* Surrey: Surrey County Council social services department (mimeo)

Thomas, D.N. (ed) (1983) *The Making of Community Work.* London: George Allen and Unwin.

Thompson, N (1993) *Anti-Discriminatory Practice.* London: Macmillan.

Thompson, W. (1995) `An examination of the structure which enables young people in care to continue education', unpublished MA in Community Education thesis, Leicester: De Montfort University.

Trades Union Congress (1996) *Underworked And Underpaid.* Labour Force Survey. London: Trades Union Congress.

United Nations, General Assembly of (1991) *The Convention On The Rights Of The Child,* adopted by the General Assembly of the UN on 20 November 1989

Voluntary Organisations Personal Social Services Group (1990) *On Different Tracks. The Inconsistencies Between the Children Act 1989 and the Community Care Act,* VOPPS. London: Family Service Unit.

Walentowicz, P. (1995) 'Rent control returns.' In *Roof,* January/February.

Wallace, C. and Cross. M. (1990) *The Sociology of Youth and Youth Policy.* London: Falmer Press.

Ward, H. (1996) 'Constructing and implementing measures to assess the outcomes of looking after children away from home.' In M. Hill and J. Aldgate (eds) *op.cit.,* 240–54.

White, J. (1994) 'User involvement in the planning of services within social services departments.' In *Social Services Research 4,* 1–9. Birmingham: University of Birmingham.

Whyte, L. (1994) 'Anti-discriminatory practice and policy.' In A. Henson (ed) *Improving Practice and Policy in Aftercare Work: A Report on the NCB/Aftercare Consortium Conference.* London, 29 November 1993. Leeds: First Key, 16–20.

Young Homelessness Group (1991) *Carefree And Homeless,* London: YHG.

Youthaid (1996) *Working Brief, September 1996.* London: Youthaid.

Subject Index

Author Index